SPEAK THE WORD
WITH BOLDNESS

Homilies for Risen Christians

WALTER J. BURGHARDT, S.J.

PAULIST PRESS
New York/Mahwah

also by Walter J. Burghardt, S.J.
published by Paulist Press

GRACE ON CRUTCHES
LOVELY IN EYES NOT HIS
PREACHING: THE ART AND THE CRAFT
SEASONS THAT LAUGH OR WEEP
SIR, WE WOULD LIKE TO SEE JESUS
STILL PROCLAIMING YOUR WONDERS
TELL THE NEXT GENERATION
TO CHRIST I LOOK
DARE TO BE CHRIST
WHEN CHRIST MEETS CHRIST

Illustrations by Norman Woehrle

Acknowledgments
The lines from "On Eagle's Wings" by Michael Joncas © 1979, is used with permission from New Dawn Music, P.O. Box 13248, Portland, OR 97213. All rights reserved.

Library of Congress Cataloging-in-Publication Data

Burghardt, Walter J.
    Speak the word with boldness: homilies for risen Christians/
Walter J. Burghardt.
        p. cm.
    Includes bibliographical references.
    ISBN 0-8091-3470-5 (paper)
    1. Catholic Church—Sermons.   2. Sermons, American.   3. Occasional
sermons.   I. Title.
BX1756.B828S64   1994
252'.02—dc20
                                                                        94-4905
                                                                        CIP

Published by Paulist Press
997 Macarthur Boulevard
Mahwah, NJ 07430

Printed and bound in the
United States of America

TABLE OF CONTENTS

PREFACE

In large measure, *Speak the Word with Boldness* continues my effort, begun on a significant scale in *When Christ Meets Christ,* to demonstrate through actual homilies that Scripture's "just Word" is not limited to a small number of obvious biblical texts. The *whole* of Scripture is social. Creation itself is God's imaginative design for a human family, a community of persons, a body genuinely one. Sin (Cain's, the tower of Babel) was not simply an offense against God; it involved the sundering of community; sin dis-membered the body. The Exodus was not simply a liberation from slavery; it was the formation of a new social order, a contrast society, a community summoned to response and responsibility. In the Hebrew prophets, concern for the poor and the marginal is pervasive. Such was the tradition that sparked the ministry of Jesus, his programmatic sermon in the Nazareth synagogue, his mission to "preach good news to the poor, proclaim release for prisoners and sight for the blind, send the downtrodden away relieved" (Lk 4:18).

The present set of homilies exemplifies two other pertinent truths. On the one hand, biblical justice is not merely or primarily an ethical construct: Give to each person what he or she deserves. Its focus is a relationship of responsibility that stems from a covenant. Its high point among humans is the second great commandment of the law and the gospel: Love your sisters and brothers as if you were standing in their shoes. In fact, love them as Jesus loved all of us—even unto crucifixion. It lies, therefore, at the core of Christianity. On the other hand, given the instinctive reaction of many Christians to the word "justice," homilies on justice can frequently be more effective if the word is not used at all, if justice in its biblical meaning is a lens through which the preacher sees all of reality.

In consequence, the reader may understand why this collection contains five homilies delivered on weekdays during my retreat/workshop *Preaching the Just Word,* and four homilies in the context of an annual convention of the Catholic Health Association of the United States that had as its theme "Heal USA, Heal US."

Walter J. Burghardt, S.J.

FROM
ADVENT
TO
EASTER

1
WITH WHAT SHALL I COME BEFORE
THE LORD?
Second Sunday of Advent (A)

- Isaiah 11:1–10
- Romans 15:4–9
- Matthew 3:1–12

Two days ago the President of the United States announced that we are sending American troops to lead a United Nations coalition force into Somalia. Why? To ensure food for the hungry. One sentence in that announcement was simple, direct, and . . . soul-searing: "When we see Somalia's children starving, all of America hurts."[1]

Good friends: As we privileged children of God prepare in song to welcome the Christmas Child or to celebrate another sacred Hanukkah with gifts to the poor,[2] let me direct your thoughts swiftly in three directions: (1) God's own cry to us, (2) how God's cry touches our children, and (3) what this demands of us as we sing our joy these holy days.

I

First, listen to God's own cry to us. It comes to us from the burning lips of the prophet Micah, fierce champion of pure worship of the Lord, fiery enemy of the corruptions and pretensions of the capital. Micah addresses all of us, Christian as well as Jew, all of us who fear the Lord:

> "With what shall I come before the Lord,
>   and bow myself before God on high?
> Shall I come before [the Lord] with burnt offerings,
>   with calves a year old?   ·
> Will the Lord be pleased with thousands of rams,

3

with ten thousands of rivers of oil?
Shall I give my first-born for my transgression,
   the fruit of my body for the sin of my soul?"
[The Lord] has told you, O mortal, what is good;
   and what does the Lord require of you
but to do justice, and to love kindness,[3]
   and to walk humbly with your God?

                          · (Mic 6:6–8)

"Do justice." Oh, not simply give to a fellow human what he or she deserves, what has been written into human law or can be proven from my philosophy. Justice for the Jew, biblical justice, was

> *fidelity to the demands of a relationship.* In contrast to modern individualism the Israelite is in a world where "to live" is to be united with others in a social context either by bonds of family or by covenant relationships. This web of relationships—king with people, judge with complainants, family with tribe and kinfolk, the community with the resident alien and suffering in their midst and all with the covenant God—constitutes the world in which life is played out. . . .[4]

"All with the covenant God." Put another way, the Jews were to father the fatherless and welcome the stranger, not because the orphan and the outsider deserved it, but because this was the way *the Lord God* had acted towards *them,* towards the Hebrew people. A text in Deuteronomy is telling: "The Lord your God is God of gods and Lord of lords, . . . who executes justice for the orphan and the widow, and who loves the strangers, providing them food and clothing. You also shall love the stranger, for you were strangers in the land of Egypt" (Deut 10:17–19).

    In a word, the Jews were to mirror not the justice of man and woman but the justice of God. Not to execute justice was not to worship God.

II

    Second, how does God's cry for justice touch our children? Now Somalia is tragedy indeed—tragedy writ large in the wasted bones of its children. But we need not jet to Somalia to touch child tragedy; it dots our American landscape. I shall not dull your minds with sheer statistics: one out of five children growing up poor in the richest nation on earth; 5.5 million under 12 hungry, 6 million underfed; 40,000 each year who do not live to age one; 2.5 million physically, emotionally, or sexually abused or neglected each year; teenage suicide tripling in 30 years; more teenage boys dead from guns than from all natural causes combined; 25% of teenagers dropping out of school. Every 26 seconds a child runs away from home; every 47 seconds a child is seriously abused or neglected; every 67 seconds a teenager has a baby; every 7 minutes a child is arrested for drug abuse; every 36 minutes a child is killed or injured by a gun; every day 135,000 children pack a gun on the way to school.[5]

Statistics dull, bore, fatigue. Read the powerful little book by Covenant House president Mary Rose McGeady, *God's Lost Children*, "dedicated to the 1,000,000 homeless children who slept on America's streets [in 1990], scared, cold, hungry, alone, and most of all, desperate to find someone who cares." Read their stories, their letters—from among the 28,000 homeless kids Covenant House rescues in a single year. Michael, kicked out of his home at 15 because he confessed himself homosexual—swallowed up by New York's sex industry. Jimmy, his father a suicide, mother dying somewhere of AIDS. Wendy in 12 foster homes, pregnant at 18. Michelle physically abused by her mother, sexually abused by her father. Five-foot-two Amy, running barefoot in the snow from a pimp threatening to kill her. Anthony, mother a hooker, father a pimp, himself "doing tricks" four times a night. Christy phoning her mother, "How are you?", only to hear, "I'm much happier now that you're out of my life."[6] Kareem, about to jump off the highest bridge he could find in New York, stopped by a cabbie, "You'll be holding up traffic." Robby, dying of AIDS: "Dying," he once said, "is easy. Living is tough." "Sometimes," says Sister McGeady, "I feel that God created the dark of night so kids can cry unnoticed."[7]

III

Third, what does all this demand of us as we sing our joy these holy days? I assume that each of us who gather here today is part and parcel of a covenant. On God's part, a divinely guaranteed promise from a Lord who alone can save; on our part, a response that is basically obedience to God's will, to God's law. Jews can look back to God's covenant with Noah and Abraham, with Moses and David, through the prophets. Christians look back to a messianic covenant sealed in the blood of Christ.

Whatever our covenant, it involves relationships—not only with the Lord but with our sisters and brothers as well. It involves the second great commandment of the law and the gospel: You shall love your neighbor at least as much as you love yourself. And loving our sisters and brothers, Jesus said, "is like" loving God (cf. Lev 19:18; Mt 22:39).

Why the stress on children, on the little ones? Because they are the most vulnerable of God's images on earth, often the most helpless. Because our children are our future: tomorrow's citizens, tomorrow's leaders, tomorrow's believers, tomorrow's parents. Because, as Pope John Paul II put it, "In the Christian view, our treatment of children becomes a measure of our fidelity to the Lord."[8] Because, as a Christian, I believe that the Son of God came among us as a child, took flesh of a teenage Jewess, was locked in loving arms from the moment he opened his eyes in a stable. Because our Lord God surely commands us as Jesus himself did, "Let the little children come to me, and do not stop them, for it is to such as these that the kingdom of heaven belongs" (Mt 19:14). Because Jesus took a little child in his arms and declared, "Whoever welcomes one such child in my name welcomes me, and whoever welcomes me welcomes not me but the One who sent me" (Mk 9:37). Because all too often there is no room in the world's inns for today's Christ child.

A guilt trip? Not at all. Am I casting a wet blanket over Christmas, dimming the lights of Hanukkah? Perhaps. But only to make our holiday a holy day, a festal day for every Christ child, for every child of Abraham. For when I look into the Christmas crib, I shall have to ask myself: What do I see in the crib? Another Moses crying in a basket among the reeds? Another Christ shivering in straw? The problem is, the original Christ child is no longer there; he has grown up, died, risen from the rock. Whom do I see? A child sexually abused? A child with Down's syndrome? A child wasted by hunger? An empty crib, because a child was prevented from ever entering it?

Good friends: As I celebrated the liturgy this morning outside of Annapolis, so much of it spoke to me as I have spoken to you. There is Isaiah's ideal king to come, who administers justice in favor of the weak and lowly. There is the Psalmist praying that God's king will "defend the cause of the poor, . . . give deliverance to the needy" (Ps 72:4). There is John the Baptist demanding in the desert that the people reform their lives, change the ways they think and act, insisting that unless their lives bear fruit, there is no point to calling Abraham their father. But most penetrating of all was the opening prayer:

"God of power and mercy, open our hearts in welcome. Remove the things that hinder us from receiving Christ with joy."

What hinders me from receiving Christ with joy? A kind of myopia, nearsightedness, tunnel vision. Seeing Christ beneath the veil of bread and wine, behind tabernacle doors, in the Christmas crib; failing to see Christ in the man or woman next to me, in the homeless addict I meet on the street, in the prisoner on death row I never meet—most importantly, in the Somalian child on the front page of today's *Post* . . . wasting away before the eyes of the world. Light one child's eyes with hope, and you will experience the joy which, Jesus promised, no human being, nothing whatever, "will take from you" (Jn 16:23).

One final question for all of us: Is it true that when we see *America's* children starving—starving for food or affection—all of America hurts? Do *I* hurt?

Our Lady of Victory Church
Washington, D.C.
December 6, 1992

2
DON'T BE AFRAID?
Fourth Sunday of Advent (A)

- Isaiah 7:10–14
- Romans 1:1–7
- Matthew 1:18–24

One of the most frequent assurances in Scripture is one you just heard from Matthew: "Don't be afraid." It dots the Old Testament and the New. The Lord said it to Abraham before cutting a covenant with him: "Don't be afraid" (Gen 15:1). Gabriel said it to Daniel when he was frightened by a terrifying vision: "Don't be afraid" (Dan 10:12). An angel said it to Zechariah, future father of the Baptist: "Don't be afraid" (Lk 1:13). Gabriel said it to Mary troubled at being greeted as "favored" by God and "The Lord is with you": "Don't be afraid" (Lk 1:12, 30). An angel said it to shepherds startled by the Christmas glory that shone round them: "Don't be afraid" (Lk 2:10). Jesus said it to Peter fearful at an amazing, net-breaking catch of fish: "Don't be afraid" (Lk 5:10). Jesus said it when the disciples thought he was a ghost walking on the waters: "Don't be afraid" (Mk 8:50). Jesus said it to Peter, James, and John flat on the ground when they heard the voice from heaven on the mount of transfiguration: "Don't be afraid" (Mt 17:7). A frightening angel who had rolled back the stone from Jesus' tomb said it to Mary Magdalene and the other Mary: "Don't be afraid" (Mt 28:5). And here you have an angel assuring Joseph: "Don't be afraid to take Mary as your wife, for the child conceived in her is from the Holy Spirit" (Mt 1:20).

As we draw ever closer to Christmas, that exhortation could be a significant facet of God's message to us: "Don't be afraid." But, like many other messages from heaven, it raises problems. So then, three questions: (1) What does it *not* mean? (2) What *does* the Lord mean when that assurance comes from above? (3) What might all this be saying to you and me this Christmas?

8

I

First, "Don't be afraid": What does it *not* mean? It is not a blanket prohibition, as if fear were a Jewish or Christian contradiction. People have good reasons to feel afraid. Mary had. She was being asked to bear a child when she had no experience of sexual relations. Joseph had a good reason. By the standards of the Torah, he was expected to expose his pregnant fiancée to the dreadful trial by ordeal prescribed in the Book of Numbers (5:5–31). The shepherds in the fields were right to be frightened. How else do you react when "the glory of the Lord" shines all around you (Lk 2:9)?

And what of us? Don't be afraid when you lose your job and your children are hungry? Don't be afraid when guns and knives, coke and crack are kings in our streets? Don't be afraid when more women are sexually abused than suffer from all other violences combined? Don't be afraid when you have no access to healthcare, to health insurance? Don't be afraid when your child goes to a school terrorized by young thugs? Don't be afraid when doctors aid the suffering to suicide? Don't be afraid when you're hungry or homeless or cancer-ridden or on death row? Don't be afraid if you're a recovering alcoholic, are addicted to heroin, are afflicted with AIDS? Don't be afraid if you're young and vulnerable, elderly and unloved, middleaged and unhappy with your life? Don't be afraid if you're dying? Hogwash!

If you need a powerful precedent for legitimate human fear, wasn't Jesus himself afraid in the garden of his agony, when he begged his Father, if at all possible, not to let him die?

II

Such questions lead to my second point. If it's true that at times we have good reasons for fear, if fear is a perfectly normal, natural, instinctive response to danger, to threat, how are we to understand the Lord's "Don't be afraid"? What is the positive side of the coin?

Let's begin with the First Letter of John—an intriguing assertion: "Perfect love casts out fear. . . . Whoever fears has not reached perfection in love" (1 Jn 4:18). But how do we reach perfect love? Here is where the Christmas story comes in. It is the promise distantly glimpsed by the prophet Isaiah: "The Lord will give you a sign. Look, the young woman is with child and shall bear a son, and shall name him Emmanuel" (Isa 7:14). What does that Hebrew word Emmanuel mean? "God is with us."

Such is the essence, the pith, of the Christmas story: God is with us. But with us in unique fashion, as never before. Not simply everywhere, as God must be . . . everywhere by God's power, by God in touch with what God has created. No, here is God's unique Son in our flesh. God born as we are born, of a woman, after nine hidden months. God fed from a mother's breast. God walking as we walk, hungry as we hunger, tired as we tire. God healing human illness with a touch, lifting the sinner from the earth, instilling courage into hopeless hearts. God betrayed with a kiss, mocked for a fool, lashed with whips, crowned with thorns, pinned to a cross like a common criminal. God rising from the rock. God remaining with us in the sacrament of his flesh and blood.

What does this say to fear? God came among us, God is with us, not for God's own good, not even to show us what a perfect baby looks like. God is with us to save us. This is what the name Jesus means. Remember today's Gospel: "You [Joseph] are to name him Jesus, for he will save his people . . ." (Mt 1:21). And what is salvation? A liberation, a process of freeing. From sin indeed; but not only from sin. Beyond and apart from sin, freedom from fear. Not from instinctive reactions. From the fears that keep us from loving God with all our mind and heart, all our soul and strength. So that we can cry, to ourselves and to others, "Have no fear, God is here."

III

So far, two realities. (1) Neither God's Son nor God's angels are playing psychiatrist when they say, "Don't be afraid." The Gospels are not a minicourse, therapy, in dissolving fear. God is not denouncing or downplaying a very natural emotion in human living. Without a certain amount of fear, I risk living recklessly: cross highways against red lights, walk down dark alleys, spend money as if dollars are going out of style, take no thought for tomorrow, risk AIDS, let my infant play with knives, don't care who buys guns. Without fear, our nation would be a target for any mad leader with an A-bomb. (2) The Gospels are concerned over those fears that could destroy our oneness with God. The antidote to such fears is the realization that "God is with us." This leads into my third question: What might all this be saying to you and me this Christmas?

Christmas, God-in-our-flesh, tells me that fear, for all its value, is not the critical characteristic of a Christian. At the heart of Christianity is love: to love as Jesus loved. My whole life is a ceaseless effort to love more and more the way Jesus loved. On the road to such perfect love I need a gift of God called . . . trust. Where do I begin? With God's own Christmas gift: God's Son trusting himself to us. He did, you know. He trusted himself to a teenage girl's body for nine hidden months. He trusted himself to a mother and foster father who never quite understood who he was and what he was about. He trusted himself to twelve intimate friends, one of whom sold him for silver, another denied with an oath that he had ever known him, another to whom he had to say at the end, "Have I been with you all this time . . . and you still do not know me?" (Jn 14:9). He trusted himself to a people of his own creation whose leaders let the Romans crucify him. He trusts himself to us—in our hands and on our tongues; if we love him, he lives in us.

What does this Christmas gift demand of us in return? Our own trust. Let the Lord gradually remove the fears that prevent perfect love. There are indeed fears about which God says to you and me, "Don't be afraid." They touch our salvation, our love: love for God now and for ever, love for our sisters and brothers, love of our own selves. So many of us are afraid: afraid of God, afraid of hell, afraid of ourselves, afraid to risk.

All too many Christians are afraid of God. In their experience, God seems so distant . . . or so majestic . . . or so despotic . . . or so uncaring. God is the God of tornados and hurricanes, of wars and laws, of vengeance and punishments. No, if such is your image of God, look down into a crib, look up at a cross. There is your God— in swaddling clothes and bloody naked. "God so loved the world . . ." (Jn 3:16), so loved you and me.

All too many Christians are afraid of hell. St. Ignatius Loyola was acutely practical. Let me "beg for a deep sense of the pain which the lost suffer, that if . . . I forget the love of the eternal Lord, at least the fear of these punishments will keep me from falling into sin."[1] But only if I forget God's love, only if I forget to love. Once more, look down into a crib, look up at a cross.

All too many Christians are afraid of themselves. I mean, they do not trust their own joy, are afraid to be happy, think that if they're too happy something bad is about to happen. No. Remember Jesus' promise: "I will see you again, and your hearts will rejoice, and your joy no one will take from you" (Jn 16:22). Your joy? Look down into a crib, look up at a cross. All for you.

All too many Christians are afraid to risk. They are like the fearful servant in Jesus' parable, the servant who was afraid to invest his master's capital, played it close to the vest, kept the capital in a safe place, only to hear his master shout, "Out of my sight, you lazy lout!" (Mt 25:26 ff.). Jesus made it quite clear: If I'm ceaselessly set on saving my life, I will lose it; only if I risk losing my life will I save it. Only if I'm willing to sacrifice whatever God asks of me for love of God and my sisters and brothers, only then am I so free of fear that I can say I love as Jesus loved.

I am reminded of a delightful bit of dialogue in Graham Greene's novel *Monsignor Quixote*. In a Spanish monastery church an American professor is quizzing a Trappist monk who has forsaken philosophy for the cloister.

> "Father Leopoldo, you are a student of Descartes. What brought you here?"
> "I suppose Descartes brought me to the point where he brought himself—to faith."
> "But to become a Trappist?"
> "I think you know, professor, that when one has to jump, it's so much safer to jump into deep water."[2]

So much safer to jump into deep water. That's what the Son of God did; look down into a crib, look up at a cross. Christmas is not a cute little baby; Christmas is a fierce, passionate God. A New Jersey pastor preached it powerfully: "What you have in Christmas is a terrible desire on God's part to 'be with us,' to be a part of the human condition: our losses, our recessions, our disappointed and fractured relationships; the deaths we've had in the past year; the difficulties, the addictions, the alcohol, the drugs, sex; things that turn us upside down. . . ."[3]

Good friends: Christmas is not an end to all fear; but it should be the beginning of a fresh love. Fresh love for a God who experienced in our flesh all that we experience—for love of us. Fresh love for our own selves—not what we have made of ourselves, but what God's love has made of us—new creatures. Fresh love for our sisters and brothers—not a vague abstraction called humanity, but each image of God we touch each day, with a word or a scalpel, with a phone call or a decision, with a look or a prayer . . . however, wherever. And all this within a fresh yearning to risk, to open ourselves to God, to God's world, to God's children.

This Friday, this "silent night, holy night," try to see in the Christmas crib a challenge and an assurance. A challenge: to love somewhat as this child loved—terribly vulnerable, but always arms outstretched to a world. An assurance: Emmanuel; "God is with us." Christmas does not automatically cast out fear. Go to Midnight Mass, carol like crazy, kneel at the manger, and fear will evaporate? No. But God is with you, God loving, God caring. So, don't . . . be . . . afraid.

> Dahlgren Chapel
> Georgetown University
> and
> Holy Trinity Church
> Washington, D.C.
> December 20, 1992

3

IN *GOD* WE TRUST?
First Sunday of Lent (C)

- Deuteronomy 26:4–10
- Romans 10:8–13
- Luke 4:1–13

Last week a thoughtful article in *Time* magazine expressed vividly the fears, the uncertainties, the angers of middle-class America.[1] I mean the 63% of the American population where families of four earn between $18,500 and $74,300. Not only is it more difficult for the average middle-class American to make ends meet than it was a few years ago. Not only do they worry about school tuitions and running out of medical insurance. Not only are they afraid of crime in the streets, of crack in their children. In the new world that has emerged with the dissolution of the Soviet Union, Americans are confused. (1) The powers we defeated in war, Japan and Germany, are challenging us economically. (2) A massive influx of new immigrants is challenging our sense of identity: Who are we? Are we still one people? (3) The baby-boomers, just about reaching mid-life crisis, are tasting the disillusion, the hopelessness, that hit "when people think their best years are behind them."[2]

Good friends, it's a good time for Lent to show its face. Fear not. I am not about to tell you how superb a thing sacrifice is, how blessed the poor are in God's eyes, what perils lurk in possessions. Not that I deny this. Even more importantly, in today's readings Moses and Jesus and Paul all highlight a virtue, a gift of God, a monosyllable which ultimately is our only antidote to the fears, the uncertainties, the anger of America in the nineties. So, let me do my usual three-step: (1) recapture the experience of Moses, Paul, and Jesus; (2) talk a bit about the momentous monosyllable each of them stresses; (3) ask how all this touches us.

14

I

First, our three speakers, our superstars. What is Moses telling his countrymen? Why is he recalling the "bad days" in Egypt? What you have here is something typical of a pattern you find in the Hebrew Testament from Genesis to 2 Kings. The pattern is (1) oppression, (2) cry for help, (3) divine action in response to the cry.[3] Listen to Moses: "The Egyptians treated us harshly, and afflicted us, and laid upon us hard bondage. Then we cried to the Lord the God of our fathers, and the Lord heard our voice . . . and brought us out of Egypt with a mighty hand and an outstretched arm" (Deut 26:6-8). Oppression, petition, relief.

Leap over the centuries to Jesus. To Jesus tempted by the devil. Yes, the Son of God tempted. For, as the New Testament Letter to the Hebrews insists, "We have not a high priest who is unable to sympathize with our weaknesses, but one who in every respect has been tempted as we are . . ." (Heb 4:15). But tempted to what, to what evil thing? Very simply, to use his power, his authority, as Son of God in his own interest, for his own purposes, apart from the mission given him by his Father. (1) You're hungry; you haven't had a bite for 40 days. Well, you're the Son of God, aren't you? So, change stones to bagels. Try it, you'll like it. (2) You want to rule the world, don't you? Isn't that why you're here? For a kingdom? So, I'll give it to you. Just fall on your face and worship me. (3) You want to make a name for yourself, don't you? You want the people to listen, the way they listen to George Burns? Well, here's your chance. Amaze the motley mob, jump like Superman from the tip of the temple.

Jesus' reply? In each instance, a reference to his Father. (1) You don't live on bread alone; you live on every word from God's mouth. (2) It's only the Lord our God a creature dares to worship. (3) Don't you dare tempt God.

Now leap a few decades to St. Paul. A comforting, consoling sentence: One "Lord of all," Jesus the Christ, "bestows his riches upon all who call upon him" (Rom 10:12). Call upon him and your life will be enriched beyond imagining.

II

So, point number two: What is the magic monosyllable Moses and Jesus and Paul imply? Trust. Not some vague word you toss about thoughtlessly: "Of course I trust you." Not a word stamped on a coin,

"In God we trust." Not a feeble wish that all just might work out. Christian trust is a wedding of three realities, three gifts. It is a hope that springs from faith and is kept alive by love.

Trust is a hope. It is a confident expectation that, no matter what happens, God will be there—God *is* there. For you. With you. But you will not enjoy that confident expectation unless your faith is founded on rock. For you know that God is with you not from some ironclad philosophical proof. You know it because the Son of God promised you—a promise sealed not with a pen but with his blood. And you hope even against hope because you're in love.

It's dear Job on the village dump, all his children killed, all his possessions gone, loathsome sores from head to foot, his wife urging him "Curse God and die" (Job 2:9), yet still trusting God. Not because God has explained to him the mystery of suffering, of evil, but because he has seen God's face; God has appeared to him. It's teenage Mary of Nazareth, asked by an angel to mother God's Son, not knowing all that God was asking of her, only that it was God who was asking—and responding in simple trust, "Let it happen to me as you say" (Lk 1:38). Whatever you want, Lord.

It's Jesus himself sweating blood in the Garden of Gethsemane: "Father, if you are willing, remove this cup from me; yet, not my will but yours be done" (Lk 22:42). Jesus crying aloud, "Father, into your hands I entrust my spirit" (Lk 23:46). Jesus dying not with absolute proof that he would rise again—dying only with hope, trust in his Father's love.

It's a true story told me by a Bahamian priest. A two-story house had caught fire. The family—father, mother, several small children— were on their way out when the smallest boy became terrified, tore away from his mother, ran back upstairs. Suddenly he appeared at a smoke-filled window, crying like crazy. His father, outside, shouted to him: "Jump, son, jump! I'll catch you." The boy cried: "But, daddy, I can't see you." "I know," his father called, "I know. But *I* can see you."

III

Now for the nitty-gritty. What of you and me? How can you and I possibly continue to hope against hope—when cancer strikes, when a career is blasted, when the pink slip comes, when my life style is threatened, when a child is murdered, when I'm utterly alone and unbearably lonely, when there's nothing left to live for? Let me simply tell you why *I* trust.

Why do *I* trust, I this strange combo of man, Christian, Jesuit, and priest?[4] Behind it, of course, lies God's good grace. But what keeps God's gift alive in me is my own day-by-day experience. I trust God because I have seen what trust can do for men and women who murmur confidently with the Psalmist, "Even though I walk through the darkest valley, I fear no evil; for you are with me" (Ps 23:4).

I have seen Martin Luther King Jr. with his dream, undimmed by a bullet, that one day "all of God's children, black and white, Jews and Gentiles, Protestants and Catholics, will be able to join hands and sing in the words of the old Negro spiritual: 'Free at last! Free at last! Thank God Almighty, we are free at last!' "[5] I have seen Solidarity in Poland, seen Polish workers without weapons, with hope only in God and the courage God gave them, overcome an army, overthrow a government. I have seen El Salvador: martyred Archbishop Romero crying "Enough!" to the death squads, my six Jesuit brothers and their two lay sisters massacred by the military because they believed with St. Paul that "If for this life only we have hoped in Christ, we are of all people most to be pitied" (1 Cor 15:19). I have seen Dorothy Day, Communist-turned-Catholic, with her houses of hospitality and her breadlines; walking picket lines, jailed for supporting Mexican itinerant workers, squaring off against a New York cardinal in defense of cemetery strikers; arguing passionately that the poor do *not* have the gospel preached to them; living with the criminal, the unbalanced, the drunken, the degraded; reflecting with Dostoevsky that "Hell is not to love any more"; loving the Church that was so often a scandal to her, loving it because it made Christ visible.[6]

More personally, I trust God because of a lady I met briefly 50 years ago: flat on her back for 25 years, paralyzed from the neck down, more alive than I, heart intent on God yet thinking only of others. I trust God because of another lady 50 years later in a D.C. hospital, totally blind, both legs amputated, smiling at me like the risen Christ. I trust God because of my own mother, at the graveside of my father and only brother, dead within three weeks of each other, and looking through her tears up to heaven, to a God she did not understand, a God she never stopped loving. I trust God because of the thousands of men and women whose lives have intersected with mine, have touched mine briefly or long, men and women who have carried Christ's cross in a hundred different ways, have died and risen time and again, men and women who have been tempted to despair but kept repeating with the Psalmist, "Even though you should slay me, I will continue to hope in you."

How have they managed to hang on? Again, ultimately by God's grace. But with that, in my experience, they have given themselves to others, their life expressed in St. Paul's impassioned outburst to the Christians of Corinth, "I will most gladly spend and be spent for you" (2 Cor 12:15). Spent for those equally or more agonizingly crucified: the aged hungry and the children abused, the drug-addicted and the AIDS-afflicted, MS and Down's syndrome, the homeless and the helpless, the unloved. In a word, they bring hope to others. Bringing hope to others, they find their own hope deepened.

But remember always, trust such as this stems from a profound faith and is nourished by limitless love. As dear old Job discovered, you don't first prove that God is worthy of trust and then come to love God. When God appeared to Job, God did not explain patiently and clearly why innocent Job was sitting atop the village dump scraping his loathsome sores and cursing the day he was born; God touched Job, and that was enough for him. The movement is simple but difficult: from experience of God . . . to love for God . . . to trust in God. You begin with love; you are touched by God; then you will throw yourself unconditionally into God's hands, cry with Jesus, "Father, into your hands I entrust my spirit" (Lk 23:46).

This is why Lent is so important. Jesus journeying to Jerusalem is not some mythical figure from the past carrying his solitary cross. Jesus carrying his cross is my father struck with cancer at 53, my mother senile at seventy. Jesus in Gethsemane is the couple in North Carolina who cannot afford to buy a house, who worry what the future holds for their two-month-old daughter Grace.[7] Jesus carrying his cross is you and I. As Christians, St. Paul declares, we are "always carrying in the body the death of Jesus, so that the life of Jesus may also be manifested in our bodies" (2 Cor 4:10). With Paul, "I carry the marks of Jesus branded on my body" (Gal 6:17). Christian life is a ceaseless journeying to Jerusalem. The journey has begun; it began when you were born. Don't walk it alone; walk it with Jesus. Now.

Franciscan Renewal Center
Scottsdale, Arizona
March 8, 1992

4
NOT KNOWING WHERE HE WAS GOING
Second Sunday of Lent (A)

- Genesis 12:1–4
- 2 Timothy 1:8–10
- Matthew 17:1–9

I wonder how many of you have read C. S. Lewis' *Chronicles of Narnia*. It is high spiritual adventure in the realm of imagination. In the land of Narnia the Christ-Lion, Aslan, reigns over his kingdom and leads a group of children into battles, into brilliance, into beauty. When the children leave this only world they have ever known, the door is shut on Narnia. In fear they answer the call to go "further up and further in." They had hoped that Narnia would last for ever. They expect to feel lost and alienated in a new land. Instead, as one of the children says, this is "more like the real thing." He explains:

> When Aslan said you could never go back to Narnia, he meant the Narnia you were thinking of. But that was not the real Narnia. That had a beginning and an end. It was only a shadow or a copy of the real Narnia, which has always been here and always will be here: just as our own world, England and all, is only a shadow or copy of something in Aslan's real world. You need not mourn over Narnia, Lucy. All of the old Narnia that mattered, all the dear creatures, have been drawn into the real Narnia through the Door. And of course it is different; as different as a real thing is from a shadow or as waking life is from a dream. [He pauses, then adds under his breath] It's all in Plato, all in Plato: bless me, what *do* they teach them at these schools![1]

"Further up and further in." With Narnia as imaginative context, let's talk about Abraham, about Jesus, and about you and me.

I

First, Abraham. There he was, once a seminomad, now settled in Mesopotamia (the part that is now in Turkey), when God spoke to him: "Go from your country and your kindred and your father's house to the land that I will show you" (Gen 12:1). About this divine command the New Testament Letter to the Hebrews has an instructive sentence: "By faith Abraham obeyed when he was called to set out for a place that he was to receive as an inheritance; and he set out, not knowing where he was going" (Heb 11:8).

Not knowing where he was going. Somewhat like the inhabitants of Narnia, Abraham was happy in Mesopotamia. Age 75, happily wed to Sarah, surrounded by loving kinsfolk, rocking contentedly on his front porch, what need did he feel to pack up and go . . . he knew not where? That act of obedience began a life that would make Abraham the father of faith, an extraordinary example to Jews and Christians alike of what it means to believe. Not simply to accept as true with his mind whatever God revealed; even more importantly, to say yes with his life to whatever God wanted.

Not knowing where he was going. Leaving home and dear ones was little more than a first act in Abraham's drama of faith. God did not inform him that a famine would force him and Sarah into Egypt. God did not tell him that Sarah would be taken into Pharaoh's harem because Abraham, afraid, would lie that Sarah was his sister, not his wife. God did not tell him that when he was a hundred years old and Sarah 91, she would be pregnant with their child—that they would laugh themselves blue at the idea neatly expressed by a Presbyterian preacher, "the idea of a baby's being born in the geriatric ward and Medicare's picking up the tab."[2] God did not tell Abraham that one day the Lord would say to him, "Take your son, your only son Isaac, whom you love, and go to the land of Moriah, and offer him there as a burnt offering" (Gen 22:2); did not tell him God would stay his hand only when the knife was poised to strike. Little wonder that St. Paul wrote of Abraham as he did to the Christians of Rome:

> . . . he is the father of all of us. . . . Hoping against hope, he believed that he would become "the father of many nations". . . . He did not weaken in faith when he considered his own body, which was already as good as dead (for he was about a hundred years old), or when he considered the barrenness of Sarah's womb. No distrust made him waver concerning the promise of God, but he grew

strong in his faith as he gave glory to God, being fully convinced
that God was able to do what [God] had promised.

(Rom 4:16–21)

II

Now turn from Abraham to Jesus. We do well to pray to Christ
gloriously risen from the dead, all-powerful to heal the hurts of our
humanness. But this Lenten season is prime time to rediscover what
we are always in danger of forgetting: that Jesus was utterly human,
that before he rose from the dead, during those 30-odd years from
Bethlehem to Calvary, he lived by faith—much as Abraham did,
much as we do.

This means that, precisely as human, Jesus did not come into
this world with a God-given scenario, "This is your life." Mary sang
sleep-inducing lullabies to him in the stable, not a forecast of his
future. A verse in Luke is all-important: "Jesus increased in wisdom
and in years" (Lk 2:52). He not only got bigger; he got smarter. He
not only learned from Joseph how to shape a plow; he learned from
Mary how to love God. He did not know in advance that after his
first sermon in his home synagogue his fellow Nazarenes would try
to hurl him off a cliff. I suspect that when the 12-year-old Jesus stayed
in Jerusalem's temple without his parents' permission, he did so on
an impulse, not from a prepared script. Remember what he said
about his own final coming on the clouds of heaven? "About that
day and hour no one knows, neither the angels of heaven, *nor the
Son,* but only the Father" (Mt 24:36).

Oh yes, this man had understanding beyond our feeble efforts
to comprehend. All I am saying is, he learned. Recall those solemn
words in the Letter to the Hebrews: "Although he was a Son, he
learned obedience through what he suffered" (Heb 5:8).

In at least one respect Jesus differed from Abraham: He knew
where he was going. His was a journey to Jerusalem . . . to die. But
the details gained clarity only gradually. And when he died, he died
not with experience of resurrection, not with some impregnable
proof that he would rise from the dead. Jesus died as we die, with
faith in his Father, with hope that he would rise. His final words are
wondrously revealing: "Father, into your hands I entrust my spirit"
(Mt 23:46). All I am, all I hope to be, I place with complete confidence
in your care.

III

Finally, you and I. For Abraham and Jesus are not two fine figures from a misty past. In the story of salvation, there is a direct movement from Abraham to Jesus to you and me. If Abraham represents the unknown factor in our faith, "not knowing where he was to go," Jesus represents the Lenten facet of our faith, our journey to Jerusalem. A word on each.

First, not knowing where we are to go. By this time you should be aware that you did not come into this world with a ready-made script for your earth-bound life. Oh yes, you knew from your catechism that you were expected to know, love, and serve God in this life, be happy with God forever in the next. You were handed the Ten Commandments and a laundry list of sins grave and not so grave. Environment and education gave you some idea of the possibilities in your life. But at the so-called age of reason, could you have written the actual story of your life? Oh not so much the externals, your job description; rather the movements, the comedies and tragedies, the ups and downs, that have brought you where you are now, made you the person you actually are. When I joined the Jesuits 62 years ago, I had no idea that my journey would take me from a small seminary in Maryland to two universities in Washington. Like Abraham, I too went forth at 75—from Georgetown to a land I knew not, to a nation that needed to be aroused to social justice by preachers newly inflamed.

The point is, the Holy Spirit never ceases to surprise us—surprises us with joy, surprises us with sorrow. The ultimate question is, how ready am I to listen to the Lord speaking to me—not in a vision but through my history, through my church, through my conscience? How ready to listen and say yes? I am constantly reminded of that intriguing episode in the Old Testament where the Lord calls to a young man, "Samuel! Samuel!" And the lad responds, "Speak, Lord, for your servant is listening" (1 Sam 3:2–10). A perceptive Protestant ethicist once reminded us that the answer so many give in similar situations is, "Speak, Lord, and your servant will think it over."

This introduces our journey to Jerusalem. You see, not only was Jesus' life one long journey to Jerusalem: "[I] must go to Jerusalem and suffer many things . . . and be killed" (Mt 16:21). He commanded us to follow him on that journey. We may not know each step in advance, but this we do know: Like the journey of Jesus, our journey goes to life through death. And death gives life not only when we emit our last earthly gasp; death gives life all through our Christian existence.

Here lies the significance of Lent. We recall and we follow. We recall. I mean we recapture what we call the paschal mystery. And what is the paschal mystery? Not simply a dying Christ; not simply a rising Christ. The paschal mystery is a dying-rising Christ. Not one or the other; both in the same Christ. You see, it is the Resurrection that makes sense out of the Passion. What we have to grasp is not only the history: Jesus died, then he rose to life again. But the mystery as well: Life leaped *from* death; the cross was the springboard for Jesus' rising. That is why, when the risen Jesus appeared to his disciples, he showed them the wounds of his dying (cf. Jn 20:26–27). The Christian mystery is one mystery: dying-rising. Two sides of a single coin.

But recall is not enough; we follow. The whole of Christian living should be a dying-rising, life through death. What sense can we make of this? Forget for a moment what we usually mean by dying: We die when we stop breathing once and for all. The Christian insight into dying is broader, richer, more profound. In the eyes of God, in the mind of Christ, in our journeying to life we die in two ways, because dying stems from two sources: from sin and from self.

From sin. Fear not: I shall not lecture you on sin. But the fact remains, there are sins we call "mortal"—the Ten Commandments include a handful: idolatry, adultery, murder. Mortal with its original Latin flavor: Such sins induce death. Oh they rarely stop the heart. The deadly thing about mortal sin is that Life leaves me—Life with a capital L. Not some vague abstraction; rather, the Life that is God, Christ, the Spirit. I no longer have a relationship of love with a living God. And that, for a man or woman for whom Jesus was crucified, that is to be dead. No matter how alive such sinners may be on golf links or tennis court, in board room or bedroom, spiritually, in God's eyes, they are dead. In mortal sin I am as dead spiritually as I will be dead physically when they bury me.

This dying to sin is a struggle you and I have been waging since our baptism, when first we rose with Christ. It is not something sheerly negative, simply *turning away* from sin, renouncing Satan and all his works and pomps. It is a *turning to* Christ, an act of contrition that is an avowal of love.

Death comes to us in a second way: dying to self. To move forward in Christ, I have to let go of where I've been. Whether it's turning 21 or 40, 65 or 80; whether it's losing my health or my hair, my money or my memory, a person I love, a possession I prize, a position I occupy; whether it's as fleeting as fame or as abiding as grace—

I have to let go. Let go of yesterday. Not to forget it; it's part of me. But I dare not live in yesterday, as if somewhere in the past my life reached its climax or my life bottomed out. It is the importance of the "now" in Christian living. I mean an acute awareness that God is here and now: in *this* task, *this* agony, *this* stranger, *this* Eucharist. Simply the unvarying verse with which a priest opens his breviary each day, the command of the Psalmist to a chosen people: "O that today you would listen to [God's] voice!" (Ps 95:7). Today—for today God speaks. Today I have to be open to whatever God asks, ready to journey to my Jerusalem the way God wants me to. Yes, to let go of yesterday is to die a little—or a lot. But it's the only way I can *grow* into Christ, *grow* into loving communion with Christ and his human images.

Good friends: Lent, journeying with Jesus to Jerusalem, is a splendid season for some fundamental reflection. Am I still mourning over a Narnia on which the door has been shut, or do I realize with Narnia's children that "All of the old Narnia that mattered, all the dear creatures, have been drawn into the real Narnia" that is today? Am I open, like Abraham, to whatever God wants, however old or young I am, however frail or sturdy, not knowing all that is to be, knowing only that wherever my particular Jerusalem, God will be there? It's a fascinating way to experience what the first Preface for Lent paradoxically calls "this joyous season."

Holy Trinity Church
Washington, D.C.
March 7, 1993

5
SPEAK THE WORD WITH BOLDNESS
Second Week of Easter, Monday (C)

- Acts 4:23–31
- John 3:1–8

Good friends in Christ: As we gather for our opening liturgy in this retreat/workshop,[1] a striking sentence from Acts has closed our first reading. Peter and John have been released from prison, commanded "not to speak or teach at all in the name of Jesus" (Acts 4:18). Their response is a flat refusal: "We cannot keep from speaking what we have seen and heard" (v. 20). They have rejoined the rest of the apostolic community and reported their experience; the community has prayed to the Lord for strength to speak God's word boldly in the face of hostile threats. And Luke concludes: "When they had prayed, the place in which they were gathered was shaken; and they were all filled with the Holy Spirit and spoke the word of God with boldness" (Acts 4:31).

Let me speak briefly, perhaps boldly, about the Holy Spirit: (1) the Spirit in the life of the original Christian community, and (2) the Spirit in this community which seeks to preach God's word, the just word, the social word, with boldness.

I

First, thumb through the early chapters of Acts, the story of the young Christian community—the apostles, their disciples, the hundreds and more who join up with them. What, above all, unites them, fashions a genuine community, enables them to speak God's word with boldness? Listen. . . .

Before he leaves them, Jesus promises his disciples: "You will be baptized with the Holy Spirit not many days from now" (Acts 1:5). Not many days later, there comes "a sound like the rush of a violent wind" and all in the house are "filled with the Holy Spirit," begin "to speak in other languages" (2:2, 4). When fellow Israelites ask the apostles "What should we do?", Peter says: "Repent, be baptized, and you will receive the gift of the Holy Spirit" (2:37–38). When Jewish authorities ask Peter and John by what power they have cured a lame gentleman, Peter proclaims Jesus as sole savior—proclaims him because he is himself "filled with the Holy Spirit" (4:8). Imprisoned, the apostles preach the gospel to the high priest, the death and exaltation of Christ: "We are witnesses to these things, and so is the Holy Spirit whom God has given to those who obey him" (5:32). The men who argue with Stephen cannot "withstand the wisdom and the Spirit" with which he speaks (6:10). It is because he is "filled with the Holy Spirit" that Stephen before his stoning sees "the heavens opened and the Son of Man standing at the right hand of God" (7:55–56). So powerful is the Spirit that magician Simon offers the apostles money: "Give me also this power, so that anyone on whom I lay my hands may receive the Holy Spirit" (8:19). Chosen to be God's instrument "before Gentiles and kings and before the people of Israel," persecutor Saul is "filled with the Holy Spirit" (9:15, 17). Peter tells Cornelius and his relatives and close friends "how God anointed Jesus of Nazareth with the Holy Spirit and with power" (10:38). It is the Holy Spirit who tells the church at Antioch, "Set apart for me Barnabas and Saul for the work to which I have called them" (13:2).

And so it goes, endlessly. For, as Paul brings out, the Spirit is an energizer, a Spirit of power: "My speech and my proclamation were not with plausible words of wisdom, but with a demonstration of the Spirit and of power, so that your faith might rest not on human wisdom but on the power of God" (1 Cor 2:4–5). Remember his prayer for the Christians of Rome: "May the God of hope fill you with all joy and peace in believing, so that you may abound in hope by the power of the Holy Spirit" (Rom 15:13).[2]

II

All of which brings us to . . . us. As my dream for the just word developed, it became increasingly clear to us at the Woodstock Theological Center that if this project is to succeed, it cannot be primarily through a communication of facts, data, information, skills. Important indeed; but still more significant is a context. I mean a spirituality, a process that converts, turns the preacher inside out, shapes a new person, puts "fire in the belly." Such a spirituality, like all Christian spirituality, is a work of the Spirit, the energizing force in the proclamation of the gospel.

This is not to suggest that we mount the pulpit or approach the podium with spirits enthusiastic but minds blank. It was to disciples in peril of persecution, not to potential preachers, that our Lord said: "Do not worry about how you are to speak or what you are to say; for what you are to say will be given to you at that time; for it is not you who speak, but the Spirit of your Father speaking through you" (Mt 10:19–20). When we speak of poverty, let it be because we have studied the frightening facts and the fearsome figures, or have even walked in the shoes of the unfortunate. When we dare touch women's issues, let it be because we have been moved by the appalling reality of second-class citizenship women "enjoy" across the earth. We cannot raise the consciousness of a congregation with empty abstractions.

What am I saying? Simply this. Preaching the just word is not *in the first instance* a matter of societal competence, of economic expertise, of political persuasion, of posture and gesture, of assonance and resonance, of a heroic style, a rich vocabulary, a presence without peer. In the last analysis, what will turn our people on is the Holy Spirit—the Spirit in us and the Spirit in them. The Spirit in us who preach. Paul was right on target: Our speech and our proclamation, to be effective, must be "a demonstration of the Spirit," so that faith rests "not on human wisdom but on the power of God." But the Spirit in the pews as well; for we are not hurling missiles at unbelievers; before us sit temples of the Spirit, needing only a Spirit-filled word to come to life.

What does this mean in the concrete? It demands that we live a life close not only to people but to God. It warns us that the age-old adage "To work is to pray" should not eliminate the calluses from our knees. It urges us to develop an intimate relationship with the Trinity within us. With Yahweh commanding us through Micah: "What does the Lord require of you? Act justly, love steadfastly, and walk humbly with your God" (Mic 6:8). With Jesus insisting that loving our sisters and brothers "is like" loving God (Mt 22:39). With the Holy Spirit, the *dunamis,* the dynamite in our lives.

I am reminded that some of our most effective preachers were persons of prayer. Augustine, for whom the preacher's real teacher is the Christ within us, who claimed that "we preach but Christ instructs."[3] The Curé d'Ars, hearing confessions from midnight to evening, listening to fractured hearts and to Christ. Fulton Sheen, spending an hour before the Blessed Sacrament each day, no matter what city, no matter how busy. The Presbyterian David Read, insisting that "the preacher is an individual with one hand stretched out toward God in faith and the other extended toward other people in understanding and compassion."[4]

Where, then, is our focus tonight? On the inexhaustible power of the Spirit to renew us, our people, the face of the earth. With that in mind, pray with me the prayer of the original Christian community, the prayer that made the room quake: "Now, Lord, look at the threats [that overhang your people], and grant to your servants to speak your word with all boldness, while you stretch out your hand to heal, and signs and wonders are performed through the name of your holy servant Jesus" (Acts 4:30).

St. Francis Retreat Center
DeWitt, Michigan
April 27, 1992

6
WERE NOT OUR HEARTS ON FIRE?
Third Sunday of Easter (A)

- Acts 2:14, 22–28
- 1 Peter 1:17–21
- Luke 24:13–35

Today's Gospel raises an intriguing question: How does one come to recognize Christ? Let's try to find out: (1) from the two disciples on the road to Emmaus; (2) from the Catholic experience of liturgy; (3) from a wider, tantalizing, engrossing experience that takes us out of our pews and into the world.

I

We begin with the two disciples of Jesus. Terribly discouraged disciples. Disciples whose refrain is "We were hoping" (Lk 24:21). All they can think about is a Jesus they had known, had followed, a Jesus who had promised them a kingdom, had been captured and condemned and crucified, a Jesus now seemingly stone cold in death. And so they are leaving Jerusalem, for Jerusalem is the city of dashed hopes. Even when another Jew joins them, discouragement prevails. They can talk only of a fairyland past, of "a prophet mighty in deed and word" (v. 19) come to an untimely end. Even the empty tomb reported by women and fellow disciples fails to excite them.

What changes them? There are three stages. The first stage? A stranger joins them. A new presence. Jesus indeed, but not recognized. A stranger to whom they open their saddened hearts, their hopelessness.

The second stage? A lesson in Scripture; a double lesson. To begin with, Jesus chides them: Don't they realize from their own beloved Scripture that the Messiah must suffer[1] before entering into

29

his glory? Then Jesus interprets for them what the whole of the Hebrew Testament has to say about him. And their hearts burn: "Were not our hearts on fire within us as he was speaking to us on the road and opened to us the sense of the Scriptures?" (v. 32). And still they do not recognize him.

The third stage? Jesus takes bread, blesses it, breaks it, and gives it to them. Jesus performs the same basic actions he had employed when multiplying the loaves for thousands and at the Last Supper: He took, he blessed, he broke, he gave. Then it is that the disciples recognize him. A significant word, this "recognize." It means to know someone again, someone one has seen before. But they do not recognize him because of what they see of him, his face, his eyes: "Ah yes, now I see a resemblance to the man who multiplied the loaves." It is with the gift of faith, stimulated by his actions, that they recognize the risen Christ. And though the hour is late, they rush back to Jerusalem to tell the Eleven and their companions, to explain "what had happened on the road and how he became known to them in the breaking of the bread" (v. 35).

The lesson in the story? Once he has risen to his Father, Jesus will be present to his disciples no longer in his visible humanity but in the breaking of the bread.[2]

II

Move on now to our Catholic experience of liturgy. I don't know if you caught it as you heard the Gospel: The three stages in the disciples' experience foreshadow three stages where Christ is present to us in our Eucharistic liturgy, three ways in which we can recognize him.

The first stage? The reality that transpires as soon as we gather together. Never forget that striking declaration of Jesus, "Where two or three are gathered in my name, I am there among them" (Mt 18:20). To have the risen Christ in our midst, we do not have to wait for the Consecration. When we sang the gathering song, David Haas's resounding "God Is Alive," Christ our Lord was there. Not only within each of us as individuals; he was present in the community, in our coming together. It reminds me of the Hebrew Shekinah, the radiance and glory of God that was manifested in the storm cloud, manifested in the cloud and fire over and in the tabernacle, manifested in the cloud on Sinai's summit, and ever so often in Jewish history. As Jesus was present to Cleopas and his companion on the road to Emmaus, even though they did not recognize him, Jesus is present to us the moment we come together. But this time there is no good reason not to recognize him.

The second stage? Vatican II phrased it simply, yet startlingly: Christ "is present in his word, since it is he himself who speaks when the holy Scriptures are read in the church."[3] Has this penetrated my Christian consciousness? Am I aware that when God's own Book is proclaimed, God is addressing me, Christ is speaking to me? Do I listen the way Moses listened to the Lord on Sinai? Do I echo young Samuel in the Old Testament, "Speak, Lord, for your servant is listening" (1 Sam 3:9–10)? Do I even listen the way the Samaritan woman in John's Gospel, hardly a friend of the Jews, listened to Jesus at Jacob's well? The liturgical texts are not primarily readings in religious history. Oh yes, they can be difficult. A snippet from St. Paul, utterly without context, perhaps hastily mumbled, may not sound like Christ; but there he is, speaking to my heart. But my heart must be open, yearning, thirsting to be filled.

The third stage? The body and blood of Christ. Not only when a priest takes bread, blesses it, breaks it. In all its glorious mystery, when the blessed and broken bread is given; when the same Christ rests on your palm or on your tongue, enters your flesh and your spirit, to transform you into his likeness, to instill into you a life beyond your ability to dream. The burning question: Do I thrill to his presence within me? Do I recognize him, recognize that here again is "God with us," God within us? Do I react with the First Epistle of Peter, "Although you have not seen him, you love him; and even though you do not see him now, you believe in him and rejoice with an indescribable and glorious joy" (1 Pet 1:8)?

III

So then, three ways to recognize Christ, prefigured in the two discouraged disciples plodding to Emmaus, realized even more remarkably in our Eucharist: Christ in our assembling, Christ in our hearing, Christ in our table fellowship and in our flesh. Now let me move you to a wider experience of Christ.

One of my favorite books is titled *The Faces of Jesus*.[4] It shows, in photo and text, "all the ways men have dreamed it down the years, painted it and sculpted it, scratched it into the teeth of whales, stitched it into wool and silk, hammered it out of gold."[5] "All those faces—they come drifting back at us like dreams: the solemn child in his mother's arms, the young man scattering words and miracles like seed, the old man eating for the last time with his old friends, the Jew retching out his life from the cross of his shame.''[6]

A remarkable re-presentation. But for me the volume has an unintended advantage. It has inspired me, compelled me, to see the faces of Jesus, to recognize Christ, everywhere I look. I drop in on Children's Hospital, look into a bassinet, see the face of Bethlehem's Child on a victim of Down's syndrome. I pass a local playground where black teenagers are flying through the air like Michael Jordan, and I see the joyous Jesus of early Nazareth. I learn that a dear young friend, graduate of Georgetown, has just died of AIDS, and I see the tortured eyes of Gethsemane's Jesus, hear him begging his Father, "Don't let me die!" I touch the corner of Wisconsin and M, and in a ragged, shivering imitation of humanity I spy the naked Crucified. Once a month I look upon your faces, and I see the faces of Jesus from Bethlehem through Nazareth and Jerusalem to Calvary and beyond, Jesus ceaselessly dying and rising.

There it is, what the Hebrew Testament and the Christian Testament call the image of God on the face of humanity. Pray God that we recognize it more and more intensely as the days move on, that we see the face of Jesus as our face. For this is not fantasy; it is the biblical proclamation that God made the human in God's image, that sin marred this image almost beyond recognition, that the Son of God borrowed our flesh to reshape us in the likeness of Christ. Not some of us; every single human born into this world. And despite the pervasive presence of sin, despite the hatred and violence, despite all the injustice that disfigures the face of humanity, there is simply no one who is totally severed from Christ, ceases utterly to be in his image.

In closing, let me move from a face to a voice. Earlier this month a remarkable black lady went to her Lord at 96. Remarkable not for her age. Remarkable rather because, as Arturo Toscanini told her, "Yours is a voice such as one hears once in a hundred years." Even more remarkable because "when she sang, the walls [of racism] came tumbling down."[7]

You see, for decades Jim Crow laws kept the divine contralto of Marian Anderson from being heard on America's operatic stage. Barred from segregated Constitution Hall, she sang on Easter '39 before 75,000 blacks and whites at the foot of Lincoln's statue. Concert halls and hotels she had to enter through service entrances. Yet she never raised her voice save in song.

What lent her this incredible grace under stress? What kept her strong? Her profound faith. Whence the passion in her songs? Largely from the burdens she carried. She had come to recognize Christ in the spirituals she started to sing at six. She recognized Christ in the contradictions she confronted. She recognized Christ on the faces of all who heard her voice.

Good friends: Can you imagine what would happen to our tortured country if we Catholics could spy the face of Christ on all without exception whose paths we cross? All manner of walls would come tumbling down. And our hearts too would burn within us. For we would be struggling to realize the high-priestly prayer of Jesus, that we "may all be one" as he and the Father are one, so that all men and women may know God's love, may come to recognize and to love the Christ who died for them.

Holy Trinity Church
Washington, D.C.
April 25, 1993

7

A NEW COMMANDMENT?
Fifth Sunday of Easter (C)

- Acts 14:21–27
- Revelation 21:1–5
- John 13:31–35

Any day now, I have a difficult visit to make. Several weeks ago I learned from a young man's grandmother that he has AIDS, that he hasn't long to live, that he is alienated from the Catholic Church that he feels has let him down. I wrote to him, good friend that he's been since his Georgetown days, and asked if I might visit with him. I assured him I had no ulterior motives, no hidden agenda, no "conversion" in mind; I just wanted to show my feelings face to face. He phoned to say . . . yes. And now—now I simply don't know what I shall say to him.

It is in this context that I have shaped my homily on Jesus' declaration, "A new commandment I give to you . . ." (Jn 13:34). I confess, it was difficult to put together "three points." But here they are; really my feelings. (1) I am saddened. (2) I am puzzled. (3) I am hopeful.

I

First, I am saddened. You see, my friend with AIDS brings me face to face not simply with an illness but with a person—and in him with uncounted thousands of flesh-and-blood persons. It recalls vividly an unforgettable day four years ago in Nashville, Tennessee. An Anglican minister was addressing the 73rd Assembly of the Catholic Health Association of the United States. To an audience that often wept openly Canon William Barcus said:

I stand here with you—as a brother to you, a churchman, a man with AIDS. A man who regrets nothing of the love and goodness he has known, who stops now to notice flowers, children at play. . . . A man who loves his church from his heart, from every molecule in him.

In the course of his address Canon Barcus recalled a 1944 photo essay in *Life* magazine:

It was about the red foxes of Holmes County, Ohio, who lived in the woods and ate mostly mice and crickets, but sometimes also chicken and quail. This, the story explained, "made the brave men of Holmes County angry because they wanted to kill the quail themselves." So one Saturday about 600 men and women and their children got together and formed a big circle five miles across. They all carried sticks and started walking through the woods and fields, yelling and baying to frighten the foxes, young and old, out of their holes. Inside this diminishing circle the foxes ran to and fro, tired and frightened. Sometimes a fox would, in its anger, dare to snarl back, and it would be killed on the spot for its temerity. Sometimes one would stop in its anguish and try to lick the hand of its tormenter. It too would be killed.

Sometimes, the photo showed, other foxes would stop and stay with their own wounded and dying. Finally, as the circle came closer together, down to a few yards across, the remaining foxes went to the center and lay down inside, for they knew not what else to do. But the men and the women knew what to do. They hit these dying wounded with their clubs until they were dead, or they showed their children how to do it. This is a true story. *Life* reported and photographed it. The good Christian people of Holmes County considered it sport and it still goes on.

I stand before you today [Barcus continued] as one weary of running, as one wounded myself, and I say to the churches, the churches first, and then to the government, the silent government, and then to the world: "What have you done to my people? What have you done to your own people—beautiful people . . . ?"

My people are being destroyed, and your people, and all our people together. Not only by an illness called AIDS, but by a darker illness called hatred. . . . The Christ, Jesus, the compassionate lord of life and lord of more forgiveness and lord of more hope is the one we have vowed to follow and be ultimately guided by. We must tell that to our smugly self-righteous brothers and sisters. . . . For if we do not, their souls will perish in the circle of misunderstanding and scorn they teach so many as they club and scream their disdain for the outsider, the misunderstood, the different. . . .

Sadly, too many of them, too many with AIDS, have wondered if they had any alternative but to go to the center of the circle and lie down and die. Where are you in that circle? Where are we? Where would Christ be? . . .

For all of us within an awakening church . . . I say to the world, "Help us. Join us." To you as church . . . I say from long despairing peoples of all kinds, "Help us. Please help us. Be the gospel alive!"[1]

II

Canon Barkus leads inevitably into my second point: I am puzzled. Why? Because I experience a gulf, a chasm, that all too often yawns between who we Christians actually are and what sort of Christians Christ wants us to be.

You see, for a significant number of Christians AIDS is God's vengeance on the immoral, the homosexual, the lesbian. It is God's Black Death on the promiscuous. "Serves them right!" I am afraid that this attitude runs afoul of at least two genuinely Christian realities. First, these good folk presume to read God's mind on a host of men, women, and children. They are like the friends of Old Testament Job. His friends see him stripped of his wealth, bereft of his children, afflicted with "loathsome sores from the sole of his foot to the crown of his head" (Job 2:7), even bid by his wife, "Curse God, and die" (v. 9). So they insist: You must have sinned, otherwise God would not be just in treating you like this. Second, the attitude gets terribly close to the Pharisee in the temple: "God, I thank you that I am not like the rest of humans, extortioners, unjust, adulterers . . ." (Lk 18:11).

Today's Gospel tells us in incomparable accents where the Christian begins: not with condemnation but with love. Three facets of this love emerge from the words of Jesus: It is a commandment, it is a gift, and it is new.[2] A word on each.

Strange, isn't it, that love can be commanded? It can be commanded because it is demanded by the covenant between Christ and Christians, the covenant Christ sealed with his blood: "This cup which is poured out for you is the new covenant in my blood" (Lk 22:20).[3] The point is this: If we are to live as a chosen people, there are certain stipulations, certain conditions, you and I have to observe. We are accustomed to see these stipulations, these conditions, in terms of the Ten Commandments, what we are forbidden to do if we want to be good Catholics, if we are to remain within the structure, if we are to be faithful to the covenant, to the God of the covenant. Don't worship false gods; don't miss Mass on Sunday; don't take another's life; don't play fast and loose with sex; don't take what doesn't belong to you; don't lie about another or sully someone's reputation; don't lust for another's spouse. Don't, don't, don't. . . .

But the "don'ts" are not the pith and marrow of Christianity. Every "don't" simply specifies some activity that is the other side of Christianity's most precious coin; it is some threat to love, or the reverse of love, or a refusal to love. It brings love out of the clouds, puts flesh and blood on the skeleton, brings love alive. Such refusal to love runs through the Gospels: the priest who sees the half-dead victim of robbers and passes by on the other side; Judas selling his Lord for 30 pieces of silver; Peter denying to a servant girl that he has ever known Jesus; the elder son refusing to share his repentant brother's party; Herod beheading the Baptist to please a dancing girl; the Sadducees who tried to catch Jesus in a contradiction; the scribes and Pharisees who neglected justice and mercy. What makes these actions sins is ultimately that they are refusals to love.

But this love which Jesus commands is more than a commandment; it is a gift. You don't acquire it by human effort, by wanting it, by being "the best that you can be" through your unaided efforts, pulling yourself up by your bootstraps. It comes from the Father through Jesus to those who believe in him. The source of such love is Jesus; you can have such love only because Jesus loves you. Only because his love was so all-embracing that he laid down his life for you, an act of love that gave life, his life, to you and me.

But how can the commandment to love one another be "new"? After all, were not the Israelites commanded to love their neighbors as they loved themselves (Lev 19:18), even to love the foreigner dwelling among them (Lev 19:34)? Jesus' commandment is "new" because it is part and parcel of the "new covenant" (Lk 22:20). Love is the basic, fundamental condition of the new relationship between Christ and his sisters and brothers.[4] So intimate is this love to be, so striking, that in Jesus' mind it should command the world's attention, challenge the world to recognize God's love for all: "I in [my disciples] and you [Father] in me, that they may become completely one, so that the world may come to know that you sent me and that you have loved them even as you have loved me" (Jn 17:23). What is so new in this love? The partners in this covenant are not separated by a radical inequality—God and humans. God has become our brother in the flesh.[5] And the love we have for Jesus is the love we must now share with our sisters and brothers.

III

My third point: I am hopeful. Why? Not because AIDS is on the decline; it is not. Rather because so many of our Catholic people, so many such as you, are moving out to the crucified images of God who cry clamorously or mutely for our love. It is not only Mother Teresa. She is indeed a living example to all of us. I recall just one of the derelicts in Calcutta she took to her hospice. He was dying, a man so covered with maggots as to be physically repulsive. The sisters cleaned him up, and Mother Teresa held him in her arms. He looked into her eyes and said: "All my life I've lived like an animal; but today I'm going to die like an angel."

Today unnumbered men and women are reaching out to the outcasts of our society. Some of you know Jesuit Father Angelo D'Agostino, medical doctor, psychiatrist, who went to Africa in his sixties. He discovered that more and more babies were being brought to an orphanage by police who had found them abandoned on the street, in garbage bins; and many had tested positive for HIV. The government could not care for them, and the World Health Organization predicted that in five years there would be 3000 such babies in Kenya. So D'Ag is building a hospice in Nairobi, lining up staff, food, medical supplies, other necessities. To make the hospice a place with an atmosphere of loving care, D'Ag and his associates "are training immediate caregivers, single mothers, of which there are so many in Kenya, structuring the place so that it will look and function as a traditional African village with many small huts with four or five babies being cared for by a housemother."[6]

All this, and so much more, is impressive reason for hope. Not only for the AIDS-afflicted but for the less obvious victims of AIDS. I mean so many of us for whom AIDS has for all too long carried a stigma, a sign of moral blemish—somewhat as leprosy did for centuries. We have kept the diseased at arm's length, even banned them from civilized society—today's untouchables. I still recall vividly a song sung by Barbara Cook at the Kennedy Center three years ago—a song composed in part by a long-term AIDS victim. Two lines in particular laid powerful hold on me:

> Love is all we have for now,
> what we don't have is time.[7]

It's true not only of the AIDS-afflicted; it's true of all of us. Each of us—this whole body St. Paul calls the body of Christ—has so much pent-up love—love struggling, yearning, to burst forth from us. And time is desperately short. We sense it all around us, near and far: the L.A. tragedy,[8] the poverty in the richest country on earth, the violent death that haunts our streets, the hatred ceaselessly bubbling beneath the surface. Time is terribly short. And we dare not do nothing while we wait for the day when all creation will be freed of imperfection, when *God* "will wipe away every tear" from the eyes of the crucified (Rev 21:4).

Strangely, I'm not quite as worried as before about what I shall say to my friend with AIDS. No need to say anything. I shall simply be there . . . with him . . . for him. "Love is all we have for now."

Manresa-on-Severn
Annapolis, Maryland
May 16, 1992
also
Dahlgren Chapel
Georgetown University
and
Holy Trinity Church
Washington, D.C.
May 17, 1992

8
NO GREATER LOVE
Fifth Week of Easter, Friday (C)

- Acts 15:22–29
- John 15:12–17

I speak to you this high noon on a highly personal note, with uncommon brevity.[1] For, as the apostles and the elders wrote to the believers of Gentile origin in Antioch, Syria, and Cilicia, "It has seemed good to the Holy Spirit and to us to impose on you no further burden than these essentials" (Acts 15:28).

In this project that engages us—Preaching the Just Word—what is the quintessential? Love your brothers and sisters. Love them at least as much as you love yourself. This, the second great commandment in the law and the gospel, this commandment is, Jesus said, "like" the first (Mt 22:39). Loving our brothers and sisters is like loving God. But the gospel adds something striking to the law: Love your sisters and brothers as Jesus has loved you (Jn 15:12). In your situation and mine the command no longer lives in glorious abstraction. It is splendidly, fearfully, gloriously concrete. How do we love as Jesus loved?

1) We share his incarnate *mission*. Preaching the Just Word, living the Just Word, is our loving role in Jesus' programmatic declaration of his mission in Nazareth's synagogue: "The Spirit of the Lord . . . has anointed me to bring good news to the poor, . . . to let the oppressed go free" (Lk 4:18).

2) We share Jesus' mission as *servants,* "slaves" if you prefer the stronger translation. If "the Son of Man came not to be served but to serve" (Mt 20:28), then we dare not imitate the rulers Jesus experienced, the rulers we experience, those who "lord it" over their people, are "tyrants over them" (v. 25). Nor do we ape John Gielgud, valet to Arthur indeed,[2] but with nose ever haughtily in air. If I may

40

add a phrase to the prophet Micah, we need to "walk humbly" not only "with [our] God" (Mic 6:8); we must walk humbly with our people.

3) We share Jesus' mission as *suffering* servants. Here perhaps is the pith and marrow of our ministry. From your own touching confessions these five days, you have experienced what it means to serve as Jesus served: even unto crucifixion. That greatest of all loves which Jesus lauded, to lay down life itself for those we love, is rarely a single act: St. Sebastian a dart board for pagan arrows, Archbishop Romero dead from an assassin's single bullet. It is even more difficult to lay down your *whole* life for those you love. Such is our gethsemane, and it forces from us time and again Jesus' own cry from bloody sweat: Please, please, God, "remove this cup from me" (Lk 22:42). Living the Just Word is a ceaseless journeying to Jerusalem, a daily dying/rising. "This is my body, [and it is] given for you" (Lk 2:19). It is in dying that we come to life. Not only on the final cross— "Father, into your hands I entrust my spirit" (Lk 23:46)—but from womb to tomb, what Karl Rahner once called "dying in installments."

Go forth, then, with fresh confidence, aware with St. Paul that you "can do all things," but only "through [the Lord] who strengthens" you (Phil 4:13). And the Lord will strengthen you, if . . . if you cast all your hope on him.

My sister and brothers: Through the years that lie ahead, God lead you, God feed you, God speed you.

Manresa-on-Severn
Annapolis, Maryland
May 22, 1992

9
CELEBRATE OUR JOY
Sixth Sunday of Easter (A)

- Acts 8:5–8, 14–17
- 1 Peter 3:15–18
- John 14:15–21

My theme for this homily does not derive directly from the biblical readings just proclaimed to you. It takes its rise from the prayer that opened our liturgy this evening: "Ever-living God, help us to celebrate our joy in the resurrection of the Lord . . . ." To *celebrate* our joy assumes that we *have* it. Where is this Easter joy to be found? What exactly is supposed to give us joy? Is joy still realistic when so much misery surrounds us from our own streets to the bombed-out buildings in Bosnia?? Any serious attempt to justify joy, to make it real, has to begin with the resurrection of Jesus, must move from there to our own resurrection, should then confront some genuine obstacles to joy.

I

First, the resurrection of Jesus. Here is where joy is rooted. St. Paul saw this clearly, stated it shockingly: "If Christ has not been raised, then our proclamation has been in vain and your faith has been in vain"—empty, without content, without basis, without truth. "We are even found to be misrepresenting God, because we testified of God that He raised Christ" (1 Cor 15:14–15). If Christ is not alive, gloriously alive, alive in the fulness of his humanity right now, go home. For our Creed makes no sense—"On the third day he rose again"; the words of consecration, "This is my body," are spoken over a dead Christ; and the wafer you receive in your hands or on your tongue, "The body of Christ," is sheer bread, nothing more.

42

But the fact is, the Jesus who gasped out his life on a bloody cross, the Jesus who lay lifeless in the arms of his mother, is dead no longer. Remember that marvelous closing scene in the musical *Godspell*? Like the apostles and Mary Magdalene running around the audience like crazy, you too can shout for joy, "He's alive! He's alive!"

I suspect some of us may have difficulty recapturing for ourselves the tearful joy of Jesus' mother when he stood before her gloriously alive;[1] the reverent delight of Magdalene when he said so simply, "Mary" (Jn 20:16); the awed amazement of the apostles when he came through the locked door and "showed them his hands and his side" (Jn 20:20); the quiet happiness of the seven on the shore when he said, "Come and have breakfast" (Jn 21:12); perhaps even the disbelief of Thomas before he exclaimed with all his heart, "My Lord and my God!" (Jn 20:28).

But it is precisely this kind of joy we must recapture. For a profound spirituality, it's just not enough to accept the resurrection of Jesus with my intellect, even inspired by faith. At some moments I should feel it in my flesh, get goose-pimples on my skin, erupt with a joy that cannot be contained. I ought at some point react like the Greek inventor Archimedes, racing naked into the street and shouting "*Eureka!* I have found it!" Have I found the risen Jesus, not simply as an object of belief, not only as an article of the Creed, but as a vibrant man alive with the glorified wounds of his passion? There lies Christian joy unconfined.

II

This leads directly into my second point: my own resurrection. I am not speaking simply or primarily of the resurrection that awaits us after death. I mean the Entrance Song the liturgy commends for this Sunday, a verse borrowed from Isaiah: "Speak out with a voice of joy; let it be heard to the ends of the earth: The Lord has set His people free, alleluia!" (cf. Isa 48:20).

The Lord has set His people free? A question intrigues me. If George Gallup were to poll the Catholic population, what percentage would say that Catholicism has set them free? How many would point to the restrictive Ten Commandments, the 1399 canons in the Church's law, the Catholic Hospital Directives, the sexual morality from abortion to in vitro fertilization, the petty particulars in our worship, and so on into the night?

I suggest that we have to probe deeper. What you will hear in today's Easter Preface points the way to more profound understanding. There we proclaim that in this Easter season we praise God "with greater joy than ever," that "the joy of the resurrection renews the whole world." Why? Because

> In [Christ] a new age has dawned,
> the long reign of sin is ended,
> a broken world has been renewed,
> and man and woman are once again made whole.

Not that sin is a thing of the past; rather, sin no longer reigns like a despot, a tyrant, over us. With the grace that comes from the crucifixion and resurrection, we are not the slaves of sin; we can overcome. If we sin, we do so freely. If we are genuinely sorry, we are forgiven. Not that brokenness is utterly healed; rather that with the grace of Christ we need no longer be torn within, schizophrenics, repeating St. Paul's anguished presentation of human history: human history without Christ and then human history with Christ. Without Christ:

> I do not understand my own actions. For I do not do what I want, but I do the very thing I hate . . . . I do not do the good I want, but the evil I do not want is what I do . . . . I delight in the law of God in my inmost self, but I see in my members another law at war with the law of my mind, making me captive to the law of sin that dwells in my members. . . .

Then with Christ: "Who will rescue me from this doomed body? Thank God! [It is done] through Jesus Christ our Lord!" (Rom 7:15:25).[2]

On a more positive note, mull over Jesus' promise in today's Gospel: "Because I have life, you also will have life" (Jn 14:19).[3] The Christian stress in your existence and mine should not rest on sin. Not that sin has fled entirely; rather that the reason why Jesus came, why he lived and died, why he made it possible for us to triumph over sin, was, in his own words, "that [you] may have life and have it to the full" (Jn 10:10).

This "life," what is it? Listen again to today's Gospel, the promise of Jesus: "You will know that I am in my Father, and you are in me, and I am in you" (Jn 14:20). And he will go on to say: "If [you] love me, [you] will keep my word, and my Father will love [you], and we will come to [you] and make our home with [you]" (v. 23). It is simply the thrilling declaration of what it means to be alive in Christ. Not a strong heartbeat, fine muscle tone, energy to burn. It is the triune God dwelling in you as in a home, making of you a temple of God as truly as is the tabernacle in this church. St. Paul insists on it: "You are the temple of the living God" (2 Cor 6:16). "Do you not know that you are God's temple and that God's Spirit dwells in you? . . . God's temple is holy, and you are that temple" (1 Cor 3:16–17).

This is what it means for man and woman to be "once again made whole": Your flesh and your spirit are alive with the presence of the living God, of the risen Christ. This is not romantic poetry; this is Gospel truth. Little wonder Paul could cry, "If [you] are in Christ, you are a new creature" (2 Cor 5:17); this state in which you live is "a new creation" (Gal 6:15). If you and I could only conquer our Anglo-Saxon embarrassment about our feelings, we might well race around the streets of northwest Washington shouting not simply "*He's* alive!" but "*I'm* alive! I'm *alive!*"

III

And so to our third point: What obstacles stand in the way of such an experience, such deeply felt Christian joy? Some awfully powerful ones. Try telling a poor mother to rejoice as she cradles her malnourished child, helpless to feed his hunger. Try Easter joy on 36 million refugees across the world. Try selling Easter joy to Catholics who are frustrated by the Church that is supposed to reveal and implement the freedom the gospel proclaims: marriage laws, annulment hang-ups, liturgies that fail to inspire, homilies dull as dishwater, an all-male priesthood, pastoral insensitivity, priestly pederasty.

In 52 years of priesting, I have felt it all, been terribly discouraged by the human failings, my own and others', that keep us from experiencing the joy that filled the flesh and spirit of Jesus as he rose alive from the rock that unique Sunday morning. I do not come to you with a hatful of answers. I do know that the joy Jesus promised to his disciples and to us, "You have sorrow now; but I will see you again, and your hearts will rejoice, and your joy no one will take from you" (Jn 16:22)—such joy is possible for everyone who believes, is God's gift to all of us if only we will surrender our whole selves totally to him. Rather than try to prove this, let me tell you a movingly true story.

This past Thursday I received a letter from a brother Jesuit, a fellow of the Woodstock Theological Center located at Georgetown University. He recalled how last year elaborate surgery had been done on his right leg to remove a tumor and build a new knee. Aggressive chemotherapy followed. Rehabilitation began and went well, and he moved ahead fairly rapidly from wheelchair and crutches to a cane. A favorable end seemed in sight, with only checkups and cat-scans ahead to report progress and monitor any metastasis. Hopes were high on metastasis, because the tumor when removed in December had been found 99.9% dead. But when the first check was done on March 10, spots were found on his chest. Major surgery was done immediately to remove material from both lungs. The pathology report: metastasis. Another cat-scan, at the end of April: two new areas of activity in the right lung. And now, aggressive chemotherapy one week a month. . . . He writes: "And so the journey continues. I struggle to make it a pilgrimage." Then he shared with us one particular prayer: "You helping, Lord, I can do the next thing. Let me be heartfelt in doing it, and so find joy, and love."

Be heartfelt in doing the next thing, and so find joy, and love. Allied to this, I can add only one suggestion more, from my own personal existence. Joy, the joy of Jesus, the joy of being alive in Christ, is least likely to possess me when I let life revolve around *me*—my hiatus hernia, my hurt feelings, lack of appreciation, slights, rebuffs, an unfavorable review of my latest book, the hundred-and-one daily challenges that make us turn in on ourselves. Joy returns only when I turn outward, as Jesus did—turn to others, especially the less fortunate images of Christ who experience far more of his crucifixion than of his resurrection. Joy returns when I can bring a smile to a child who has rarely felt love, work with a teenager drug-addicted, hug a once-vigorous adult AIDS-afflicted, bring hope to one of the downtrodden who see no future. Or just be reasonably human to someone I don't especially like.

Good friends, besides the traditional taxes and death, there are two other realities of which we can be certain: (1) God will ceaselessly surprise us, and not always delightfully; (2) no matter how unwelcome the surprise, God will always be there—a Father (or Mother) who shaped us for joy, a Jesus who died that we might experience his joy, a Holy Spirit who is the dynamism within us that engenders joy.

Before Easter ends, resolve that for you it will never end. An infallible sign that Easter is still yours is the joy that lights your whole being because you are alive. Alive in Christ. Let's *celebrate* that joy now by sharing joyously in the central act of our worship: God with us in our gathering, Jesus alive on our table, in our hands, on our tongues, in our hearts.

Holy Trinity Church
Washington, D.C.
May 16, 1993

ORDINARY TIME

10

WHAT IN GOD'S EYE HE OR SHE IS
Second Sunday of the Year (A)

- Isaiah 49:3, 5–6
- 1 Corinthians 1:1–3
- John 1:29–34

In today's readings two prophets come together neatly: Isaiah and John the Baptist. They come together with a surprisingly similar message. A message that touches not only the people who heard them in person but us later folk who hear them from a book. So then, let's focus on (1) Isaiah, (2) John, (3) you and me. Put another way, three questions: (1) What does the Old Testament prophet have to say? (2) How does this mesh with the New Testament? (3) What might all this say to Christian living today?

I

First, the Old Testament prophet.[1] Here is a messenger of God preaching during the latter part of the exile in Babylon, around 550 before Christ. To whom is he preaching? To "a people discouraged, dazed, and destitute, severely tempted to apostasy. [This] people in exile must be consoled, not punished; their faith must be sustained, not further tried."[2] They must even see themselves after the exile as possibly a world religion, leaping beyond their native soil. It is in this context, within this situation, that you must listen once again to our passage—but this time with ears utterly open to the Spirit:

> [The Lord] said to me, "You are my servant,
>   Israel, in whom I will be glorified."
> And now the Lord says,
>   who formed me in the womb to be His servant,

51

        to bring Jacob back to Him,
            and that Israel might be gathered to Him. . . .
        He says:
        "It is too light a thing that you should be my servant
            to raise up the tribes of Jacob
            and to restore the survivors of Israel;
        I will give you as a light to the nations,
            that my salvation may reach to the end of the earth."
                                            (Isa 49:3, 5–6)

This is the second of the famous four Servant Songs. To whom is the Lord speaking? Who is the servant here? All faithful Israelites, but especially the disciples of the prophet—in a very particular way, the prophet himself.[3] In what sense is Israel to be "a light to the nations"? Listen to the Lord in Isaiah: "You are my witnesses" (Isa 43:10). Witnesses in what sense? By your tenacious survival and by your still more wondrous resurgence, you will witness to the world that Yahweh alone is God, that Yahweh alone is savior.[4]

This was true before Christ, and it remains true after Christ. Before Christ was born, the Israelites bore witness to the world around them. Witness to what? To the reality and the power of their God. How? In their escape from Egypt and the tyranny of Pharaoh, in their seemingly endless desert march to the Promised Land, in their return to Jerusalem after the captivity in Babylon, in their return time and again from their sinfulness and their idolatry, in their efforts to live the first great commandment of the law, to love the Lord their God with all their heart and mind, with all their soul and strength.

After Christ was born, a fascinating fact. From the 12th century on, the more common view among the Jews has been to see in Isaiah's Servant the Jewish people as a whole, or at least the righteous element among them; and in the suffering of the Servant, not only the agony of the Babylonian captivity, but all the sufferings of the Jewish people to the time of the particular rabbi discussing the text. For down into our own time the Jewish people have witnessed to their God: through every Jewish ghetto ever structured by Christians; every forced baptism; every Crusade to liberate the Holy Places; every Good Friday massacre; every forced exodus like 1492; every portrait of Shylock exacting his pound of flesh; every accusation of Christ-killer and God-killer; every Dachau and every Auschwitz; every death for conscience' sake; every back turned and shoulder shrugged; every sneer or slap or curse.

My reaction? Not a patronizing "Some of my best friends are Jews." Rather, St. Paul's pointed question and resounding reply: "Has

God rejected His people? By no means!'' (Rom 11:1). I confess, I do not know what God has in mind for them, whether they will ever recognize Jesus as their Messiah. I do know, from a half century of experience, that they are not simply to be thanked for giving us Jesus and his mother. If we have minds to recapture Jewish history, if we have eyes to see real Jews, if we have ears to hear the agonizing cries from ghettos and gas chambers, we may begin to understand God's promise to them, "I will give you as a light to the nations" (Isa 49:6).

II

Our second prophet, John the Baptist, introduces us into the New Testament. I am not sure I would have fraternized with John, even though he was related to Jesus. His "garment of camel's hair with a leather belt" (Mt 3:4) was not the kind you wear to a Redskins game. His diet of "locusts and wild honey" brings no saliva to my lips. A teetotaler, he would likely axe every barrel of Bud on our beaches. A reformer, he keeps emerging from the wilderness shouting "Repent!" (Mt 3:2).

Still, I cannot escape him. Why? Because, like Isaiah, he is a witness: "I myself have seen and have testified that this is the Son of God" (Jn 1:34). Because his whole life has a single focus; he keeps pointing to Jesus.

All his life he pointed to Jesus. You remember how Mary, newly pregnant, rushed to the hill country to help her kinswoman Elizabeth six months with child. How, at her greeting, the child John leaped for joy in Elizabeth's womb. Unseen, unheard, he was already pointing to Jesus. You remember how he told the priests and Levites, "I am not the Christ. Among you stands one whom you do not know. . . . I am not worthy to untie the thong of his sandal" (Jn 1:20, 26–27). Always "He must increase, but I must decrease" (Jn 3:30). Today's Gospel is a perfect example. With the Jews surrounding him, questioning him, anxious to learn just who and what he is, John sees Jesus coming in his direction, declares simply yet profoundly, "Look! Here is the Lamb of God; here is the one who takes away the sin of the world" (Jn 1:29).

Even in death John pointed to Jesus. Herod thought he had seen the end of John when he had him beheaded. Not much later Herod was puzzled; marvels had been told him of a man named Jesus. His response? "John I beheaded; but who is this about whom I hear such things?" Luke adds, "And [Herod] tried to see [Jesus]" (Lk 9:9). Yes, even in death John pointed to Jesus.

Little wonder that the evangelist John inserts the baptizer John into the Prologue that opens his Gospel: "There was a man sent from God, whose name was John. He came as a witness to testify to the light [to God-in-flesh], so that all might believe through him. He himself was not the light, but he came to testify to the light. The true light, which enlightens everyone, was coming into the world" (Jn 1:6–9).

III

Now for you and me. Like the Jewish people, we are called to bear witness to God, to God's presence in the world, to God's love for the world. Like John the Baptist, we have for mission to point to Christ.

We point to Christ in myriad ways. Augustine and Aquinas pointed to Christ with their theology, the six Jesuit martyrs and their lay associates in El Salvador with their blood. Gerard Manley Hopkins pointed to Christ with his poetry, Michelangelo with his "Pietà." A Trappist can point to Christ from the silence of a pigsty, a Jesuit (God forgive him) is more likely to talk about Christ. John of the Cross pointed to Christ from Carmelite contemplation, cancer-ridden Sister Thea Bowman from the wheelchair she propelled across the country. Politicians can point to Christ from the pinnacles of power, professors by touching young minds to the true, the beautiful, and the good. Doctors point to Christ when they lay healing hands on a broken body in process of redemption, lawyers when they link love of law to the law of love. Scientists point to Christ when they make technology serve God's people, environmentalists when they reverence the nature that speaks of Christ. This extralong weekend we honor Martin Luther King Jr., who pointed to Christ by eschewing violence and loving those who hated him. And—I've said this before—perhaps the most unforgettable Christian I have ever met was a lady who for 25 years pointed smilingly to Christ from a bed of all but total paralysis.

Clearly, there are countless ways of witnessing to Christ. Yet precisely here we uncover a paradox, if not an out-and-out contradiction, in our everyday existence. It is only rational creatures, creatures with intelligence and love, who fail to point to the God in whom they believe; it is Christians who do not see that they are created to

witness to Christ. Do you remember what St. Paul proclaimed to the
Christians of Rome? "Ever since the creation of the world, [God's]
eternal power and divine nature, invisible though they are, have
been understood and seen through the things [God] has made"
(Rom 1:20). Psalm 19 announced it in syllables that the centuries
have ceaselessly sung: "The heavens are telling the glory of God"
(Ps 19:1). If I may paraphrase Paul and the Psalmist in my own
rhetoric, God saw that the visible could image the Invisible, that a
whirlwind could reflect God's power, a mountain mirror God's majesty, surging waves God's irresistibleness, a star-flecked sky God's
breath-taking loveliness. Yes, each blade of grass, each panther
prowling the forest, each wondrous waterfall is God's struggle to
paint God's own portrait. The way we strange folk called theologians
phrase it, there are "traces" of God in everything God has fashioned—vestiges of God, God's footprints.

And we? We are not vague, distant traces of an all-powerful
Creator. Scripture shouts that we are *like* God, have been shaped
"in the image of God" (Gen 1:27). For centuries theologians have
wrestled with that awesome declaration from Genesis: What can it
possibly mean? We have discovered our likeness to God in the
breadth of our intelligence, in our God-given ability to love as Jesus
loved, in the freedom we have to choose what we will love, in our
power to imagine, to create, to shape our world; yes, even in our
grace to suffer somewhat as the God-man suffered, to cry to God
like him from the depths of our gethsemane, "Remove this cup
from me; yet, not my will but yours be done" (Lk 22:42). And when
all the deep thinking exhausts me, I fall back on Jesuit poet Hopkins
singing that the just man, the just woman, "acts in God's eye what
in God's eye he [or she] is":

> Christ. For Christ plays in ten thousand places,
> Lovely in limbs, and lovely in eyes not his
> To the Father through the features of men's faces.[5]

God plays in our world through God's images, through us. The point
I want to make is this: In the eyes of God, the genuine witness is not
so much the what as the who. You point to Christ by who you *are*.
You point to Christ by being Christlike. Not slavish imitation, walking
in sandals to crucifixion in Jerusalem. You point to Christ by living
what he lived: "I seek [to do] not my own will but the will of the
One who sent me" (Jn 5:30).

You know, you will rarely hear a more exciting compliment than when someone says to you, "You remind me of someone. You remind me of . . . Jesus." That's not pious mush; that's our Christian vocation.

Holy Trinity Church
Washington, D.C.
January 17, 1993

11
PREACH THE GOSPEL
AND CAST OUT DEMONS
Second Week of the Year, Friday (A)

- Hebrews 8:6–13
- Mark 3:13–19

For practical reasons this "farewell discourse"[1] must be brief. Pungent perhaps, but brief—if only to "get me to the plane on time." So then, immediately into Mark. His focus? The selection of 12 special friends of Jesus, from Peter who would deny him, through Thomas who would doubt him, to Judas who would betray him. Three buzz words: (1) preach, (2) exorcise, (3) apostle. Not in vague abstraction; rather, in the context of priesthood.

I

First, a priest, like the original apostles, is commissioned by Christ "to preach" (Mk 3:14). In fact, Vatican II declared that proclaiming the gospel is our "primary duty" (*primum officium*).[2] Since Latin enjoys neither a definite nor an indefinite article, you may debate till the cows come home: Is preaching *the* primary duty of a priest or *a* primary duty? No matter; at least it should rate high, even if uncomfortably high, among priestly priorities.[3]

But does it? All too many of our genuinely devoted faithful tend to agree with the split between proclamation and ongoing life that disturbed the Catholic president of the University of Rochester, George Dennis O'Brien. In a book entitled provocatively *God and the New Haven Railway and Why Neither One Is Doing Very Well,*[4] he noted that most people on the train station are not likely to see church service as "one of the livelier, more salvational times of week." Their appraisal is more likely to be "Saturday Night Live, Sunday Morning Deadly."

And yet St. Paul insists that faith comes through hearing; no hearing, no faith. Apart from PVS, permanent vegetative state, I see no valid justification for the unprepared homily. Not time, not other duties, not even most illnesses. A priest friend of mine in Connecticut is one of the most powerful preachers in my experience. MS, speech impediment, several other afflictions—these are simply gifts of the Holy Spirit; they give him added dynamite to proclaim the gospel as *God's* Word on feeble human lips. Oh yes, it takes sweat and blood and tears. Prepare in dread earnest and it will murder sleep, bleed your ulcer, induce diarrhea. But it may not be declined, under peril of maiming your ministry. Hours of agony indeed, but also that moment of ecstasy when God's light goes on in the eyes of an individual or a community.

Do not tell me that our Catholic people do not like sermons. What they do not like is a bad sermon. And a bad sermon is not merely laying another clerical egg; a bad sermon can force faith to flicker, can harm hope, can lessen love. Bad sermons are driving thousands of Catholics to the Pentecostals. Why? Because they have fire in the belly.

II

Second, Jesus sent the apostles to cast out demons. Exorcising devils of the biblical stripe is a rare event in our day, and scholars of all stripes debate whether fallen angels are actually prowling our earth in search of souls. But one devilish reality is undeniable. I mean idols that undermine or supplant the one true God. The molten calf the Israelites worshiped in the wilderness while Moses dialogued with the Almighty on the mountain is symbolic of the gods that people our world, at times infest even our temples.

I am not pushing priest/preachers to play Savanarola, to flay the believing folk in front of us. I am not applauding the passionate young seminarian in the movie *Mass Appeal* raging against the blue hair of women, their mink hats and cashmere coats. But, as disciples of Jesus, must we not remind our people of the peril that pervades possessions and power? It took a brain cancer to open the eyes of powerful politician Lee Atwater, open his eyes to the 80s as the decade of insatiable acquisition; he died repenting his own. It was a Supreme Court, not the Sermon on the Mount, not our sermons, that decreed an effective "No longer" to white supremacy, to black slavery, to second-class citizenship for women. Must we be silent while power structures rape the earth that sustains us, destroy legally 1.6 million developing humans each year, keep every fifth child in abject poverty, hold 37 million Americans without healthcare, balance the scales of Lady Justice in favor of the moneyed, yes even gas or hang criminals for vengeance' sake? Shall we be silent when rugged individualism threatens not only our country but our church community?

The examples are legion; they dot the front pages of our papers each day. With the gospel of Christ in our hands, what shall we say to the idols that are conquering our culture, wasting our families?

III

Third, the priest as apostle. An apostle was one who had seen the Lord, could bear witness to the risen Christ. That is why, when the Eleven had to choose someone to take the place of Judas, we hear Peter proclaiming to 120 of his brethren: "One of the men who have accompanied us during all the time that the Lord Jesus went in and out among us, beginning from the baptism of John until the day when he was taken up from us—one of these must become a witness with us to his resurrection" (Acts 1:21–22). They had to select someone who had walked with Jesus, talked with him, listened to him, suffered with him, experienced his cross and his rising from the rock.

Those unique days are long gone. Jesus no longer walks the ways of Palestine, is not visible in Palm Beach or St. Paul, Minnesota, cannot be handled in Harlem or Honolulu. And still, an apostle in a genuine sense is a man or woman who has seen the Lord. Not indeed pressed flesh with him, but has actually experienced him. Has not only come to know *about* Jesus, the way, say, a theologian might, but has come to *know him,* the way Peter, James, and John did; I mean, a knowing that is loving. And loving him, wants to bear passionate witness, testimony to a living Lord.

This is what made apostles of countless women and men down the ages: Sir Thomas More and Archbishop Oscar Romero, Teresa of Avila and Thérèse of Lisieux and Teresa of Calcutta, Dorothy Day and Dr. Tom Dooley, Cardinal Newman and Bishop Neumann, Mother Seton and Mother Cabrini—the list is endless. Each had experienced God, had touched and been touched. Each realized in actual living the acute insight of metaphysician Jacques Maritain: The height, the acme, the pinnacle of human knowing is not conceptual, it is experiential. Very simply, man/woman *feels* God. And so for you and me. A priest is an apostle. But not automatically by ordination. We are indeed commissioned by a special sacrament to preach the good news and cast out today's devils, today's idols. But we preach effectively, we expel demons actually, only if we have experienced our good Lord, feel his presence lighting up our darkened intelligence, putting fire in our bellies.

Let's pray for that, my brothers. It's crucial to our priesthood. It's particularly critical at a time when priesthood is not the most attractive of vocations, when priests are dartboards for every sort of accusation, when discouragement can be a nightly recurrence, when all too many thousands of our brothers have decided that the privilege is not proportionate to the pain.

Dear Lord, in this farewell Eucharist, grace us to see you more clearly, love you more dearly, follow you more nearly. Force us freely to *feel* your presence—in our gathering together, in the Word proclaimed, in the bread transformed into your body, in the Host within our hearts. Then send us forth to proclaim news that is excitingly good, to cast out of ourselves and our people the idols we have erected in your stead, to witness to your risen reality because we have experienced you . . . alive!

Our Lady of Florida Spiritual Center
North Palm Beach, Florida
January 22, 1993

12
SMALLEST OF SEEDS,
LARGEST OF SHRUBS
Third Week of the Year, Friday (A)

- Hebrews 10:32–39
- Mark 4:26–34

Today the Holy Spirit sends you forth, sends you on mission.[1] Not for the first time. Most of you were sent forth when you were ordained to ministerial priesthood, a few when ordained as permanent deacons, all of you at baptism. For, as Léon-Joseph Cardinal Suenens insisted 25 years ago, the greatest day in the life of a pope is not his coronation but his baptism, the day of his mission "to live the Christian life in obedience to the gospel."[2] As you sally forth once again, filled afresh with the just Word in God's own Book, I commend to you a swift meditation on today's remarkably pertinent readings: first Mark, then Hebrews.

I

In proclaiming the gospel, you and I plant a seed. What seed? The Word of God. As we humans plant it, with our human weaknesses, it is a small seed. It does not always fall on fertile soil, for the ground is often thorny, often rocky; at times the soil has no depth. So many of our hearers couldn't be less interested. I recall the pessimistic advice of Jesuit William O'Malley: "Presume disinterest. Presume that [your audience] would rather feed their children to crocodiles than listen to you."[3] Some are actively hostile—to the message or the man, to what smacks of politics or a sexism intrinsic to a male priesthood.

And still the seed must be planted. Oh yes, all sorts of satans will come and carry off what was sown; men and women will listen joyfully in the beginning but will falter under pressure or persecution; lust for possessions or the anxieties of sheer survival will choke the seed from the States to Somalia. Jesus himself experienced all of this: fellow Nazarenes casting him over a cliff after a sermon in their synagogue, relatives shouting he was mad, men in power plotting to kill him. But as with Jesus, so with us, there are always those who listen to the Word, take it to heart, and bear fruit. You've experienced it; God has used your words to melt hearts of stone.

Precisely here lies a crucial reality, a critical realization: It is always God who gives the increase. Channels of grace we are indeed, but grace is God-given or it is not given at all. It is in God's good time that "the smallest of all the seeds on the earth . . . springs up to become the largest of all shrubs" (Mk 4:31–32). It is in God's good time that preaching the just Word brings about a world more just, flowers into a fuller reign of God over human hearts.

Not without us. Hence the need for men and women who turn to the Lord each day, men and women who day after day hone the talents large and small that God has given us, men and women with fire for God and people in their bellies, men and women who yearn to see Jesus more clearly, to love him more dearly, to follow him more nearly.

In the context of the kingdom, today's parables, the parable of the Growing Seed and the parable of the Mustard Seed, put heavy emphasis on God: God's action is hidden, is gradual, is "without visible cause."[4] Therefore, Jesus implies, don't be discouraged, don't be anxious, don't be impatient! And this brings us back to the reading from Hebrews.

II

As with the Christians of the first century, so with us who have committed ourselves to proclaiming a tough gospel of God, a gospel that turns our dominant culture on its head, makes the centerpieces of our society the homeless and the hopeless and the helpless, the imprisoned and the impoverished, the refugee and the retarded, the minority and the marginalized, the child still in the womb and the aged in life's twilight. Like the Christians extolled in Hebrews, we too "have endured [or will endure] a hard struggle with sufferings" (Heb 10:32), have been or will be "publicly exposed to abuse" (v. 33) for simply preaching Christ or for preaching him badly. Some, like Eileen,[5] have "even joined in the sufferings of those in prison" (v. 34). But the inspired author encourages us: "Do not surrender that confidence of yours . . . . To do God's will and receive what was promised, you need patience" (v. 36). The "just man [and the just woman] will live by faith, and if [they] draw back, [God] takes no pleasure in [them]" (v. 38).

My dear friend Father John Courtney Murray, dead these 25 years, was principal architect of Vatican II's Declaration on Religious Freedom. But for a decade before that significant but modest emergence of the kingdom—Murray said it brought the Roman Catholic Church abreast of the 19th century—he suffered intensely from the wrath of Roman power. That is why I treasure his frequent farewell to me: "Courage, Walter! It's far more important than intelligence." And his inspired insight: "As with the bishops in council, so with us: We begin with a large amount of confusion and uncertainty, must therefore pass through a period of tension and conflict, but can expect to end with a certain measure of light and of joy."

Once again, the courage is not of our own making—an Anglo-Saxon stiff upper lip. *This* courage comes only from God. It stems from that thrilling declaration in the First Epistle of Peter: "Blessed be the God and Father of our Lord Jesus Christ! By His great mercy He has given us a new birth into a *living hope* which draws its life from the resurrection of Jesus Christ . . . . Although you have not seen him, you love him; and even though you do not see him now, you believe in him and rejoice with an indescribable and glorious joy" (1 Pet 1:3, 8).

Sally forth, then, as the earliest Christians sallied forth. With confidence, because it is God who gives the increase to the people to whom you proclaim the gospel. With courage, because it is precisely through suffering that your words kindle a flame in your people. With joy, inexpressible joy, because you share—all of you, ordained and lay—in the priesthood of Christ, in the passion of Christ, in the apostolate of Christ. Can you imagine a more profound joy, a more exciting joy, this side of heaven?

FINAL BLESSING
From Isaiah 43

Thus says the Lord who created you, who formed you:
Be not afraid, for I have redeemed you;
    I have called you by name, you are mine.
When you pass through the waters, I will be with you;
    and through the rivers, they shall not overwhelm you.
When you walk through fire, you shall not be burned,

and the flame shall not consume you.
For I am the Lord your God, your Savior;
   you are precious in my eyes, and I love you.
Be not afraid,
   for I am with you.
Lead out the people who are blind, though they have eyes,
   who are deaf, though they have ears.
You are my witnesses,
   my servants whom I have chosen.
Remember not the events of the past,
   or consider the things of old.
See, I am about to do something new;
   now it springs forth; do you not perceive it?

San Pedro Center
Winter Park, Florida
January 24, 1993

13

BEFORE YOU ARE LIFE AND DEATH
Sixth Sunday of the Year (A)

- Sirach 15:15-20
- 1 Corinthians 2:6-10
- Matthew 5:17-37

I don't know how you reacted—or even if you reacted at all—to the Old Testament reading: "Before [you] are life and death, and whichever [you] choose will be given to [you]" (Sir 15:17). Tell that to the waves of Haitians vainly trying to escape hunger, fear, and gunfire. Tell that to the Muslims in Bosnia, dying by the thousands from Serbian massacre. Tell that to the children of Somalia starving to death, legs like storks'. Tell that to the Sudanese, a half million dead from war and famine. Tell that to the people of Armenia, prosperous under Russian rule, threatened again with genocide by their neighbors. Tell that to the children of America, one out of five "living" below the poverty line. Tell that to the hundreds of men on death row for vengeance' sake.

Choose life? There is something of a contradiction here. It is not solved by saying that Ben Sira was speaking to faithful Jews, not to the unfortunate down the ages. The words are addressed to all of us who claim to be alive. So then, three questions: (1) What is this "life," what is this "death," which Ben Sira claims we have the power to choose? (2) What, if anything, does the New Testament add to the Old? (3) How does today's Gospel concretize all that?[1]

I

First, Sirach's "life and death." "Life" here does not mean primarily the period from conception to your last breath. Ben Sira is not saying that, if you want to, you can choose to live like Moses for

65

120 years, or like Grandma Moses for 101. What "life" means Moses told the Israelites while they were struggling toward the Promised Land: "loving the Lord your God, obeying [the Lord], holding fast to [the Lord]; for that means life to you" (Deut 30:20). This is what the God of this chosen people meant by being alive. And "death" in our text is not my last gasp on earth. "Death" is idolatry in its myriad modes: not only the Israelites in the desert worshiping a golden calf, but our contemporary idols from possessions to popularity to power. In God's eyes, to die is to set up a creature in place of God.

That is why the Psalmist can say that the Lord's "steadfast love is better than [sheer] living" (Ps 63:3). That is why the more spiritual of the Israelites preferred above all else "the happiness of living his [or her] entire life in [God's] temple where one day before [God's] face, consecrated to [God's] praise, 'is worth more than a thousand' [Ps 84:10] elsewhere."[2] That is why from the darkness of exile Ezekiel could cry out: "As I live, says the Lord God, I have no pleasure in the death of the wicked, but that the wicked turn back from their ways and live, turn back from your evil ways" (Ezek 33:11). To be truly alive was to turn to God. And listen to the prophet Amos: "Thus says the Lord to the house of Israel: Seek me and live" (Amos 5:4). For Israel, to be alive was to be searching for God.

II

Second, what, if anything, does the New Testament add to the Old? Very simply, life at its acme is life in Christ. This is not pious sentimentality; it is the only thing that makes Christian sense. Let me explain.

You know what it means to be alive on a sheerly natural level, simply as a human being. You are not genuinely alive simply because there is life in you. This powerful insight was captured decades ago in a novel by Gabriel Fielding. As the review in *Time* magazine put it:

The title of this exciting new novel [*In the Time of Greenbloom*] sounds like an archaic phrase in celebration of spring. But Greenbloom is a man, not a season. Greenbloom is awareness, sentience, ceaseless war on man's most deadly enemy, which is not cancer or heart disease, but habit—all the routines of thinking, feeling and doing that enable humans to get through life without living it.[3]

I am not genuinely alive simply because there is life in me. Simply because I watch a time clock from nine to five, or a Late Show from eleven-thirty to one. Simply because my standard of living is high, my cholesterol low. Simply because I offer the Sacrifice of the Mass each day, or am perpetually poor, chaste, and obedient. Simply because I sit at a CEO's desk or build bridges, wash diapers or trump aces. Simply because I eat and dance, weep and laugh, curse and bless. Simply because I am going through the motions of living—"all the routines of thinking, feeling and doing that enable humans to get through life without living it."

The point is: I am not genuinely alive simply because I am not medically dead. What I do must have meaning for me. Whether I do it once or a thousand times, be it dull or exciting, comedy or tragedy, entertainment or crucifixion, what I do must be humanly done. I mean, it must be compounded of intelligence and love. There must be understanding in it, and heart. Otherwise 90 years are no better than nine—only longer. Otherwise I can be replaced—by another machine.

But in the Christian scheme of things, understanding and heart are not quite enough. Every dictator from Herod to Hitler, from Attila the Hun to Saddam Hussein, has had purpose and passion, has been amazingly alive, whether he has focused on newborn babies in Bethlehem or on aged folk in Auschwitz, on powerful Romans or on defenseless Kurds. Sinners can be astonishingly alive, especially in their sin: Saul "breathing threats and murder against the disciples of the Lord" (Acts 9:1); young Augustine "in love with love"[4] in semipagan Carthage; every fictional devil with the morals of James Bond. Unbelievers are often amazingly alive: an artist at her easel, an archeologist at his digs, a man or woman who thrills to love. Here is life, and not routine; here are mind and heart, purpose and passion. And still it is not enough. For, in the Christian vision, to live is to "know the only true God, and Jesus Christ whom [God has] sent" (Jn 17:3).

But, as the apostle John makes clear, to know God, to know Christ, is not a matter of mind, cold intellect, book knowledge. John put it bluntly: "Whoever does not love does not know God" (1 Jn 4:8). I do not really know God unless I love God; I do not really know Christ unless I love Christ. Oh yes, I can know *about* God, *about* Christ, from intense study; but this is not the same as knowing *them*, not the same as a close encounter, an intimate relationship. I shall not get to heaven because I am a theologian, or even because some of you generous folk give "high fives" to my homilies. I shall get to heaven only if I love God, if I love Christ, above all else, only if I love the human images of God and of Christ at least as much as I love myself. It is then that mind and heart, purpose and passion, reach Christian heights; it is then that I am alive in Christ. It is then that, as the New Testament declares, my "life is hidden with Christ in God" (Col 3:3), I "share in God's nature" (1 Pet 1:4), the Spirit of God "dwells in" me (Rom 8:11), and "nothing in all creation can separate [me] from the love of God in Christ Jesus our Lord" (Rom 8:38). It is then that I can say with St. Paul, "For me, living is Christ" (Phil 1:21).

A fifth-century pope and preacher, Leo the Great, used to challenge his listeners, "Remember your dignity." May I too urge you, "Remember your dignity"? Whoever you are, whatever your station in society, however much you lack in mind or body, in personality or power, through a God-man who died for you you have been graced to choose life—to live the life that Christ lives.

III

This suggests my third question: How does today's Gospel concretize all that, bring it down to the nuts and bolts of everyday living? Our brief Gospel passage[5] is part of the Sermon on the Mount that has confronted us these past few Sundays. Now you may debate till doomsday whether that "sermon" contains only absolute commands, or is a mixture of commands ("Don't commit murder or adultery") and counsels ("Never swear an oath"; "Don't let your fasting be known to others"). A legitimate discussion for some disenchanted evening, but not the core of the Christian question. The heart of the matter is not, what must I do to get into heaven, how little can I do and still sneak past St. Peter's portals? The heart of the matter is, what does it take to be a disciple of Jesus, to see him more clearly, love him more dearly, follow him more nearly? What does it take to be what the disciples of Jesus, you and I, were told to be in last Sunday's Gospel, "the salt of the earth, the light of the world"?

Precisely here the going gets rough. For Jesus is not satisfied if I never commit an external action that violates God's law: if I never take an innocent life, if I never steal someone else's wife. Jesus gets to the roots of immoral activity: what goes on in the human heart. He knows how often violence stems from anger, the emotion that triggers the violence, the feelings that overwhelm reason. If you don't believe it, you haven't been watching your Movie Channel or the nightly news. And so Jesus goes beyond what has been commanded before: "You have heard the commandment imposed on your forefathers, 'You shall not commit murder . . . .' I say to you, 'If you are angry with your brother or sister, you will be liable to judgment' " (Mt 5:21–22). That is why Jesus insists: before worship, friendship; before litigation, reconciliation. That is why St. Paul could counsel his Christians in Ephesus, "Don't let the sun go down on your anger" (Eph 5:26). Wise counsel—for married life, in your office, on the corridors of Georgetown, wherever.[6]

Jesus knows that sexual immorality is not merely an external act. It is not only the visible act of forbidden intercourse that is destructive. Equally destructive is the lustful heart—perhaps even more destructive. Jesus put it bluntly on another occasion: "Out of the heart come evil intentions, murder, adultery, fornication, theft, false witness, slander. These are what defile a person" (Mt 15:19–20). Today's front pages confirm the Christian gospel: To look lustfully is worlds apart from looking lovingly.

These are but two examples of "Choose life," life in Christ, Christian living that goes literally to the heart of the matter. Lent is just ten days away. If you find yourself searching for a Lenten penance both provocative and potentially productive, forget the Slim-Fast, "I Can't Believe It's Yogurt." Mull day by day through the *whole* Sermon on the Mount, Matthew 5 to 7. Discover what it means to be blessed, happy, fortunate in God's eyes; how you can possibly love not only those who admire you but those who hate your guts; how to pray with fresh insight for God's will however much it hurts, for forgiveness on such as have hurt you; how to store up treasures not on earth but in heaven; how to enter life by the narrow gate; how to build your house not on sand but on rock. It's cheaper, and far more effective, than phoning the late-night psychics for an intimate chat.

Good friends in Christ: An Off-Broadway play called *Jeffrey* features a gay young actor-waiter. He grew up thanking God for the joy of sex; now he curses God because "life is suddenly radioactive."[7] Terribly sad, of course; beyond me to experience or to judge. But what is still sadder is a widespread Christian failure to recognize a different, a richer radiant energy, the Christlife that radiates within each of us who has been baptized into Christ. If you are living it consciously now, thank God. If not, then for your joy now and for ever . . . choose life. Not the edge of living; surrender any idols that hold you captive. Choose life in its fulness; choose life in Christ, life with Christ, life for Christ. As we New Yorkers say, "Try it, you'll like it."

Holy Trinity Church
Washington, D.C.
February 14, 1993

14
WOE TO YOU WHO ARE RICH?
Sixth Sunday of the Year (C)

- Jeremiah 17:5–8
- 1 Corinthians 15:12, 16–20
- Luke 6:17, 20–26

Good friends: Over the past month, I experienced a terrible temptation. A temptation difficult to resist. No, it was not sexual; it wasn't
that pleasant. I was tempted to let today's Gospel go, focus on Jeremiah. Why not enjoy the *prophet's* blessing and woe? "Blessed is the
man or woman who trusts in the Lord." "Cursed is [woe to] the man
or woman who trusts in humans, . . . whose heart turns away from
the Lord" (Jer 17:7, 5). Great homiletic stuff. Why ruffle your Sunday
feathers with woe on you if you are well off financially, woe if you
shop at Sutton Place Gourmet, woe if your laugh meter is "off the
wall," woe if everybody likes you? And then wash my hands of it,
blame it all on Jesus.

The problem is, I cannot skip Luke today and pretend I am
preaching the Christian gospel.[1] Not when I am directing a national
project called *Preaching the Just Word,* an effort to move the preaching
of social-justice issues more effectively into all the Catholic pulpits of
our country. But is it now my God-given task to reproach the rich,
savage the well-lined stomach, go for the jugular if you are joyful?
The problem is agonizingly real, for it asks questions basic to Christian
living. So then, suppose we do three things: (1) find out what Luke's
Jesus was saying then, (2) go on to ask what the risen Jesus might be
saying to us now, and (3) try our hand at rephrasing Luke's beatitudes
for our time, our situation.[2]

I

First, what was Luke's Jesus saying then? Here you must be extraordinarily careful. You cannot cut Luke into a thousand pieces, take a paragraph here or there, study it in isolation, and conclude: Ah, here is the real Jesus.

You see, Luke is puzzling. On the one hand, hardly another New Testament writer save "James" speaks so bluntly about material possessions. On this score all too many Christian disciples left Luke less than ecstatic. On the other hand, Luke leaves us puzzled: Who is the real Jesus? There is the radical Jesus: Give it *all* up! Unless you "say good-bye to *all*" you have, you "cannot be a disciple of mine" (Lk 14:33). All of it. "You cannot serve both God and money" (16:13). "It is easier for a camel to pass through the eye of a needle than for a rich man to enter the kingdom of God" (18:25)—the largest of Palestinian animals and the tiniest of openings the Jews knew. It is to the poor that the kingdom of God belongs (6:20). He himself "had nowhere to lay his head" (9:58).

Then there is the moderate Jesus. He wants you to use possessions prudently. One prudent way: Give alms (11:41). Then remember Zacchaeus, small in size but big in bucks: "Look, Sir," he says to Jesus, "half of what I own I give to the poor." Not all I own; half. Jesus' reply? "Today salvation has come to this house" (19:8–9). He had well-to-do friends—Lazarus, Martha, Mary. Galilean women of means provided for him and the Twelve (8:3). This Jesus reminds us of John the Baptist, usually quite radical as he munches locusts in the wilderness. The crowds plead with him when baptized by him, when moved to repentance: "What shall we do?" His reply? Do you have two coats? Give one to the poor (3:10–11). One.

Well now, will the real Jesus please stand up? Which is it to be, no riches or some? Give it all away, or share some of it? Not easy to say. Even Scripture scholars are puzzled. But a liturgy is not a classroom; a homily is not a lecture. And so, while the experts are trying to make exegetical sense out of the paradox, let's see what the paradoxical Jesus might be saying to us today.

II

On the one hand, the radical Jesus must never cease to challenge us. You see, nothing, absolutely nothing, should take precedence over Christ in my life. But history, my history, tells me that there is a peril in any possession, whether it's an adult's million-dollar home or a child's "raggedy Ann," whether it's the presidency or a pastorate, whether it's profound knowledge or a touch of power, my law firm or my ad agency, my books or my stamp collection, my health or my wealth—whatever I "own." The peril? Simply that it's mine, and it can become the center of my existence. It can organize my life, manipulate me, strangle me—to the point where nothing else matters, nobody touches this. When that happens, Christ takes second place. I don't listen, I don't hear his invitation or his command: to give it all up or only half, to care and to share, to let go. The radical Jesus poses a perennial question: What rules my life? Who is king of my heart?

On the other hand, the moderate Jesus fixes my eye on something splendidly positive. I mean the gift I have in anything I possess, anything I "own." Ultimately, whatever is mine (save for sin) is God's gift. Even if it stems from my own fantastic talent, that talent itself owes its origin to God. But a gift of God is not given to be clutched; it is given to be given. The idea is summed up in a thrilling verse from the First Letter of Peter: All Christians should employ (literally, "deacon") the many-splendored charisms they have from God for the advantage of one another, "as good stewards of God's dappled grace" (1 Pet 4:10).

Therein lies the glory of our gifts, therein its Christian possibilities. The theology I have amassed through half a century is not merely *my* theology, packed away in my personal gray matter for my private delight. It is meant to be shared, at times even refuted—if you dare! Each of you is a gifted woman or man—gifted in more ways perhaps than your modesty will admit. It matters not what your specific possessions are: millions or the widow's mite, intelligence or power, beauty or wisdom, faith and hope and love, gentleness and compassion— whatever. What the moderate Jesus tells you is to use your gifts as he invites or commands you. To some he may say: Give away all you have and come, follow me. To others: Share what you possess; use it for your sisters and brothers. Remember, your most precious possession is yourself. Give it away . . . lavishly.

III

This suggests my third point. Let's turn Luke's woes around, rephrase them for today. It could be a profound experience, might even disclose what sort of Christians you and I are.

It's true, in Georgetown the radical Jesus might still say baldly: Woe to you who are rich in money, because you profit from a sinful social structure. Woe to you who are rich in intelligence, because you waste it like the prodigal or use it only to make megabucks. Woe to you who are rich in time, because you squander it in self-pity or to get "bombed." Woe to you who are well-fed, because you are "a privileged part of the way food is unequally spread among humans."[3] Woe to you who are filled, because you rarely experience your own emptiness. Woe to you who laugh, because you joy not in the gifts of the Spirit, you joy in what you have made of yourself.

But I would rather turn the woes around. Blessed, fortunate, happy[4] are you who are rich, rich in money or power, in talent or time, because you can do so much for the poor, can lift the yoke of the oppressed. But blessed only if you have the mind of the poor, the mind of Christ. Only if you recognize that you may not do what you will with what you have. Only if you realize that you are stewards, that whatever you "own" you hold in trust. Only if you employ your power for peace, your wisdom to reconcile, your knowledge to open horizons, your compassion to heal, your hope to destroy despair.

Blessed, fortunate, happy are you who are full now, who are sleek and well-fed, because you are strong enough to feed the hungry, to touch empty stomachs with compassion. But blessed only if you have the mind of the hungry, the mind of Christ. Only if you do not take your food for granted. Only if you are uncomfortable as long as one sister or brother cries in vain for bread or justice or love. Only if you experience your own emptiness—how desperately you need the hungry, how far you still are from God. Blessed are the full, if you are always hungry.

Blessed are you who laugh now, because you can bring the joy of Christ to others, to those whose days are woven of tears. But blessed only if you can laugh at yourselves, if you don't take yourselves too seriously, if human living doesn't revolve around you and your needs, your hiatus hernia and your latest rebuff. Only if you take delight in all God's creation, in snow and star, in blue marlin and robin redbreast, in Rodin and Dolly Parton and Veal française, in the love of man or maid, in the presence of the Trinity within you. Only if laughter means that you let go—let go of all that shackles you to yesterday, to dead hopes, imprisons you in your small selves. Blessed are you, because you are free.

Finally, dare I say "Blessed are you" to the 60 million poor in America, to the billion who will go to bed hungry tonight, to the blacks in D.C. who find it hard to laugh? In some ways, yes. Blessed are you because God loves you, because Christ has a special place in his heart for you. Blessed are you because somehow—I know not how—somehow the blessings of God's kingdom will be yours; sometime—I know not when—sometime you will laugh and leap for joy. Blessed are you because now God alone can fill your emptiness. Blessed are you because you prick my conscience, because you reveal to me my nakedness, my poverty in God's eyes, my borderline Christianity, the way I, like the priest in the Gospel, pass you by "on the other side" (Lk 10:31). Blessed are you because you are living the crucified Christ I so often avoid.

Good friends: Homilies to hundreds can do no more than graze your real-life existence as the gospel touches it. So, it is time for each of us to ask ourselves, to mull over, a bruising, healing question: What are my beatitudes? Blessed am I yes, fortunate indeed . . . but why? How would Christ close this sentence to me: "Blessed are you because . . ."?

Holy Trinity Church
Washington, D.C.
February 16, 1992

15
LOVE YOUR ENEMIES?
Seventh Sunday of the Year (A)

- Leviticus 19:1–2, 17–18
- 1 Corinthians 3:16–23
- Matthew 5:38–48

Love your enemies? Pray for those who persecute you? My dear perse-cuted Kurds in Iraq, shower your love on Saddam Hussein? Arme-nians once again threatened with genocide, think kindly of the Azer-baijani blockading you? Refugees watering the ways of Bosnia, say "Bless you" to the raping Serbs? Children of Somalia, think lovingly of the warlords wasting you? Survivors of Auschwitz, love the Nazis who exterminated six million of your fellow Jews? Survivors of Hiro-shima, love the Enola Gay bombardier who irradiated uncounted thousands of you? General Noriega, cast your eye lovingly on the George Bush who whisked you from your Panama empire to an Amer-ican jail? Mother and father, love the beast who ravished your child?

Good friends, the breath-taking command of Jesus raises not only a challenge but a problem. A crucial problem, for it focuses on the core of the Christian reality. It highlights a critical four-letter word: love. So, let's muse on three trouble areas: (1) the word "love," (2) the love Jesus preached, and (3) our own love of the enemy—the enemy that is "not us."

I

First, the word "love." If words could sue for verbal abuse, "love" would fill our courts with their anguish. For love is the golden jubilee of a wedding, and love is a one-night stand shaped of chemistry and alcohol. Love is a child born of total self-giving, and love is good safe sex. Love is erotic joy between equal partners, and love is pornographic power and possession. Love is God giving a Son to a cross for us, and love is what Bostonians feel for the Celtics. Love is a tough self-sacrifice, and love is a sexy TV pitch for diamonds, tooth paste, mouthwash. We love Siamese cats and Subaru cars; we love pepperoni pizza and a souped-up Harley; we love the sun on our skin and the chill of a strawberry daiquiri. Another way of saying "good-bye"? "Love ya."

I am not trying to lock love into a strait jacket, a single meaning. One beauty of English is the shapes a word can take, its nuances, shades of meaning: Just think of cross, of faith, of resurrection. But love is in peril of losing its legitimate meanings when it comes to mean anything at all . . . or nothing.

And still it's true: Love is difficult to define. A pulpit is not the place for a history, for a disquisition on Plato's love-as-longing or Aristotle's love-as-friendship. But it does demand that we focus on what Christianity has contributed to the concept. If I want to grasp the inner essence of love, I would do well to look first to God: who God is and what God has done. Who is God? Here the basic newness was pithily expressed in the First Letter of John: "God is love" (1 Jn 4:8). God's secret life reveals a loving community of divine Persons, wherein there is indeed I-and-thou but never mine-and-thine. What has God done? God's outreach reveals a powerful God who shaped a universe to mirror divine love, an imaginative God who fashioned male and female to image God's love, a compassionate God who gave an only Son to a torturous cross not from necessity but from an excess of love, not for a limited elite but for every man and woman from Adam to Antichrist.

A Roman Catholic tradition, from Dionysius the Ps.-Areopagite through Thomas Aquinas to John Courtney Murray, sees a twin force in love, whether human love or divine. On the one hand (to borrow Murray's rhetoric), love is a centripetal force: Love makes for oneness; the lover produces another self. On the other hand, love is a centrifu-gal force: Love makes for ec-stasy; love carries the lover outside him-self, outside herself; the lover becomes self-less.[1] Such is love divine; such should be love that is genuinely human.

II

Let's move to Jesus, to the love Jesus preached. You know, Jesus loved the law of Moses. Some Christians tend to speak disparagingly of Jewish law, the Torah, the Five Books of Moses; so many of us identify the Prior Testament with a divine despot, strict justice over-powering mercy, an erroneous understanding of "an eye for an eye." But in the Jewish tradition the great guiding principle of Jewish law is love. Not love in high abstraction; rather, a love that reaches up to a living God and out to bone-and-blood brothers and sisters.

Back in the early days of our Jewish-Christian era, Rabbi Akiba, a remarkable scholar and saint, claimed that the whole of Jewish law was summed up in a single verse from Leviticus: "You shall love your neighbor as yourself" (Lev 19:18). For him, the purpose of law was to teach love of neighbor—a love that had to be taught, had to be commanded, because no blood tie links us to the man and woman next door. More than that, Rabbi Akiba was martyred by the Romans because he refused to cease teaching the Torah. As he was being executed, he said he now knew the meaning of the verse "You shall love the Lord your God with all your heart, and with all your soul, and with all your might" (Deut 6:5). It means, you are to love God even if God takes your life.[2]

It is this kind of love that Jesus preached—preached it from his Jewish background and from his unique intimacy with his Father. When a Pharisee asked him, "Which commandment in the law is the greatest?" he responded, "Love God with all your heart, soul, and mind." Then he added a second commandment, "Love your neigh-bor [at least as much] as you love yourself." This commandment he commended with a phrase that should adorn every refrigerator door: This commandment "is like" the first (Mt 22:34–39). Loving your neighbor is like loving God. Not to love the human images of God is not to love God.

More than that, Jesus made quite clear what he meant by "neigh-bor." It was not only the family next door in Nazareth, but the scribes and Pharisees in Jerusalem. Not only fellow Jews in the fold, but the despised Samaritans. Not only the common folk who "spoke well of him" and resonated to "the gracious words that came from his mouth" (Lk 4:22), but his relatives who thought he was off his rocker. Not only Lazarus and his sisters who could serve up a gourmet meal, but the sinful woman who bathed his feet with her tears and the paralytic imprisoned on his cot, the despised toll collector and the leper ostracized from society. Not only the John who rested his head on Jesus at the supper, but the Peter who denied him and the Thomas who doubted him and the Judas who sold him for silver.

And then that sentence which must have perplexed his hearers: "Love your enemies, pray for your persecutors" (Mt 5:44). Not only the exhortation in Proverbs, "Do not rejoice when your enemies fall"

(Prv 24:17). Not only Elisha telling the king of Israel, "You shall not slay [the defeated Syrians] .... Set bread and water before them ... and let them go to their master" (2 Kgs 6:22).[3] From Jesus, a clear command to love. Love the Pompey who captured Jerusalem? Love your Roman masters, the soldiers that hold you and your land in bondage?[4] Love Pilate? Love Herod? Did Jesus actually love the Herods who sought his infant life and beheaded his kinsman the Baptist? The answer is ... yes indeed! But to grasp its inner meaning, we must move to ourselves—to ourselves and the enemy that is "not us."

III

Last week's issue of *Time* magazine featured two articles on love and its chemistry.[5] Granted their limited scope—romantic love and the recent interest of biologists and anthropologists—it still is a discouraging commentary on our cultural priorities when the story of love is restricted to evolutionary roots, brain imprints, and biological secretions, when only the penultimate sentence suggests that love is "a commingling of body and soul, reality and imagination, poetry and phenylethylamine."[6] Not a word about a kind of love that centuries ago Rabbi Akiba realized has to be taught, has to be learned, because in those instances no blood ties, no chemistry, link us to the other; because the only ties are our common humanity, the redemption of all of us by a God-man on a bloody cross, and the fact that, despite sin, God's image can never be totally obliterated in any human by the mark of Cain.

Of such realities is fashioned a Christian love of enemies. Not an easy love. A first difficulty: What does such love mean? Not what love of friendship means: We are attracted to each other, we feel affection for each other, we are fused in soul—what Augustine of Hippo called "one soul in two bodies."[7] It is not identical with forgiveness: I must somehow love terrorists who have bombed a bus filled with children, even if it makes no sense to forgive them while they still rejoice in their carnage. What, then, am I like when I love those who hate me?

Soon after the war in the Persian Gulf, I gave a baccalaureate homily at the Air Force Academy in Colorado Springs. I insisted that only one thing could justify their uniform: that they are peacemakers. What basic quality underlies a peacemaker? A profound respect for life. So deep a respect that no man's death, no woman's death, is an unqualified blessing, a good thing in every way. It goes back to God's own declaration in the book of Ezekiel: "As I live, says the Lord God, I have no pleasure in the death of the wicked, but that the wicked turn from his way and live" (Ezek 33:11). It is a respect for life that molds every Christian into a man or woman of compassion. Com-passion: I "suffer with" those who hate me, who seek my life. And I pray for them. Pray that they may turn from their ways and live. I hate what they do; I do not hate those who do it—Stalin, Saddam Hussein, the serial rapist.[8]

I said above that this is something I must be taught, must learn; it is not inherited, not a function of my genes. But the learning process is at once sticky and startling. When the chips are down, when reason fails to sway me, when I see no trace whatsoever of the image of Christ in the other, then I love those who hate me, who destroy my dear ones, who starve the world's children, simply because Jesus tells me to.

But learning from Jesus is not sheer obedience to a command. In Jesus I see with my own eyes, hear with my own ears, love of enemies in action—the "love of another kind" that Amy Grant sings. I stand beneath a cross and hear a God-man murmur through blood-stained lips, "Father, forgive them" (Lk 23:34). Forgive whom? Not only the Herod who treated him with contempt and the Pilate who handed him over to crucifixion; not only the leaders who scoffed at him and the soldiers who mocked him and the criminal who derided him. Listen to Paul: ". . . while we were still enemies, we were reconciled to God through the death of God's Son" (Rom 5:10). A sobering thought: The enemy is not totally "out there." We—all men and women from Eden on—we are the enemy transformed by Christ's love. With that in mind, dare we still divide the world between "us" and "them"? Can we possibly play Christ to our little world if we do not struggle to imitate the Christ of Calvary?

Here we find "good news" indeed. You see, what makes love of enemy possible in my life as well as in Christ's is not my high I.Q.; it is the God of compassion active within me, the God who *is* Compassion, the God who, says the Psalmist, "does not deal with us according to our sins, nor requite us according to our iniquities" (Ps 103:10). The grace to love our enemies is there for us—even the grace to grasp the grace. Once again, very simply, "for God all things are possible" (Mt 19:26).

A perceptive author has recently written:

> . . . what [Jesus] taught about loving enemies is fundamental, not
> peripheral, to the church and its understanding of its own exis-

tence. Indeed it is fundamental to the survival of the human race.
Unless humans learn to live with their enemies, indeed, unless we
learn to love our enemies, our days on this earth are numbered.[9]

It is not only our ravaged earth that threatens our existence; so too
does our failure to love, our innate or our learned habit of loving
only those who love us. It threatens not only our physical existence
but our life in Christ, Christ living in us, our ability to cry with St.
Paul, "It is no longer I who live, but it is Christ who lives in me"
(Gal 2:20). And remember, only love can destroy hate. I am reminded
of Augustine's insight: "There is nothing that invites love more than
to be beforehand in loving; and that heart is overhard which, even
though it were unwilling to bestow love, would be unwilling to return it."[10]

Dear Lord: Impregnate us with the grace to act as your children
should, to love our enemies as you love them—you who make your
"sun rise on the evil and on the good," you who send "rain on the
righteous and on the unrighteous" (Mt 5:45). Grace us to experience
what you command: to imitate your holiness, to be holy somewhat as
you are holy. Grace me to start not overseas with an autocrat in Iraq,
but in my own back yard, in my office, in my classroom, in my parish.
Wherever I live and move and breathe, grace me to love as your Son
loved, the Jesus who lived for sinners and died even for those who
crucified him, who lives and rules with you and the Holy Spirit, one
God, for ever and ever.

The Memorial Church
Harvard University
Cambridge, Mass.
February 21, 1993

16

HAPPY TRINITY AND SUFFERING HUMAN?
Trinity Sunday (C)

- Proverbs 8:22–31
- Romans 5:1–5
- John 16:12–15

Trinity Sunday? A homily on healthcare?[1] Can there possibly be a greater distance than the gulf between the life Father, Son, and Spirit live in heavenly happiness and the life lived by 37 million Americans without access to healthcare? Strange as it may sound, quite the opposite is true; there is no gulf, save for the gulf we humans make. The community that is the Christian Trinity and the community of our sick and dying are intimately connected. To make sense of this outrageous affirmation, let me put together three realities: (1) the happy Trinity, (2) the suffering human, and (3) the Catholic Health Association.

I

First, a word about the Trinity. Fear not: I shall not solve the most difficult of Christian mysteries; I shall not bore you with technical theology. But I feel I must tell you of a God who does not dwell in outer space, "far from" what poet Thomas Gray called "the madding crowd's ignoble strife." Our Trinity, God Three in One, is a God *for us.*

To begin with, our God is a Father. Remember the prayer Jesus left us, the Our Father? *Our* Father. Yours and mine and everyone else's since human life began. Or, if you prefer the moving language of Pope John Paul I, God is not only Father; God is "even more so Mother, who wants only to be good to us," loves us even when we are bad. This Father/Mother shaped each one of you out of nothing—sorry, out of love. Not that God had to. It is simply that love

82

has an all but irresistible urge to go out of itself, to share—even God's love, especially God's love.

How much did this Father/Mother love us? So much, John the Evangelist tells us, that God sent an only Son that we might not perish but have life without end. "In this is love," the First Letter of John exclaims, "not that we loved God but that God loved us," "sent [God's] Son into the world so that we might live through him" (1 Jn 4:10, 9). If you think the world is a mess now, see it as God saw it from beginning to end, from Adam to Antichrist, and instead of letting it go literally to hell, sent Jesus to save it. Not a cold gesture of international amnesty: All of you are forgiven. No. God's Son born a baby as we are born, from the body of a woman. God's Son an adolescent who learned as we learn—learned from Mary and Joseph how to love God, how to love the people of Nazareth. A flesh-and-blood Jew who was convicted as a criminal, was lashed with whips and crowned with thorns, died murmuring from bloody lips "Father, forgive . . . ." A God-man who left us without his smile and tears but left himself under what looks like bread, tastes like bread, and is not bread. A God-man who left us his mother to be our mother.

Not only that. When Jesus returned to his Father wearing our flesh, he did not leave us orphans. He sent us his Holy Spirit, to teach us about God and ourselves; to be our Dynamo, our Power, in our journey to Jerusalem; to live in us as in a temple of God. In his own words the night before he died, "I will ask the Father, and [the Father] will give you another Helper, to be with you for ever. This is the Spirit of Truth . . . . You know [this Spirit], because [this Spirit] abides in you, and [this Spirit] will be in you" (Jn 14:16–17).

Trinity Sunday, good friends, is not *God's* feast; it is ours. Today we celebrate "God with us." However humbly you think of yourself, however much you may regret what you do *not* have, never forget the supreme gift that is yours, more precious and more lasting than the diamonds that are supposedly for ever. You are a living tabernacle: God is alive in you—Father/Mother, God's unique Son, and Their Holy Spirit.

II

Now move from God-with-us to . . . us, to the suffering human. Why did God take our flesh? To heal it. Not to take away the ills that afflict body, mind, and spirit. These remain part of the human situation even after Jesus' resurrection. There is so much we cannot explain, so much that baffles philosophers and theologians, saints and mystics. I do not know how to reconcile a good God with crib deaths, Down's syndrome, an infant born with AIDS, thousands killed in a Guatemala earthquake, hundreds of thousands perishing in Soviet death camps, six million Jews gassed by Nazis, untold millions destroyed by war, a family wiped out in a car accident, my only brother dead at 27, and so on into the night. No homily can transform such tragedies into triumphs; no homily can pry open the mystery of evil, why bad things happen to good people.

What, then, dare I do? Simply tell you what *God* has revealed to us about the *religious* meaning of sickness and of healing in the context of salvation.[2] You see, Jesus came across sick people wherever he went: blind and deaf and mute, paralyzed or possessed, fevered or hemorrhagic, lepers and a woman unable to stand straight for 18 years. Some he cured; most he did not.

What did Jesus see in sickness? An evil brought on by sin. Not necessarily the personal sin of the sick, but always an evil that entered the world through the Sin that dominated the world, a sign of Satan's power over men and women. Remember what he said to his people: "Ought not this woman, whom Satan bound for 18 long years, be set free from this bondage on the Sabbath day?" (Lk 13:16). Sickness is a symbol. I mean a sign pregnant with a depth of meaning suggested rather than clearly stated—like a crucifix, for example. What does sickness reveal in God's plan? The state in which a sinful world finds itself: spiritually blind, deaf, paralyzed.

Why did Jesus heal at all? To reveal his power; to show himself more powerful than the forces of evil; to tell us that the kingdom of God is here, God's rule over human hearts. Not here in its fulness; only the beginning of God's rule. Not that sickness and evil would disappear with his first coming. Jesus heals to reveal the spiritual cure he came to work in us.

And St. Paul goes further, gives a thrilling positive shape to suffering. By taking upon himself our ills during his passion, Jesus has given them a new meaning. What we suffer can have redemptive value, can be a saving force for ourselves and others. It can unite us to the suffering Christ. "We are afflicted in every way, but not crushed, . . . always carrying in the body the death of Jesus, so that the life of Jesus may be made visible in our mortal flesh" (2 Cor 4:8, 10). Whereas Job could not grasp in any way the meaning of his suffering, the Christian can say to the world with St. Paul: "I am now rejoicing in my sufferings for your sake, and in my flesh I am completing what is lacking in Christ's afflictions for the sake of his body, the Church'' (Col 1:24).

The mystery does not disappear; we do not completely understand. But this we do know: If I unite my sufferings with the Christ of Gethsemane, with the Christ of Calvary, I am not only deepening my own oneness with him; I am sharing in the plan of God whereby others are brought from sin to salvation, from unbelief to belief, from death to life. This realization is indispensable for genuine Christian living in a world where evil seems all too often to triumph, where genocide and massacres and terrorism make much of the world a jungle, where deadly "accidents" make no human sense. It does not explain the gas chambers of Auschwitz or the fiery frustrations of L.A.[3] What it does do, or should do, is compel us to link all human suffering to the cross of Christ. Not to play it down; not to keep from feeling it; only to keep from wasting it, from tossing it into a garbage disposal of meaninglessness.

III

All of which compels my third point: What has this to say to the CHA? Suffering calls for healing, sufferers for healers. But you are not engaged in a purely secular service, good as such service is. You have a significant adjective in your title. I like to think that, for you, the adjective "Catholic" modifies both "Association" and "Health." It modifies Association because at its best it links you to a universal Church in what you believe, the way you worship, how you live. But it modifies Health as well, because it suggests that health is broader than the body, deeper than a physical cure, a reality more comprehensive than is recognized even by admirable practitioners of today's holistic medicine. For you, from the hospital administrator to the early-morning linens dropper, to heal is to engage in the ministry of salvation, to co-operate with a human person working out his or her salvation. Health for you is Catholic.

This means that you would do well to be impregnated with a paragraph from a first-rate novelist and Presbyterian preacher. Frederick Buechner compared humanity to an enormous spider web:

> if you touch it anywhere, you set the whole thing trembling. . . .
> As we move around this world and as we act with kindness, perhaps,
> or with indifference, or with hostility, toward the people we meet,

we too are setting the great spider web a-tremble. The life that I touch for good or ill will touch another life, and that in turn another, until who knows where the trembling stops or in what far place and time my touch will be felt. Our lives are linked. No man [no woman] is an island. . . .[4]

This insight is particularly pertinent for you in the health apostolate. You are ceaselessly touching humanity, the human person—touching men and women not only with scalpel and CAT scan, with stethoscope and angiostomy, but with incomparable care, with reverence for a body that encases an image of God, with love for a human person struggling to link this crisis with his or her reason for living. The touch of your hand, the love in your eyes, this busy moment given totally to this anxious heart, at times even responding to a mute cry, "What does it mean to die?"—here is how you can, without preaching, help another human person integrate this gethsemane into a Christlife.

But this is not where it ends. Touch a person and you set the spider web a-tremble. The person you touched will touch another, that other still another, "until who knows where the trembling stops." For all its hates, for all its wars, for all its dread smallness, for all its colors and smells, this thing we call humanity is still one body, still the body God shaped in the image of Christ,[5] still struggling, as Paul put it, to "grow up in every way . . . into Christ" (Eph 4:15), and through Christ into the Trinity.

Yes, the Trinity. For by this time I trust you have glimpsed how all-important is the Trinity in your efforts to heal this scarred, unhealthy nation. It is our fathering/mothering God who called you to this mission you share with the Son of God in flesh, the Christ who proclaimed in Nazareth's synagogue, "The Spirit of the Lord is upon me, because [the Lord] has anointed me to bring good news to the poor, has sent me to proclaim release to the captives and recovery of sight to the blind, to let the oppressed go free" (Lk 4:18). We need not despair; quite the contrary. For, as St. Paul proclaimed to the Christians of Rome and to you in today's second reading, "hope does not disappoint us, because God's love has been poured into our hearts through the Holy Spirit who has been given to us" (Rom 5:5). It is this Trinity that lives in you and in the unfortunates you struggle to heal. It is this God One and Three who gives you the power to be better than you humanly are. It is this Trinity that makes it possible for you to bring healing not only to broken bodies but more especially to broken persons, to your local community, to your nation that may be "the home of the brave" but is not yet "the land of the free."

Dear healers in and with Christ: On this feast that celebrates not only God One in Three but God-with-us, I ask you to do yourselves three favors. I ask you to celebrate the gift that is yours: God *within* you. I ask you to recognize the mission that is yours: to touch a gigantic spider web at one small point and know that the image of God you touch with your healing, with your love, will touch another, and that other still another, till it ends only God knows where. And I ask you never to forget what St. Paul in his own distress told the Christians of his time: "Whenever I am weak, then I am strong" (2 Cor 12:10); for "I can do all things through [the Lord] who strengthens me" (Phil 4:13).

This is *your* feast, good friends. Celebrate it—for your sake, for your country's sake, literally for Christ's sake.

Disneyland Hotel
Anaheim, California
June 14, 1992

17

NABOTH OR AHAB? A LESSON IN GREED
Monday after Trinity Sunday (C)

- 1 Kings 21:1–16
- Matthew 5:38–42

Against all the odds, the story you have just heard from the First Book of Kings is not impertinent to the theme of this Catholic Health Association convention: Heal USA, Heal US. First the story; then USA; finally US.

I

First the story: Naboth and Ahab; a small landowner and a powerful king. Naboth owns a vineyard he has inherited from his fathers. Ahab wants Naboth's vineyard—wants it for a vegetable garden, wants it because it is near his house. He is willing to make what seems a fair exchange: either a better vineyard than Naboth now owns, or the money value of the vineyard. What could be fairer? Naboth's response? Religious horror: "The Lord forbid that I should give you my ancestral inheritance" (1 Kgs 21:3), what I have inherited from my fathers. And that refusal is safeguarded in Jewish law: the law that protects patrimony, property inherited from ancestors.[1]

Ahab returns to his palace in a royal snit. Like a peevish child, he throws himself on his satiny bed, turns his face to the wall, refuses to eat. His wife, dear practical Jezebel, manages to squeeze the reason out of him. The way he tells it, that cheap little farmer refused my money, refused another vineyard—refused me! He says nothing about Naboth's religious feelings, nothing about the law on nonalienation of patrimony. Jezebel swings him around, pulls the pillow off his face: What kind of a king are you? Get your butt out of bed, toss cold water on your face, order a pepperoni pizza from Domino's, laugh up a storm. I'll get you that vineyard.

And indeed she does. In the king's name, she writes to the elders and nobles of Naboth's city. She sets it up so that in the assembly where Naboth sits at the head two known good-for-nothings accuse him of cursing God and cursing the king. Naboth is dragged outside the city, is stoned to death. Jezebel passes the good news on to her husband: See, I told you so. Not to worry. Naboth is dead, his vineyard is yours, go down and take it.

II

Let's turn to the USA. What links that royal couple to our country as we move through the nineties? Well, what was it that motivated Ahab and Jezebel? It is one of those seven sins which in the Christian tradition came to be called "capital" sins. Capital in the sense of principal: They are sources from which all sorts of other sins spring. One of the seven is a mean monosyllable: greed. What is greed? A keen, excessive craving to acquire, to get something for myself beyond what reason would counsel.

I am not about to claim that America is simply greedy, that all of our fair country is lusting for all it can get. But I do resonate to Pope John Paul II when he deplores a "civilization of 'consumption' or 'consumerism,'" which "makes people slaves of 'possession' and immediate gratification," which "involves so much 'throwing-away' and 'waste.'"[2] If a papal encyclical leaves you cold, listen to a remarkable statement of Lee Atwater, the architect of presidential politics who almost singlehandedly turned the Bush campaign around in '88. Dying of a brain tumor at 40, this gifted man made this poignant confession:

> The '80s were about acquiring—acquiring wealth, power, prestige. I know. I acquired more wealth, power and prestige than most. But you can acquire all you want and still feel empty. . . . It took a deadly illness to put me eye to eye with that truth, but it is a truth that the country, caught up in its ruthless ambitions and moral decay, can learn on my dime.[3]

The consumer mentality is an addiction our commercials spur, on which they thrive. We are being told quite frankly by some defenders of the free market that, for capitalism to work, you have to be greedy. And events conspire to confirm that conviction. To bail out the greedy cheats of Savings & Loan, each hour you taxpayers are shelling out 33.7 million dollars—enough to revamp the healthcare system of the United States in a month. Greed doesn't spare any group: not Wall Street's Boeskys, not real estate's Keatings, not tel-evangelism's Bakkers, not the private purveyors of weapons to the world, not even the medical profession.

III

Now what of US, of the CHA? We Catholics are warned by fellow Catholics and by sympathetic non-Romans that we are not a credible, believable church unless we practice what we preach, that a church unjust within can hardly persuade others to shape a more just society. One prime example is . . . healing. There is so much to heal: not only rickets but the malnutrition that brings it on; not only an infant's addiction but her pregnant mother on drugs; not only third-degree burns but the slums that rear uncaring or frustrated parents; not only low black survival in Harlem but the racist slavery that kills the spirit; not only bodies mangled by violence but the hatred that produces it. The calls on our compassion go far beyond the open wound, beyond the OR, beyond the nursing home. But we shall not contrib-ute significantly to the healing of our country unless we ourselves are ceaselessly being healed.

This morning the Word of the Lord speaks to us of one specific illness, a virus that afflicts all strata of our society. I mean greed, the itch to acquire, the yearning to get. Is it a problem for Catholics? Ideally, one would expect not, since we claim to be a single body, the Body of Christ, wherein "if one member suffers, all suffer together with it" (1 Cor 12:26). But I shall never forget Robert Bellah's chal-lenge to us Catholic theologians some years ago. Claiming that our country is plagued by a resurgence of late-19th-century rugged indi-vidualism, where the race is to the swift and the savage, he told us that research reveals little if any difference between Catholics and our non-Catholic neighbors. That night, alone in my room, I wept.

I make no accusations; a homily is not a guilt trip. It isn't easy to speak of ourselves as greedy—not when times are tough, jobs at a premium, children to feed and educate. I simply look at myself. The morning I left Annapolis for Anaheim, I opened my closet: 14 sweaters! Gifts indeed, but really, how cold can a celibate Jesuit get? I read of the food thrown away in hotels and homes each day, and I weep over the waste that could feed all the hungry in Calcutta. A fan pays a scalper $250 for a pro basketball ticket, and a child's stomach rumbles in hunger. I know, we are incredibly generous; and still the rich get richer and the poor get poorer.

Remember how Naboth refused to surrender his ancestral patrimony, the inheritance from his fathers—even died for it? We too have inherited a rich vineyard—not only 19 centuries of social teaching, but even more importantly "God's love poured into our hearts through the Holy Spirit who has been given to us" (Rom 5:5). Within us is not some intellectual muscle but a power that is a person, the Holy Spirit. Here is our power to love as Jesus loved, to say no to things and yes to people, to keep from turning luxuries into necessities, to walk every so often in the shoes of the unfortunate. In the power of this Spirit, may we adopt from this day forward Naboth's response to the powerful and greedy of this world: "The Lord forbid that I should give you my ancestral inheritance"?

Disneyland Hotel
Anaheim, California
June 15, 1992

18

IF YOU LOVE THOSE WHO LOVE YOU....
Tuesday after Trinity Sunday (C)

- 1 Kings 21:17–29
- Matthew 5:43–48

Today's Gospel is a powerful challenge to the Catholic Health Association. On the face of it, it has terribly little to say to healthcare practitioners. "You have heard that it was said, 'You shall love your neighbor and hate your enemy.' But I say to you, Love your enemies and pray for those who persecute you, so that you may be children of your Father in heaven" (Mt 5:43–44).

What you must remember is that this short paragraph is part of a larger complex. I mean the Sermon on the Mount. In all likelihood, what Matthew gives us as a "sermon" delivered on a steep hill along the shores of the Sea of Galilee is actually a compilation of sayings of Jesus, some of them uttered on other occasions. And a snippet like the four verses on loving your enemies is part and parcel of Jesus' most thunderous message, the second commandment of the gospel, "Love your sisters and brothers at least as much as you love yourself" (cf. Mt 22:39). In that context let's see what those four verses might say to you and me. Two principal questions: (1) What is Jesus saying to Christians in general? (2) What might Jesus be saying to Christians in healthcare?

I

First, what is Jesus saying to Christians in general, to any and all disciples of Christ? Something very modern, very contemporary, something of which we all have experience: It's relatively easy to love someone who loves us, and to show that love in our actions. I recall how easy I found it to teach youngsters who responded to my teaching. I have found it easy to love attractive people, people with agreeable personalities, men and women who lap up my homilies, laugh at my humor, agree with my theology, think that my project *Preaching the Just Word* is the greatest thing to hit this country since McDonald's 99-cent cheeseburger.

My problem is loving people who don't love me. Not so much the Muslims in Iran; they are so far removed from my daily life that at times they seem unreal, live in a different world. I am thinking rather of people I am in contact with. I find it difficult to love theologians who take pot shots at me, especially in print; ultraconservatives who blast the bishops for pastorals on peace and the economy that they claim are none of the hierarchy's business; the evangelizing Falwells and Bakkers and Swaggarts with their mesmerizing TV influence on millions; all sorts of politicos and Fortune 500s who think America can be saved by big business. Even the lady who recently wrote to me after a misleading newspaper quotation: "Shame on you, Reverend!"

What Jesus tells me is that this MO (*modus operandi*) is not particularly Christian. Don't even atheists, hardened sinners, Mafia types, drug dealers love those who love them? The Christian facet of love is to love as Jesus loved. How did he love? He took our flesh and nailed it to a cross not only for Mary of Nazareth but for Mary of Magdala, not only for beloved disciple John but for apostate apostle Judas, not only for the women who wept as he carried his cross to Calvary but for the men who jeered him as he hung in agony on the wood. His love was for outcast lepers as well as for socially acceptable Lazarus, for the self-righteous Pharisee in the temple as well as for the repentant publican, for Pilate who washed his hands of him and Herod who mocked him as well as for the simple shepherds on the hillside and the adoring astrologers from the East.

I am suggesting that we listen to the Lord Jesus as he commands us to imitate his Father in heaven, the Father who sends sun and rain on all God's children, however far they stray. I am suggesting that we take seriously the exhortation of Jesus that closes today's Gospel: "Be perfect, therefore, as your heavenly Father is perfect" (Mt 5:48). This is indeed sanctity at its loftiest level. It goes beyond revenge. It rises above the silver rule, "Do not do to others what you would not have them do to you" (Tob 4:15). It exceeds the golden rule, "Do to others as you would have them do to you" (Mt 7:12). It is an invitation to moral heroism, to high holiness.

II

Second, what is Jesus saying to Christians in healthcare? Our "enemies" are not, for the most part, enemies in the usual sense, men and women thirsting for our blood. I am thinking rather of those who simply make it difficult for us to heal USA. It's easy enough to love Maurice Strong, the Canadian oil executive who organized the U.N. Earth Summit in Rio de Janeiro, because he wants nothing less than "historic civilizational change," in which "both rich and poor will turn away from the craze for consumption and begin to live within their environmental means."[1] But how do you love Michael Milken, the financier who presided over a $200 billion market and is now in jail for gigantic scams? How can you love the abortion clinicians, the doctor who practices "mercy killing," the profit manufacturers who buy up nonprofit hospitals, the Catholic health institutes that don't like CHA, the head-hunters and vigilantes in Rome who restrict your life-giving efforts, perhaps even the imaginative feminists who carry banners proclaiming "Eve was framed"?

How love them? Love is not, at bottom, a nice, gooey, touchy-feely thing. Genuine love is not easy to define. Still, one wondrous way to love, one profound proof of love, is to . . . listen. Search out: Where do those who disagree with us hurt? Even when they cry out in anger, what hurt does the anger cover over? The arsonist in L.A., the teenager after an abortion, the Catholic women clamoring for ordination, the blacks enslaved to a capitalism that has no place for them, the gay and the lesbian, at times the American Civil Liberties Union.

If you really listen, you pay a price. Archbishop Weakland of Milwaukee had his wrists slapped by Rome for *listening* to prochoicers. If you listen, you take on another's burden when you have enough troubles of your own. If you listen, really listen, you give yourself to another—not only ears but mind and heart—and that is an act of love. If you really listen, someone may fall in love with you, and that may be a burden you do not care to endure.

On the other hand, if you really listen, the issues that divide our country, the controversies that hinder healing, may submit to rational discussion, rather than the inflamed passions that preclude reasoning. They may even be open to the influence of the Holy Spirit. But only if we listen. Take the abortion controversy. It has gone beyond rational discussion. The stances have been taken, there is nothing to discuss; what remains is power: organize, rally support, put politicians on the spot. No matter what their consciences dictate; no question of listening to their views; if you're not with us, you're out.

No, good friends in Christ. Not so for disciples of the Jesus who spent his earthbound life listening. He listened not only to his Father in heaven, not only to Mary and Joseph, but to a woman taken in adultery and a man possessed; listened to Pharisees who criticized his own and his disciples' eating habits and Herodians who tried to trap him on taxes to the emperor; listened to little children who nestled in his arms and a rich young man with all too many possessions; listened to a blind man who asked for his mercy and a woman who had hemorrhaged for 12 years; listened to a sinful woman who bathed his feet with her tears and the apostle Judas who he knew would betray him; listened to all sorts of people who cried out to him from the crowds.

Love your enemies? Let's change the rhetoric. Let's ask: Am I ready to treat men and women who disagree with me, or do not like me, or maybe hate me, as brothers and sisters shaped in God's likeness, as truly children of God as I am, folk of flesh and blood for whom the Son of God died on a shameful cross?

We can get dreadfully caught up in our individual and corporate jobs, in domestic duties; the demands are many and burdensome. But to heal US and to heal USA, we have to lift our eyes to horizons near and far. To immediate demands indeed, to our specific tasks, but over and above these, to our country's cry for a fresh vision, to the uncounted millions who find our Catholic vision myopic, our opposition to contraception unintelligible in the context of overpopulation, our antipathy to abortion heartless where women's health is at issue, Rome's stand on sterilization unreasonable, and in general see our church as a problem rather than an ally in restoring the health of our nation. Why is it that so many do not see us as life-giving, as a people who care? Love our *enemies*? No. Listen to our sisters and brothers, hear why they hurt, try to understand where they come from.

This is not an appeal to sacrifice principle. Disagreements, like the poor, I fear we shall always have with us; and we dare not compromise where God's will is clear to us. I am suggesting one way in which we in the CHA can begin to heal ourselves and our scarred nation, can begin to be "perfect as [our] heavenly Father is perfect." As an exercise in love, listen. Listen to Jesus; listen to one another; listen then to the hurts in the hearts of those who follow different drumbeats—no longer enemies, just sisters and brothers.

Disneyland Hotel
Anaheim, California
June 16, 1992

19

GO INTO YOUR ROOM
AND SHUT THE DOOR?
Wednesday after Trinity Sunday (C)

- 2 Kings 2:1, 6–14
- Matthew 6:1–6, 16–18

As we leave Anaheim to return to the areas of our health apostolate, the Lord we serve has some sage advice. The trouble is, the Gospel just read to you sounds dreadfully antisocial, not the sort of counsel you seem to need for a national organization, certainly not a program you can use to heal a country: "Go into your room and shut the door" (Mt 6:6). To grasp Jesus' mind intelligently, to avoid misunderstanding, you have to see (1) what Jesus is talking about—what he is not saying, what he is saying—and then (2) how this touches our Catholic Health Association life.

I

First, what is Jesus talking about? Our works of justice,[1] our charitable giving, our prayer life, our fasting. These are simply examples of Christian living. What does Jesus say about such actions? To begin with, what is he *not* saying? He is not saying that you and I should do everything Christian in private. Justice: When you get to the office, hide behind your word processor; don't let anyone know what marvelous things you are doing for the Catholic Health Association; let someone else sign your letters; sign with a pseudonym. Charitable giving: Don't let anyone know you've given food to the hungry, drink to the thirsty, clothed the naked and taken a stranger into your home, visited the sick and the imprisoned. Prayer: Keep it private, just between you and God; stay away from the weekend Eucharist, unless you can arrange for a private home Mass. Fasting: Don't you

96

dare let anyone know you've kept the Good Friday fast. Take those ashes off your forehead when Lent begins.

What, then, is Jesus saying? Whatever you do, do it primarily to further a living, personal relationship with God. You may indeed be doing it before men and women—on a crowded street, in a gigantic cathedral, in a noisy office. Before men and women, but for God. Not so as to be seen, not to take the credit or bow to the applause. Simply to please our dear Lord. It is what St. Paul told the Christians of Corinth: "whatever you do, do everything for the glory of God" (1 Cor 10:31). Oh yes, I can still echo Paul when he says, "I try to please everyone in everything I do, not seeking my own advantage, but that of the many, so that they may be saved" (v. 33). Briefly, whatever I do, (1) I try to be of service to others; (2) I do not serve for my own purposes, do not seek my own benefit; (3) I do it ultimately for God, to come closer to the Lord who is literally my Life.

Such have been the disciples of Christ down the ages. Ancient Antony, father of monasticism, 105 when he died, balancing love for Christ with love for the thousands who stormed his cell.[2] Today's Teresa, helping thousands of Calcutta's despised to die with dignity, yet ceaselessly proclaiming "I am but a little pencil in [God's] hand," insisting that the poor are "God's greatest gift" to her, because "I have an opportunity to be 24 hours a day with Jesus."[3] And the untold sung and unsung millions in-between Antony and Teresa, men and women like you.

II

What does all this say to the CHA, to your apostolate and mine? Here, on the basis of the Gospel, I leave with you perhaps the most important facet of your health apostolate. True, *everything* you do in CHA is important: administration and ethics, surgery and nursing care, health projects—the whole wide, admirable range of your activities. They are highly important for the physical, moral, and spiritual health of the nation we love. For they bring you into contact with people—rich and poor, powerful and powerless, impregnable and vulnerable, healthy and ailing, supportive and adversarial, lovable and detestable. They bring you into contact with things—the marvels of modern medicinal technology that you touch to ailing males and females—for example, the echogram I experienced last week.

All this is important, indispensable for America's health. What today's Gospel stresses is something even more significant: your personal relationship with God. How real, how strong, how intimate, yes how passionate is your relationship of love with a fathering/ mothering God, with a Jesus wondrously alive in his risen flesh, with a Holy Spirit who lives in you as in a temple, as in a tabernacle? But, you ask, what has this to do with healthcare? Three strong connections.

1) Your commitment to CHA is not just a job. CHA healthcare is a vocation. I mean a call from Christ to continue his work of healing. And so it is your own way to be healed, to be "saved," to reach God—not only hereafter but here and now. Your work week is not a spiritual hiatus between Sundays, a gap in your pilgrimage to God. Here is where you work out your salvation. Here is the living-out of your weekend Eucharist, your movement from church to world, from altar to sickbed, from Christ to his images. But, you move out from *Christ,* not simply from competence and compassion.

Briefly, a call from Christ calls for closeness to Christ, like John reclining next to Jesus at the Supper. Here is your one Savior, here your prime Teacher. The exciting reality is this: You don't have to search desperately for Christ. He is here, within you. Not only when he rests on your hand or tongue in Sunday Eucharist, but each moment. "Those who love me will keep my word, and my Father will love them, and we will come to them and make our home with them" (Jn 14:23).

2) Your closeness to Christ is not only crucial for *you;* it is critical for the images of Christ you serve. CHA is not a secular enterprise; CHA healing is a function of Christ's Body, the Church, the People of God. You are helping to heal men and women at a critical juncture in their movement to God, when flesh or spirit is weak, when confidence crumbles, when mortality rears its ugly head, when fear forces me to cry out with Christ in Gethsemane, "Don't let me die!" Believe it or not, in the Christian vision, where no one can say to any other "I have no need of you" (1 Cor 12:21), the grace of Christ flows through you to the weaker, ailing members of the Body. The closer *you* are to Christ, the closer another will be, the greater his strength, the larger her courage. Believe it!

3) The closer you are to Christ, the greater the chance that our country will be healed. Not only of cancer and coronaries, of AIDS and arthritis, but of hatred and violence, of consumerism and greed, of selfishness and sin. "Let your light shine before men and women, so that they may see your good works and give glory to your Father in heaven" (Mt 5:16). Let Christ shine out from you, without apology,

without embarrassment; let grace pour out of you; let God's love in you move hearts to be better than they are.

You know, you are quite remarkable people. As Pope Leo the Great once told his people at Christmas, "Christians, recognize your dignity" as God's sons and daughters. Be aware of your gifts; thank God for them; but above all, ask the Christ who died for you to move you ever closer to him. For on such closeness rest (1) your own happiness and salvation, (2) the health of the people to whom you minister, (3) the healing of America.

Go forth, therefore, conscious of the Christ within you. In that thrilling awareness, live ever more passionately for the images of Christ you serve. My prayers, my heart, will always be with you. That I promise you.

Disneyland Hotel
Anaheim, California
June 17, 1992

20
MERCY, NOT SACRIFICE?
Thirteenth Week of the Year, Wednesday (C)

- Amos 5:14–15, 21–24
- Matthew 8:28–34

A cynic might suspect that in jesuitical fashion we scheduled your retreat/workshop for this week because Amos 5 is today's first reading.[1] In point of fact, we cannot claim such farsightedness, such foresight, such shrewdness. When a coincidence like this happens, we can simply repeat with Peter on the hill of transfiguration, "Lord, it is well that we are here" (Mt 17:4). For Amos tells us graphically, pungently, how intimately worship and justice are conjoined in God's covenant with God's people. So, two points: then and now; Amos and we.

I

First, Amos. Amos is a pessimist, the least hopeful of the classical prophets.[2] He lived in a paradoxical period: on the one hand, great material prosperity; on the other, social and religious corruption. His is a raw message of judgment—Yahweh's judgment on Israel. Particularly against its leaders—king, priests, upper classes; but a judgment that would affect the whole people. Why? Because to the Israelite mind the nation was a unity, with a common destiny. Israel, he storms, will be destroyed; destruction is certain, inescapable, total. Why? Several reasons. For one thing, because they had disregarded their covenant with God. They went through the motions of worshiping; merchants were careful not to do business on forbidden days. For another, when the prophets reproached them for their disloyalty, they turned a deaf ear to them.

But the ultimate reason why Yahweh would execute judgment? Because so many of the people separated worship of God from concern for their neighbor. A distinctive feature of Israelite religion, of the covenant, lay in this: Worship of God and justice to the neighbor were intimately connected. How well the Jew related to God depended in large measure on how the Jew related to fellow members of the covenant community. But what was the actual situation in Amos' time? The merchants were impatient for the holy days to pass, so they could resume their fraudulent business. Wealthy landowners oppressed the less fortunate; they simply took over the landholdings of impoverished Israelites. What was Yahweh's reaction? You have listened to it.

> I hate, I despise your festivals,
> and I take no delight in your solemn assemblies.
> Though you offer me your burnt offerings and grain offerings,
> I will not accept them,
> and the peace offerings of your fatted animals
> I will not look upon.
> Take away from me the noise of your songs;
> I will not listen to the melody of your harps.
> But let justice roll down like waters,
> and righteousness like an ever-flowing stream.
>
> (Amos 5:21–24)

A caution here: This was not an out-and-out rejection of Israelite religion. You have here a literary device. For your collection of unusable phrases, insert "dialectic negation." Amos strongly negates, denies, nullifies one facet of religion (worship) so as to emphasize the other facet (justice, righteousness). Hosea had done the same thing: Yahweh declares "I desire steadfast love and not sacrifice" (Hos 6:6). Of course Yahweh wanted sacrifice—but not when it was offered as a substitute for the demands of the covenant, not when love of God was supposed to replace love of neighbor.

II

This summons up point number two. We shift three millennia, move from Amos and Israel to you and me, to the Christian of the 1990s. I am not as pessimistic as was Amos. For all our failings, I do not believe that God has passed a definitive judgment on the People of God, that the Catholic Church or the Christian Churches are destined for destruction—certain, inescapable, total. Still, long experience tells me that our situation has strong parallels with that which caused Amos to predict disaster. The parallel lies in the gulf that severs worship from justice.

We too enjoy a covenant with God—a covenant that was sealed not with the blood of bulls but with the blood of God's Son. That covenant is shaped of fidelity: God ceaselessly faithful to us despite our infidelities; we bound by the two commandments that sum up the law and the prophets: "You shall love the Lord your God with all your heart, and with all your soul, and with all your mind." And "You shall love your neighbor [at least as much] as you love yourself" (Mt 22:37, 39). The heresy lies in believing that the only commandment that really matters for eternity, for eternal life, is the first: Love God with your whole heart and you can let humans fend for themselves.

The First Letter of John destroys that thesis in a single uncompromising sentence: "If anyone has the world's goods and sees his brother or sister in need, yet closes his heart against him or her, how does God's love abide in that person?" (1 Jn 3:17). For a Christian, self-giving to the less fortunate is not a secular handout, a natural virtue, the virtue of justice, giving others what they can legitimately claim because it can be proven by philosophy or has been written into law. This is essential Christianity. Without it I am not genuinely a Christian. Unless I love my brothers and sisters, God's images on earth, at least as much as I love myself, I do not really love God.

What a revealing God declares to me is what Rabbi Abraham Joshua Heschel expressed so strikingly a quarter century ago:

> To meet a human being is a major challenge to mind and heart. I must recall what I normally forget. A person is not just a specimen of the species called *homo sapiens*. He is all of humanity in one, and whenever one man is hurt we are all injured. The human is a disclosure of the divine, and all men are one in God's care for man. Many things on earth are precious, some are holy, humanity is holy of holies.
>
> To meet a human being is an opportunity to sense the image of God, *the presence* of God. According to a rabbinical interpretation, the Lord said to Moses: "Wherever you see the trace of man, there I stand before you."[3]

You know, the strong words Amos put on Yahweh's lips, "I will not accept your burnt offerings," did not fade away when Christ was born. Remember what he said to the Pharisees: "Go and learn what this means, 'I desire mercy, not sacrifice' " (Mt 9:13; see Hos 6:6). Good old "dialectic negation"! Of course Christ wants sacrifice, the Sacrifice that re-presents Holy Thursday and Good Friday, the sacrifice that is Paul's charge to the Christians of Rome: "I appeal to you therefore, brothers and sisters, by the mercies of God, to present your bodies as a living sacrifice, holy and acceptable to God, which is your spiritual worship" (Rom 12:1). What Jesus is saying in strong Hebrew rhetoric is simply this: Sacrifice, whether at my altar or in your home, does not please me if it is not linked to mercy, to compassion, to justice, to practical love of today's crucified.

Thank God, millions of America's Catholics live that link between worship and justice, move from church to world, from altar to people, from the Eucharistic Christ to the Christs pinned to contemporary calvaries. The problem? Uncounted Catholics who don't believe this, resent "politics" from the pulpit, or simply have enough troubles of their own without taking St. Christopher's Christ on their shoulders. Here is our challenge: how to get all of our believing worshipers to listen to Amos and respond with fire in their bellies, "This is the Word of the Lord!"

Passionist Spiritual Center
Cardinal Spellman Retreat House
Riverdale, New York
July 1, 1992

21
PERFECT HOSTESS
OR PERFECT DISCIPLE?
Sixteenth Sunday of the Year (C)

- Genesis 18:1–10
- Colossians 1:24–28
- Luke 10:38–42

Over the years an attractive interpretation of the Martha-Mary scene has grown up. It contrasts two styles of life within Christianity: the active and the contemplative. And it has Jesus playing down the active life, extolling the contemplative. If your "thing" is action—whether feeding the hungry or preaching to a congregation, watch out! You can lose your soul that way. The perfect Christian way is contemplation, sitting at the feet of the Lord, lost in admiration, all lost in wonder.

Not quite accurate. The scene in Martha's house is far richer than a contrast between Carmelites behind a grille and Jesuits running 28 colleges and universities and 43 high schools, between mother slaving over a hot stove and her sister praying before the Blessed Sacrament, between a Trappist monk silent in the fields and a Thunderbird pilot breaking the sound barrier.[1] So, a word on the Gospel, then a word on you and me.

I

First, the Gospel passage. Several points in that short passage merit mention.

1) Luke shows us a woman sitting as a disciple at Jesus' feet, Jesus encouraging a woman to learn from him. In three ways Jesus acts contrary to Jewish cultural norms that have to do with women. He is alone with women who are not related to him; a woman serves him; and Jesus is teaching a woman in her own home.[2]

2) It seems at first glance as if Jesus is reassuring Martha. She has complained to him, "Aren't you concerned that my sister has left me alone to do all the serving? Tell her, please, to come and lend me a hand" (Lk 10:40). Jesus replies, "There is need of only one thing" (v. 42)—as if he were saying, "Never mind preparing a seven-course belly-stretcher. One dish will do." But no. Jesus' remark goes far deeper. The "one thing necessary" has nothing to do with dinner. The "one thing necessary" is listening to God's word, to God speaking. It recalls an earlier observation of Jesus, when the crowds were pressing on him, and his mother and relatives could not reach him because of the crowds. Someone cries out, "Your mother and your brothers are standing outside, wanting to see you." His response? "My mother and my brothers are those who hear the word of God and do it" (Lk 8:20–21).

> Martha wanted to honor Jesus with an elaborate meal, but Jesus reminds her that it is more important to listen to what he has to say. The proper "service" of Jesus is attention to his instruction, not an elaborate provision for his physical needs. . . .[3]

3) See how gently Jesus chides Martha: "Martha, Martha. . . ." Not a harsh rebuke. Her cooking and serving are not out of place; Jesus does not reject it. His is a soft reminder that service which forgets to listen is less than what it ought to be; listening to Jesus' word is "the better portion," "the best part" (v. 42); this is the lasting "good" that will never be taken away from the listener. From perfect hostess to perfect disciple.

II

Second, a word on you and me. Like most Americans, our life is active, at times feverish. It has to be, if only because we want to serve our nearest and dearest, serve our wider community, the brothers and sisters who depend on us for ever so many needs, from food to keep them from starving to defense against hostile countries and terrorists.

What Jesus puts before us is not a harsh either/or: either an active existence that is dangerous to our spiritual life, or retirement to a monastery. No. The danger is not in serving. The danger is a service that has no time for listening—for listening to what God might be saying to us. Saying to us how, when, where? In the quiet of our hearts, whenever Jesus says to us what he said to his disciples when they were so busy they had no time even to eat: "Come away to a deserted place all by yourselves and rest a while" (Mk 6:31). During the Eucharistic liturgy, when the Word of God is proclaimed to us and the body of Christ rests on our hands, on our lips, in our bodies. Through our histories: I mean the things good and bad that happen to us, the people of all kinds we meet each day, the events that unroll from the old USSR through Yugoslavia to South Africa, the recession in our own dear land that follows on a decade of consumerism. What do they say to us? What do they tell us about God, about ourselves, about the way God wants us to live?

Today's Gospel is addressed to Christians who are expected to be, in a traditional phrase, "contemplatives in action." In action: not retiring from the world—actively engaged in the world, but not thoughtlessly. Contemplatives: I mean men and women who are ceaselessly taking a long loving look at the real. And this at the feet of Jesus. For only at the feet of Jesus, only in contemplation, does our action become Christlike.

Pray, then, that we can link both Martha and Mary in our lives. Service indeed, but service that is fed by the words that fall from the lips of our Lord. This is the "good" life, this the life that, please God, will never be taken from us.

Manresa-on-Severn
Annapolis, Maryland
July 19, 1992

22

THE RICH IN HELL,
THE POOR IN PARADISE?
Twenty-sixth Sunday of the Year (C)

- Amos 6:1, 4–7
- 2 Timothy 6:11–16
- Luke 16:19–31

Another slam-dunk on the rich? Is this today's gospel message: Good things in this life, eternal torture in the next? If today's parable—the rich man in hell, the poor man in paradise—is really part of Jesus' gospel, his "good news," we had better uncover just what it is Jesus is saying. Not surprisingly, three scenes to my act: (1) a look at Luke on possessions and power; (2) what comes out of all this for a Christian vision, especially from today's Gospel; (3) what Luke and Jesus might be saying to you and me.

I

First, skim through Luke on possessions and power.[1] In her Magnificat, Mary praises a God who puts down the powerful from their thrones and lifts up the lowly, fills the hungry with good things and sends the rich away empty (Lk 1:53). When Mary and Joseph offer little Jesus in the temple, their sacrifice is what the law determines for poor people (2:24). Jesus begins his ministry by quoting Isaiah: "The Spirit of the Lord . . . has anointed me to bring good news to the poor" (4:18). Only in Luke does Levi (Matthew to us) leave everything when he follows Jesus (5:28). In Luke the "blessed" are simply the poor (6:20), not Matthew's poor in spirit (Mt 5:3). Only Luke provides us with the parable of the Rich Fool constantly storing up goods so that he can eat, drink, and be merry (Lk 12:16–21); only Luke has our parable of the Rich Man and Lazarus (16:19–31). Upon his conversion, little Zacchaeus offers to give half of his possessions to the poor (19:8). Luke presents Jesus like an Old Testament prophet who sides with the widow (18:1–8), with the stranger in the land (10:29–37; 17:16), with those on the margin of society (14:12–13, 21). Luke's early Christian community holds everything in common; no one, no one, is in need (Acts 2:44–45; 4:32, 34).

II

What comes out of all this for a Christian vision, especially from today's Gospel? First, and highly important: Precisely why is the rich man condemned? Not because he is rich. He is condemned because he never even saw Lazarus at his gate. He should have, but he never did. He never met his eyes. The first time he saw him was from Hades— that simple but frightening sentence, "He lifted up his eyes and saw . . . Lazarus" (v. 23).[2] One of the most terrifying dangers in possessions is that they threaten us with blindness. I don't see Lazarus and his kind. Some never see them physically; it is possible to go through four years at Georgetown, marvel at monuments like the Lincoln Memorial, enjoy Wolf Trap and the Kennedy Center, eat at Houston's or Clyde's, the Tombs or the 1789, and never see the slums behind the White House and the Capitol. Some see physically but don't really see; what they see is what they want to see: the lazy and the cheat, the drunk and the coke-besotted, the killer and the carjacker. Some see the poor physically but, like the priest in the Gospel parable of the Good Samaritan, "pass by on the other side" (Lk 10:31).

A second peril: Possessions can isolate people from community. Wealth, of course; but not only *financial* wealth. Whatever I have, whatever I own, is a peril. It's mine, and no one else gets near it. It's not only the head of United Way, abusing the generosity of Americans to line his own pockets. It's a child with her Raggedy Ann doll; "No, you can't hold her; she's mine." A law student with a brilliant mind, but no time for the fellow student, the competition; only one job open at Williams and Connolly. An ecclesiastical official at the Vatican so protective of the marriage bond that he fears women in chanceries; "bleeding hearts" could drown cold reason. A pastor who believes church, liturgy, collections, parishioners are his; parish councils are a threat to his power—they get ideas, makes noises, upset established order. An Olympic athlete who will use anything to win, even substance abuse; only the losers say "It's only a game." The whiz kid who implanted a virus that infected thousands upon thousands of computers. Captains of industry and ordinary citizens who rape our earth, pollute our waters, fume our skies. Every Saddam Hussein using every trick in the books to stay in power, no matter how many Kurds or Shiites are massacred or starve.

The Christian vision? Power and possessions are not evil in themselves. Unless acquired by force or fraud, they are a gift. But a gift to be given. The idea is summed up in a thrilling verse from the First Letter of Peter: All Christians should employ (literally, "deacon") the many-splendored charisms they have from God for the advantage of one another, "as good stewards of God's dappled grace" (1 Pet 4:10).

III

"As good stewards of God's dappled grace." This moves me to my third point: What does all this say to you and me? It suggests strongly that we consult a dictionary. A steward, the American Heritage Dictionary declares, is "one who manages another's property, finances, or other affairs." Such is the profound biblical meaning. Everything I administer as a Christian belongs to someone else. But the frightening facet of this revelation is that the "someone else" is not president or pope; the "someone else" is God.[3]

That is quite obvious in the sphere of the Spirit. When I preach, I do indeed use my own words, but it is *God's* Word I claim to proclaim, and it is *God* who gives the increase. When I pour life into a fresh-born child, it is *Christ* who baptizes, and it is *God's* life I minister. When I murmur "I absolve you," it is *God's* forgiveness I channel. It is to *Christ's* supper that I invite the faithful. I have no power over the marriage contract, am only an official witness to *God's* activity, *God* linking a woman and a man for life. And when you exercise your ministry of reconciliation, healing the ruptures that sever men and women from God, from the human images of God, and from God's earth, you bring to bear not so much your native gifts as the power and wisdom of God within you. It is *God's* life, *God's* love, *God's* reconciliation you mediate; and you mediate it only because it is God who works in you to will and to do.

But is there not something you and I actually own, something of which we are not sheerly stewards? The fruit of your toil, the laser you invented, the lawsuit you won for your client, the dollars you have earned by the sweat of your brow, my latest book of homilies, your profound concepts and my personal computer, is not this our very own? Only in a limited sense. I am not denying the right to private property. But private property is not an absolute. It is subordinate to core personal rights: the right to life, to human dignity, to bodily integrity.

This means that I may not simply do what I will with what is my own. I can be, I will be, called to account for the *use* I make of all I have. As a Christian, I can never be completely comfortable as long as one sister or brother cries in vain for bread or justice or love. As a Christian, I must tear from my lips those devastating half-truths, "Charity begins at home," "Let the shiftless shift for themselves," "They are only getting what they deserve," "Why should I give to others what has cost me blood and tears to achieve?" As a Christian, I may not squander what is my own, even clutch it possessively, in disregard of my brothers and sisters.

What to do about it? Begin with the twin peril: Possessions can blind me to the other, and possessions can isolate me from community. I recall vividly a striking short sentence of Thomas Merton: "No man gets to heaven all by himself." No woman either. We reach God through community: the human family, the Christian family, the domestic family.

Take the human family. A splendid Presbyterian preacher/ novelist, Frederick Buechner, compared humanity to an enormous spider web:

> if you touch it anywhere, you set the whole thing trembling. . . . As we move around this world and as we act with kindness, perhaps, or with indifference, or with hostility, toward the people we meet, we too are setting the great spider web a-tremble. The life that I touch for good or ill will touch another life, and that in turn another, until who knows where the trembling stops or in what far place and time my touch will be felt. Our lives are linked. No man [no woman] is an island.[4]

Take our Christian family—all who believe and hope and love. St. Paul called us the body of Christ. Why? Because the relationship that links Christians to one another is like the unity of the human body. My blood carries oxygen and food to every part of my body, carries waste products away, fights disease germs, forms a saving seal over my wounds. Within my body, beneath the epidermis, lie three million sweat glands. They cool the body, help my kidneys by flushing "the excess of salt that threatens to make of [my] body juices a pickling brine."[5] And so on and so forth. But still more marvelous is the body of Christ. Each of us can echo St. Paul: This body of Christ is so intimately linked that no Christian can say to any other Christian, "I have no need of you" (cf. 1 Cor 12:21).

Take the domestic family. In all the controversy that has swirled about "family values," in all the political hoopla generated by TV's Murphy Brown and her single-parent pregnancy, I see precious little about the family as a community of life and of love. I hear no politician daring to say that the biblical "orphans and widows" are in our day poor children and single parents, that Jesus' own "the least of these my sisters and brothers" are hungry and homeless children, are unwanted, unborn children, are crack babies and children with AIDS.

What has all this to do with possessions? Just about everything. The Catholic community that is you is legendary in the D.C. area for your devotion to the downtrodden, for your fidelity to the less fortunate. And so I need not, I dare not, "dump" on you, lay land mines of guilt under your pews. What I do suggest is increased awareness of *all* your possessions. I am not downplaying the importance of the almighty American dollar; without it this worshiping community might well cease to exist. I do say that we tend to underrate the riches that reside in the gifts, the possessions, that make us human. I mean our minds and our hearts; I mean our intelligence and our love. We are surrounded not only by monetary poverty, but by stunted minds and fractured hearts, by children sexually abused and teenagers who have never heard anyone murmur "I love you," by 30,000 humans seriously ill mentally but imprisoned in jails for lack of psychiatric facilities, by a million boys and girls who sleep on America's streets.

Recently I read a book about Covenant House, six shelters for thousands of runaway kids in Times Square and Lauderdale, New Orleans and Anchorage, Houston and Hollywood—kids coked and angel-dusted, pimped and prostituted. To hide something, to be something, or wanting to believe it's cool to be homeless, many of them have renamed themselves: Crappy, D-day, Dr. Death, Insane, Lobo, Punisher II, Raccoon, Rag Doll, Riff-raff, Sad, Satan, Skunk, Skywalker, Trash, and so on.[6]

Before we join Abraham in "paradise" and share his fun, let's lift up our eyes *now,* let's see *now.* What most of these crucified images of God beg from us is that our eyes meet theirs in understanding and affection, that we don't turn from them in dismay or disgust, uncaring or unmoved. Look with love into the eyes of just one poor human and you may change not only that life but your own. Lift up your eyes . . . and see!

Holy Trinity Church
Washington, D.C.
September 27, 1992

23
FAITH AND FAITH'S DEACONS
Twenty-seventh Sunday of the Year (C)

- Habakkuk 1:2–3; 2:2–4
- 2 Timothy 1:6–8, 13–14
- Luke 17:5–10

Today's Gospel is crucial. Why? Because it focuses on one of the indispensables in Christian living—what Jesus and Paul and the total Christian tradition ceaselessly insist is essential for any disciple of Christ. I mean that all-important monosyllable . . . faith. Today I fasten on three facets of faith: (1) faith as you find it in Luke; (2) faith as we experience it within Catholicism; (3) faith as it touches you and your call to be deacons of Christ and his Church.[1]

I

First, Luke.[2] For Luke's Jesus, faith is a fundamental facet of Christian discipleship. I suggest that Jesus portrays it best in his parable of the Sower, the parable of the seed that fell some on a path, some on rock, some among thorns, some into good soil. For there Jesus describes his disciples in a single sentence: "Those who listen to the word and hold on to it with a noble and generous mind— these yield a crop through their persistence"; these bear fruit in face of adversity (Lk 8:15). Faith begins as a listening, but it does not end there. Faith indeed begins with listening. Remember St. Paul: "Faith comes from what is heard, and what is heard comes through the word of Christ" (Rom 10:17). But listening is not enough; listening should end in what Paul calls "submission" (Rom 1:5; 16:26), what we might call a personal commitment to God in Christ.[3]

Such a commitment, Luke's Jesus declares, is indescribably powerful. It's a strange picture Jesus draws. The disciples ask him to give them more faith. The petition evokes a peculiar response: "If you had faith the size of a mustard seed, you would say to this mulberry tree, 'Be uprooted and planted in the sea,' and it would obey you" (Lk 17:6). A mulberry tree transplanted in the sea? Gross! Matthew's gospel has Jesus speaking in similar vein but with different scenery: "If you have faith the size of a mustard seed, you will say to this mountain, 'Move from here over there,' and it will be moved; and nothing will be impossible to you" (Mt 17:20).[4]

The rhetoric may be outrageous but the reality is remarkably rich. Forget about the scenery—mountains and mulberry trees; focus on the fundamental affirmation. In point of fact, Jesus' answer does not really meet the disciples' request; he does not say, "O.K., here's some more faith." He puts the apostles on the spot. What is important is not the amount of faith but the kind of faith. If it were no bigger than a grain of mustard seed, it would still have unbelievable power.[5] The point is this: With even a minuscule amount of genuine faith, men and women who listen to Jesus' word and commit themselves to him can do things impossible to naked human nature. Can you recall how Mark's Gospel ends? "These signs will accompany those who believe: By using my name they will cast out demons; they will speak in new tongues; . . . they will lay their hands on the sick, and the sick will recover" (Mk 16:17–18).

II

Second, what is this faith as we experience it within Catholicism? What is this commitment in concrete reality? In the Catholic vision it has at least two breath-taking aspects. First, it is an intellectual reality. I mean the so-called Act of Faith that was drilled into me seven decades ago by Sisters of Charity: "I believe everything the Catholic Church teaches, because you [my God] have revealed it— you who can neither deceive nor be deceived." I accept what God revealed through Christ; I accept it not because the Church says so; I accept it because through the Church God has made it possible for me to accept it. It is on God's word that I can make the most awesome declarations: "There is but one God in three divine Persons"; "The Son of God was born of the Virgin Mary"; "This wafer that looks like bread, feels like bread, tastes like bread is not bread; it is Jesus Christ, flesh and blood, soul and divinity."

Highly important for a genuinely Catholic faith. Why? Because the Son of God took our flesh and died for us to tell us something—

about God, about ourselves, about living and dying. Taking God's truth on God's word is frightfully important for any true believer. But faith is not simply a head trip. When the apostles begged Jesus, "Increase our faith" (Lk 17:5), what were they asking for? Not a catechism, a laundry list of doctrines to be accepted without delay; not the Creed we offer at Sunday Mass after the homily. Nor was Jesus about to tell them what doctrines they had to believe to enter the kingdom. What Peter and Matthew and John wanted was an increase in trust. For faith in its fulness is a surrender of my whole person. The head trip will not save me, will not save anyone. Never forget the New Testament Letter of James: "You believe that God is one; you do well. [But] Even the demons believe—and shudder" (Jas 2:19). No one has ever reached eternal life simply by reciting, with sincerity, each article of the Creed. To believe means that I yield everything, including my whole self, to God. Here it is that I risk all. Against all the odds, against all my fears, against all the objections, against (in a sense) all reason, I utter a total yes to a God whose will in my regard I frequently find difficult to understand.

A total yes in darkness. Here belief involves total trust. It is Abraham leaving country and kindred, "not knowing where he was to go" (Heb 11:8), not knowing what would happen to him along the way, knowing only that God was calling him—calling him, at age 75, to leave what he loved and to settle where God alone knew. It is Job crying out in the midst of his torments, "Though [God] slay me, yet will I trust in Him" (Job 13:15).[6] It is Mother Teresa explaining her success to an inquiring reporter: "I am like a little pencil in [God's] hand. The pencil has only to be allowed to be used."[7] It is my own mother, burying my father and only brother within three weeks of each other, not reciting the Nicene Creed, only repeating again and again "Sacred Heart of Jesus, I place my trust in thee."

Do you want an extraordinary, an unexpected example? Jesus Christ. I suspect that a fair number of Catholics do not realize that Jesus lived a life of faith. We tend to see him so absorbed in his Father, so protected by his Father, that faith played little or no part in his life. Wrong! The famous German theologian Karl Rahner brought this home to me in his last years.

> According to Scripture we may safely say that Jesus in his life was the *believer* . . . and that he was consequently the one who hopes absolutely and . . . loves absolutely. In the unity of [his] faith, hope, and love, Jesus surrendered himself in his death unconditionally to the absolute mystery that he called his Father, into whose hands

he committed his existence, when in the night of his death and
Godforsakenness he was deprived of everything that is otherwise
regarded as the content of a human existence. . . . Everything fell
away from him, even the [felt] security of the closeness of God's
love, and in this trackless dark there prevailed silently only the
mystery that . . . has no name and to which he nevertheless calmly
surrendered himself as to eternal love and not to the hell of
futility. . . .[8]

The point is this: For all that he was the Son of God, for all that
he had a unique relationship with his Father,[9] this man too died not
with experience of resurrection, not with unassailable proof that he
would rise from the dead; he died with faith in his Father, with hope
of life for ever. That is why his last words from the cross are so striking,
so faith-full: "Father, into your hands I entrust my spirit" (Lk 23:46).
He died trusting—trusting in a Father ever faithful. Remember
what his enemies said as they taunted him on Calvary? "He trusts
in God; let God deliver him now, if He wants to" (Mt 27:43). He
trusts in God. . . .

III

This leads into my third point: your life as deacons of Christ and
his Church. Let me focus on one facet of that life, the facet on which
we have been focusing for two days: your apostolate as preachers. It
is not the only facet of your vocation, but I am convinced it is as
significant for you as it is for the ordained priest. A commentary on
canon 762 of the 1983 Code of Canon Law declares: "The proclamation of the gospel is what *makes* the Church; nothing can be placed
ahead of it among the priorities of its ministers." This is your "primary responsibility."[10] Why? Because of its importance for faith, for
the faith life of your people. They kneel and stand and sit before you
hungering not only for the *Bread* of life; they hunger for the *Word* of
life. You can distribute God's Bread mechanically and not threaten
the faith of a single man or woman. You cannot proclaim God's Word
like a robot and not plead guilty of infidelity before God and your
people.

We have no statistics on how many Catholics leave us because
they are not nourished by God's Word on our lips. But I can assure
you that their number is not insignificant. Day after day we hear of
Hispanic Catholics deserting us by the hundreds for the passionate
preaching of the Pentecostals.

Your preaching is not an optional interlude between Gospel and Creed. It is your solemn obligation, as pencils in God's hand, to help increase the faith of your flock. How do that? Before all else, what must come through to your people is that *you* have faith, that you not only accept as true what God has revealed, but that you have entrusted yourself entirely to Christ, that you can sing with the Psalmist (Ps 25:1–2):

> To you, O Lord, I lift up my soul.
> O my God, in you I trust.

Second, what is your story? Have you come through a valley of darkness? Can you tell your struggling people that you have wrestled like Jacob with God and that like Job you will trust God even were God to take from you all that is dear to you, even were God to slay you? Even without a single explicit "I," is your homily your own pilgrimage of faith?

Let me not seem to stress the perils in your preaching. Even more important is the privilege and the promise. In the midst of Christ's Church you exercise what is arguably the most significant function for the faith of the Catholic people. Am I downplaying the Eucharist? I do not think so. The Eucharist is indeed our central act of worship. But I find it difficult to forget a startling observation made a couple of decades ago by French Dominican Yves Congar, one of the most learned and respected theologians in the Church: "I could quote a whole series of ancient texts, all saying more or less that if in one country Mass was celebrated for thirty years without preaching and in another there was preaching for thirty years without the Mass, people would be more Christian in the country where there was preaching."[11]

Dear deacons of Christ: Your people are ceaselessly begging, "Increase our faith." Some mutely, others clamorously; some humbly, others angrily; some gratefully, others resentfully; but all want to come closer to Christ. Their yearning is the ancient prayer preserved in the musical *Godspell:* "Dear Lord. these three I pray: to see you more clearly, love you more dearly, follow you more nearly." To promote this process, such is your vocation. Oh yes, it is God who gives the increase. But God does not operate in a vacuum; God uses men and women, by divine decision needs Christians like you, to speak of God and our pilgrimage to God in language that heals while it burns, challenges while it comforts, stimulates while it reconciles.

Here and there your ministry may be loaded with land mines:

the view from the pew, the resistance in rectories. In your stoning, you just might have to pray with your archetype Stephen, "Lord, do not hold this sin against them" (Acts 7:60). And then, with God's warm blessing, go on increasing the faith of your folk. For your consolation, know that my own admiration for you is uncommonly high. Never forget the wise words of Gamaliel, "a teacher of the law, respected by all the people," as he addressed the Jewish council on the subject of the original apostles: "If this undertaking is of God, [no one] will be able to overthrow [it]" (Acts 6:39). Believe it, dear deacons, your undertaking is of God.

St. Joseph's Church
Tacoma, Washington
October 3, 1992

24
I FELT ONLY GRATITUDE. . . .
Twenty-eighth Sunday of the Year (C)

- 2 Kings 5:14–17
- 2 Timothy 2:8–13
- Luke 17:11–19

Today I shall spell out a six-letter word. It's a slender monosyllable basic to human and divine living. Without it, in any and every language, we would revert to barbarism. The six-letter monosyllable is . . . thanks. I begin with today's Gospel, move to a significant Catholic insight, and close with some pertinent (or impertinent) suggestions for you.

I

First, the Gospel. I wonder whether, in my swift reading of today's Gospel, you might have missed the irony, the pathos, of this episode. Ten lepers indeed, but only nine were Jews. The odd fellow was a Samaritan, unwelcome in Jerusalem, uncomfortable in its temple. Remember the revealing sentence in John's Gospel: "Jews do not share things in common with Samaritans" (Jn 4:9)? This Samaritan was welcome only to nine Jews, welcome because with Hansen's disease (if that's what it was) all ten were outcasts, all ten huddled together on the margin of two societies—as Luke puts it, "along the borders of Samaria and Galilee" (Lk 17:11). Ironic too, pathetic because only the Samaritan returned from his healing to the living temple of the New Covenant, the Jew Jesus. Only the Samaritan came back to say "thanks." Thanks not only for removing his leprosy, his alienation from the rest of God's children, restoring him to human society. Even more importantly, thanks for the faith that removed his alienation from God, restoring him to divine friendship. Jesus' part-

118

ing sentence is unforgettable: "Your faith has brought you salvation" (v. 19).[1]

II

This leads into my second point: a significant Catholic insight.
Negatively, what *not* to say thanks for. Jesus summed it up in his
pungent parable of the Pharisee and the toll collector praying in
the temple. Remember the prayer of the Pharisee? "I thank you,
God, that I am not like the rest of humankind—robbers, evildoers,
adulterers—or even like this toll collector. I fast twice a week; I pay
a tithe on all that I acquire" (Lk 18:11–12).

What was wrong with the Pharisee's thanksgiving? Not the details.
Jesus did not deny a single boast, did not say, "You lie! You've had
sex with your best friend's wife; you've done some insider trading at
the Tel Aviv Stock Exchange; you fast on Wednesdays, but never on
Fridays; and you give only a 20th of your produce for the support of
the temple." Where, then, did his fault lie? In the Pharisee's emphasis
on "I," on himself. Not only does he attribute his virtue to his own
powers; he sets himself apart from the assembled worshipers. "His
virtue is as destructive of real community as was the wealth of the
rich man"[2] who never saw hungry Lazarus lying at his gate. This is
not to bless God; this is not to give God the glory; this is not to thank
God—except to thank God for making him different.

This attitude is poles apart from that of America's most remarkable Trappist, Thomas Merton. A quarter century ago he described
a shattering, liberating experience. He had been a monk for 16 or
17 years. Walking through the shopping district of Louisville in Ken-
tucky, he suddenly felt he was waking from a dream. A dream that
he was somehow separate, isolated in a special world; the illusion that
by taking vows monks become a different species of being. Yes indeed,
the monk belongs to God; but, as Merton put it, "so does everybody
else belong to God. We just happen to be conscious of it, and to
make a profession out of this consciousness. But does that entitle us
to consider ourselves different, or even *better,* than others? The whole
idea is preposterous." Then follows a splendid, shivering outburst:

This sense of liberation from an illusory difference was such a relief
and such a joy that I almost laughed out loud. And I suppose my
happiness could have taken form in the words: "Thank God, thank
God that I *am* like other men, that I am only a man among oth-

ers." . . . It is a glorious destiny to be a member of the human race, though it is a race dedicated to many absurdities and one which makes many terrible mistakes; yet, with all that, God Himself gloried in becoming a member of the human race.[3]

How ought God's intelligent creatures to express thanks? By praising God for two breath-taking gifts. First, God has made us what we are, men and women fashioned in God's own image. Second, God thought so much of what we are that God's own Son *became* what we are, bone of our bone, flesh of our flesh. In the lovely couplet of the English poet John Donne:

> 'Twas much that man was made like God before,
> But, that God should be made like man, much more.[4]

III

My third point is more direct, daringly personal. I dare to suggest three splendid ways of giving thanks to God that God would love to see in you and me.

Suggestion number 1 stems from a remarkable rabbi, Abraham Joshua Heschel. Several years before his death in 1972, Heschel suffered a near-fatal heart attack from which he never fully recovered. A dear friend visiting him then found him woefully weak. Just about able to whisper, Heschel said to him: "Sam, when I regained consciousness, my first feeling was not of despair or anger. I felt only gratitude to God for my life, for every moment I had lived. I was ready to depart. 'Take me, O Lord,' I thought, 'I have seen so many miracles in my lifetime.' " Exhausted by the effort, Heschel paused, then added: "That is what I meant when I wrote [in the preface to his book of Yiddish poems]: 'I did not ask for success; I asked for wonder. And You gave it to me.' "[5]

Thanksgiving through wonder. Wonder at what? Wonder at simply being alive, at experiencing so many marvels day after day. Wonder that a child can be shaped of your flesh and spirit. Amazement that with a flicker of eyelids or a leap of imagination you can cross oceans and see a Soviet empire collapse, Eastern Europe shake off the shackles of its slavery. Delight that you can love another human person as much as you love yourself, or even more. Surprise that your ears can recapture Mozart or Streisand, your nose nuzzle the fragrance of a rose, your fingers sculpt a statue or trace the lines on a dear one's face. Awe that God can rest within you, transform you into an image of Christ, that like the Samaritan leper God's gift of faith is bringing you to salvation. You may not have asked for wonder, but the Lord has given it to you. Grasp it in gratitude!

Second, a tough type of thanks. I mean "I thank you, Lord, for the cross you have laid on my shoulders, for the gift of sharing in your passion." For if we believe with Paul that "the cross is the power of God" (1 Cor 1:18), we must proclaim with him to our fellow Christians, "I am now rejoicing in my sufferings for your sake, and in my flesh I am completing what is lacking in Christ's afflictions for the sake of his body, the Church" (Col 1:24). No suffering need be wasted. If we are to heal a broken world, it has to be the way Jesus healed. In the Christ of Calvary, God heals because God feels, because "in Christ the burdens of the world become God's burdens too...."[6]

It may well be the most difficult "thank you" God asks of us. Not only on the final, breathless cross, but on every cross erected along the way. Pain of flesh or of spirit—diverticula or disappointments, a sudden stroke or a lingering cancer, dying hopes or the death of a dear one, the insecurities of youth and the trembling of the aging—whatever it is that pricks our pride, assails our lustiness, intimates our mortality, takes the joy from our very bones, here is where the faith-full follow Christ most faithfully. Here is where we must murmur with him, "Father, into your hands I entrust my spirit" (Lk 23:46). Here too is Heschel's "I asked for wonder." Wonder that God's Son asks us to join him as he lifts our world from today's cross—your cross and mine.

Third, our central act of thanksgiving: I mean the Eucharist. For Eucharist *means* thanksgiving. But the Eucharist is a genuine thanksgiving only if we ourselves become eucharists for the life of the world. Four verbs in each consecration spell out the rhythm in Christian discipleship. What Jesus did to ordinary bread at the Supper, that Jesus does to ordinary flesh and blood, to you. Jesus took, Jesus blessed, Jesus broke, Jesus gave. In giving you life, Jesus *chose* you to follow him. In your baptism Jesus *blessed* you, consecrated you to be his disciple. In your suffering Jesus "*breaks*" you, burns out the damnable concentration on self, remolds you to himself, shapes you as a man or woman for others. And so, wherever you are, Jesus *gives* you—chosen, blessed, and broken—gives you to a whole little world for its salvation. As the bread is transformed into Christ's body, do you feel your own flesh transformed into Christ, to share in his work of redemption?

Good friends: Worth pondering today are Jesus' three questions as the Samaritan knelt at his feet, the Samaritan with flesh cleansed of leprosy and eyes opened in faith[7]: "Were not ten made clean? The other nine, where are they? Can it be that none has been found to come back and give glory to God but this foreigner?" (Lk 17:17–18). Perhaps, as we proceed to welcome little Elizabeth and Lara into our community of faith,[8] these two newborn believers will open *our* eyes to the daily wonder of our existence, to what the Church proclaims as the triumph of the cross (of our cross), so that this Eucharist and every Eucharist will be a fresh return to the Christ who heals our own leprosies, a resounding song of thanksgiving in harmony with the outburst of the Psalmist:

> It was you who created my inmost self,
>   you knit me together in my mother's womb.
> For all this I praise you:
>   for the wonder of myself,
>   for the wonder of your works.
>   (Ps 139:13–14)

Holy Trinity Church
Washington, D.C.
October 11, 1992

25
DESTROY THIS TEMPLE AND . . . ?
Thirty-third Sunday of the Year (C)

- Malachi 3:19–20
- 2 Thessalonians 3:7–12
- Luke 21:5–19

If today's Gospel confused you, take heart! One of Catholicism's most learned biblical scholars tells us, "There are almost as many interpretations of [this discourse] as there are heads to think about it."[1] Since a homily is not a lecture, I shall not take you on a head trip over what Scripture experts call Jesus' eschatological discourse. And still we dare not avoid this Gospel altogether, focus instead on St. Paul's intriguing observation, "Anyone unwilling to work should not eat" (2 Thess 3:10). So, three questions: (1) What was Jesus talking about then? (2) What might Jesus be saying now, in a different context? (3) How might you and I respond to today's Gospel today?

I

First, what was Jesus talking about then? If we look simply at today's Gospel, he was predicting the destruction of Jerusalem (he would go on later to foretell the end of the world).[2] Some of his listeners had been exclaiming ecstatically about the beauty of Jerusalem's temple. You may remember that in the year 588 before Christ the king of Babylonia, a tongue-twister named Nebuchadnezzar, laid siege to Jerusalem. Not only did he waste the city and deport its citizens to Babylonia; he destroyed utterly the magnificent temple that had been shaped by Solomon over seven years. After the Jews returned from that despairing captivity, they rebuilt the temple on the site of the old. It was more modest, did not have all the splendid appointments of Solomon's structure. In fact, Herod the Great began

123

to refurbish it in the year 20 before Christ. He erected new foundation walls, enlarged the surrounding area to twice its former dimensions.[3] Work on the reconstruction continued for decades. Recall in John's Gospel how the Jews exclaimed to Jesus in disbelief, "This temple has been under construction for 46 years, and will you raise it up in three days?" (Jn 2:20).

It is of this glorious temple that Jesus prophesied, "the time is coming when not a stone of it will be left upon a stone that will not be torn down" (Lk 21:6). It was the curtain of this temple that "was torn in two, from top to bottom" (Mt 27:51) when Jesus died. It was this temple that was destroyed by the Romans in 70 A.D., its treasures and furnishings carried off to Rome as trophies by triumphant general Titus.

II

Enough about the temple in ancient Jerusalem. The problem with today's Gospel is that "it refers to a first-century crisis that no longer obtains today."[4] After 19 centuries, what can we learn from this Gospel? What was it that concerned Jesus as he predicted the destruction of Jerusalem's pride and glory? Obviously, he did not want to see the temple in ruins; as a genuine Jew, he loved it. Here Mary and Joseph presented him to the Lord; here he sat among the teachers, "listening to them and asking them questions" (Lk 2:46). But what can the 20th century learn from the admiration the Jews had for their lovely house of God and the warning of Jesus that this house of loveliness would not last? (1) A lesson from human history. (2) The most important facet of religion. (3) A footnote about the end of our world.

First, a lesson from human history: Life is a constant movement, fluctuation, between good happenings and bad. You don't need a theologian to tell you that; Scripture is a prime witness. The Israelites experienced it. They had their Exile and their Exodus, their enslavement in Egypt under harsh taskmasters and their passage to freedom through the Red Sea. They murmured against God in the wilderness, and they blessed God when they entered the Promised Land. Their prophet Amos told them that because of their infidelities God despised their festivals and took no delight in their solemn assemblies, refused their sacrifices, would not listen to the melody of their harps (see Amos 5:12, 21–23). And their prophet Isaiah has God declaring to them when they think themselves Godforsaken:

Can a woman forget her nursing child,
   or show no compassion for the child of her womb?
Even these may forget,
   yet I will not forget you.
See, I have inscribed you on the palms of my hands.
(Isa 49:15–16)

Second lesson: the most important facet of religion. It is not a temple of stone. Recall the strong warning of the prophet Jeremiah: "Hear the word of the Lord, all you people of Judah, you that enter these gates to worship the Lord. Thus says the Lord of hosts, the God of Israel: . . . Do not trust in these deceptive words: This is the temple of the Lord, the temple of the Lord, the temple of the Lord" (Jer 7:2–4).

No, the temple never saved a single Jew. Listen again to the words of Yahweh on the lips of Jeremiah:

> Here you are, trusting in deceptive words to no avail. Will you steal, murder, commit adultery, swear falsely, make offerings to Baal, and go after other gods that you have not known, and then come and stand before me in this house, which is called by my name, and say "We are safe!"—only to go on doing all these abominations?
>
> (Jer 7:8–10)

What, then, did save the Jewish believer? Listen once more to Jeremiah's Lord:

> If you truly amend your ways and your doings, if you truly act justly one with another, if you do not oppress the alien, the orphan, and the widow, or shed innocent blood in this place, and if you do not go after other gods to your own hurt, then I will dwell with you in this place. . . .
>
> (Jer 7:5–7)

What saves? The temple of God that is the human person beloved of God, in love with God, in love with the human images of God.

Third lesson: a footnote about the end of our world. Not ours to know, or be concerned about, just when this world will end. Jesus spoke of signs—signs that would herald the destruction of the temple, signs that would signal the end of the world. He predicted wars and quakes, plagues and persecutions, famines and martyrdoms; signs in the sky, on earth, in the seas. Since then, we have never lacked for self-proclaimed prophets who knew exactly when Christ's signs were here, when he would return to inaugurate his kingdom. Some said 156, others 1000, others 1260. Again and again, in my own lifetime, thousands have gathered on the hills of the world to greet their Savior. A TV evangelist has laid out the precise battle line of Armageddon, the great battle to be fought at the end between the powers of good and evil. A decade ago, in a Virginia college, I was assured by a student that all the signs in the Book of Revelation are here for all to see (except a myopic Jesuit).

Without exception, these good Christians have focused on the signs, have discovered them everywhere—from an oppressive Roman Empire, through the Huns and Saracens, to the atom bomb, the AIDS epidemic, and the Gulf War. What they have failed to ponder is a simple declarative sentence uttered by Jesus Christ: "About that day and hour no one knows, neither the angels of heaven, nor the Son, but only the Father" (Mt 24:36). He did add a logical recommendation: Since Christ is coming "at an unexpected hour," you must "be ready [always]" (v. 44).

III

That sentence, "Be ready," leads neatly into my third question: How might you and I respond to today's Gospel today, react to our own "temple experience" of glory and destruction? Along the lines of the three lessons I sketched. First, human and Christian living is a ceaseless struggle, a fluctuation between joy and sorrow, success and failure, the manic and the depressive, highs and lows, bad things happening to good people (yes, good things happening to bad people). There is an inescapable tension in Christian living between sanctity and sinfulness. Like the Church, each of us is by God's grace holy, but always in need of reformation, conversion, new life.

In my younger days we tended to see Christian spirituality as a gradual, steady ascent, ever onwards ever upwards, to what was called "Christian perfection," with the ways and stages marked out in advance by a theology of the spiritual life. It makes more sense to see myself "as someone who is led by God's providence in [my] life history through continually new and surprising situations, in which [I] can never say from the outset what will happen and how [I] must cope with it."[5] Our way to God is more a matter of faithful following, with the courage to expect the unexpected, to respond to the unexpected not from 3 × 5 file cards but in total openness to a God who, like Augustine's Beauty, is ever ancient, ever new. Then the spiritual life becomes not a fearful scaling of icy slopes but a glorious adventure in which you and I can predict only two things with confidence: (1) The Holy Spirit will constantly surprise us and (2) however unexpected the event, God will always be there.

Second, the most important facet of our religion is not this temple of stone. Lovely though it is, house of God though it is, it does not automatically save you. The more important temple is the temple St. Paul commended to the Christians of Corinth: "Do you not know that you are God's temple and that God's Spirit dwells in you? . . . God's temple is holy, and you are that temple" (1 Cor 3:16–17). That is why Paul was so furious with fornicators: "Do you not know that your bodies are members of Christ? . . . Do you not know that your body is a temple of the Holy Spirit within you, [the Spirit] which you have from God, and that you are not your own? For you were bought with a price; therefore glorify God in your body" (1 Cor 6:15, 19–20).

This house of God houses a precious tabernacle; that tabernacle houses the body of Christ. And so we bow before it, bend our knee before it. Have you ever thought that, in wondrous Christian reality, each of you can, may, should bow in reverence before each other? For each of you houses God within you. You might keep that in mind today when you murmur to one another, "The peace of Christ."

Third, let not today's signs shatter your peace of mind, threaten you with the world's ending, with Christ coming on clouds of glory to judge you for eternity. "About that day and hour no one knows," not even the pastor of Holy Trinity! I suggest rather that you live always *as if* . . . as if Christ is coming today. Not in fear and trembling, but with the quiet joy that stems from your realization that the Christ who is coming is already within you; that he meets you in the Christophers, the Christ-bearers, who surround you here and at home; that he touches you in the hungry you nourish, the naked you clothe, the stranger you welcome, the sick you console, those you visit imprisoned behind iron bars or walls of loneliness.

Good friends in Christ: The destruction of one magnificent temple can build up gloriously the temple that is you—if you have eyes to see, if you take time to reflect on it, to ponder its deeper meaning. Since Vatican II was so thrillingly correct in proclaiming that Christ himself "speaks when the holy Scriptures are read in the church,"[6] don't hesitate to ask our dear Lord what it is he is saying to you. Not so much what he is saying to *me*–that much I've just revealed to you. Rather, what is Christ trying to tell *you?* Listen to him . . . please listen.

Holy Trinity Church
Washington, D.C.
November 15, 1992

WEDDING HOMILIES

26
POET, LUNATIC, LOVER
Wedding Homily 1

- Genesis 1:26–28, 31
- Romans 12:1–2, 9–18
- John 2:1–11

Kathy and Tim: Within the Catholic Church there are all sorts of paradoxes. A paradox, you recall, is a *seeming* contradiction. One of the humorous paradoxes within Catholicism is the custom whereby a couple just setting out on the adventure that is marriage are addressed by a man who has resolved not to. But during a half century of priesting, this paradoxical task has afforded me some of the most delightful moments in ministry.

Today let me go out on something of a limb. I want to apply to Kathy and Tim, and to all of the married among you, what a splendid Protestant preacher once said of the religious man, the religious woman. A religious person, he mused, is "a queer mixture" of three persons: "the poet, the lunatic, the lover."[1] After 50 years of wedding-watching, I am convinced that if wedded life is to touch the heights of happiness God intended for you, each of you has to be a queer mixture of three persons: poet, lunatic, and lover. Sound "off the wall" to you? I hope so. A word on each word.

I

First, to make a marriage work, you must have something of the poet in you. Oh, I don't mean you write verses to each other: "How do I love thee? Let me count the ways./ I love thee to the depth and height/ My soul can reach. . . . / I love thee to the level of every day's/ Most quiet need. . . . / I love thee freely. . . . / I love thee purely. . . . / I love thee . . . with my childhood's faith./ . . . I love thee

131

with the breath,/ Smiles, tears, of all my life!—and, if God choose,/ I shall but love thee better after death."[2] No. I simply pray that the poet may always be part of you. For poets are not people who can compose cute rhymes. Poets are persons of profound *faith*. I mean, they see beneath the appearance of things, see with new eyes. It's Mary singing her Magnificat with God's Son in her body: "The Mighty One has done great things for me, and holy is His name" (Lk 1:49). It's Jesuit Gerard Manley Hopkins comparing our Lady to the air we breathe: We "are meant to share/ Her life as life does air."[3] It's medieval lady mystic Julian of Norwich wondering why a little thing, "the size of a hazelnut," did not "suddenly fade away to nothing, it was so small," then seeing why, seeing in it three properties: "God made it, God loveth it, God keepeth it."[4]

You see, faith is not some vague, abstract thing you call on when reason deserts you, when you find yourself behind the 8-ball in an argument with an atheist. Faith is a gift, a God-given gift, that enables you to see more than meets the eye. With this gift you see a criminal on a cross and cry "My Lord and my God!" With this gift you see what looks like bread and murmur "O Lord, I am not worthy." With this gift you see in a devastated AIDS-afflicted the image of God. With this gift you know that the cold flesh of a dear one will rise again unto life without end.

Now that is the gift your wedded life demands. For without it you risk taking each other for granted. You see only as far as the eye can see. You lose the wonder of the other, see only skin-deep. You see only what the rest of the world sees: the blemish, the peccadillo, the mole, the twitch, the irritant. Time covers over what the passage from Genesis just proclaimed to you: This other was made by God, was made like God, was made for you. You risk seeing only what grows old, grows gray, grows feeble. You lose sight of all that caught your young eyes, your poet's eyes, the transparent beauty within.

Pray, then, for the poet within you, to see with the eyes of faith, with the eyes of Christ. Pray that, as the years move on, you will see in the other what God sees. Someone indeed very human, with all the graces and flaws that mark whatever is earth-bound. And still someone remarkably divine, because a human image of an imaginative God . . . another Christ.

II

Second, to make a marriage work, you need something of the lunatic, a fair measure of lunacy. I don't mean "off your rocker." I mean the wild idea, the foolishness of the cross, the mad exchange of all else for God, for each other, for each of God's images; for herein lies your Christian *hope*.

You see, from a sheerly human viewpoint, it makes little sense to commit your whole life to a single human being. Little wonder that half of American marriages break up. And yet you do so commit. Not because you can prove that you will celebrate a golden anniversary with swarms of children and grandchildren munching your cake and cuddling in your arms. You give your whole self, give lavishly, because this is how a disciple of Christ gives.

Remember, it made little human sense for God's only Son to take your flesh and mine, little human sense for him to be born of a woman as you and I are born, little human sense for him to save us from ourselves by dying in shame on a cross between two thieves. The point is, God is incredibly lavish in giving. God never asks, "How much do I have to give?" God did not say, "I've got it! We'll redeem the world in Bethlehem, beside a lovely manger. Forget that crucifixion stuff; that's just too much." You heard the miracle at Cana. When the wine ran out, Jesus made wine out of water. Not a quart, not a fifth. About 150 gallons! Wine better than the wine the guests had been drinking. An abundance that in the Old Testament symbolizes the joy of the final days. "The mountains," says the prophet Amos, "shall drip sweet wine, and all the hills shall flow with it" (Amos 9:13).[5]

Christ's cross makes one thing crystal-clear: To be a Christian, a disciple of Christ, is to give. Not simply money; your whole self. This is gloriously symbolized in Christian marriage. "I take you ... for better for worse, for richer for poorer, in sickness and in health until death." Nothing is held back. Such is Christian hope: hope against all the odds, because you trust not in humans but in God, not in what the world holds out however glamorous but in the mercy of a God who promises you not another Garden of Eden but God's grace, God's love, God's strength, God's own poetry.

Such is the hope that follows on your total gift today. It calls for a wild exchange—all you are and all you have, given to God, given to the other you now love so passionately. As an older wedding exhortation phrased it, "Not knowing what lies before you. . . ." Knowing only that, whatever happens, God will be there . . . for you.

III

Third, to make a marriage work, the poet and the lunatic have to wed with the lover. Oh, not the lover you find on the "soaps," on TV's "Love Boat," in the pornography that mocks genuine love. I mean the realism Tim and Kathy found in Paul's letter to the Christians of Rome; for herein lies your Christian *love*.

What is Paul's "Let love be genuine" (Rom 12:9)? Just before that exhortation he had a significant reminder: "We, who are many, are one body in Christ and individually we are members of one another" (v. 5). What does this mean in the concrete, in raw reality? He tells you. If someone injures you, don't curse him; say "God bless you." If your enemy is hungry, take him to McDonald's; thirsty, give him a Bud. Someone harasses you? "So far as it depends on you, live peaceably with all" (v. 18). Then a tough one: Open your home to strangers.

Now don't get hung up on details. Don't ask Paul how he would open his home to strangers if he lived in New York. Behind Paul's examples lie Jesus' two primary commandments. The "great" commandment is, indeed, "Love God" above all else. But "a second is like it": Love other humans at least as much as you love yourself (Mt 22:36–39). Loving your sisters and brothers is like loving God.

What does this say to Kathy and Tim? The love you lavish on each other must go out. For if your love turns totally inward, exclusively to each other, it risks dying. One of the miracles of marriage is a fresh mission from God: to share your love, your two-in-oneness, with others. Not only with an "in" group, those who like you and share your likes. Especially to the disadvantaged, those who do not enjoy your freedoms, are imprisoned by so many shackles, find living itself a terrible burden.

Wherever you look, there is living death. Not only the 20 million starving in the Horn of Africa. All around you. Wherever your eye falls, there it will light on an image of God replaying Christ's crucifixion—from the AIDS-afflicted to women abused. One out of every five children in our fair land is born into poverty; one out of every three little blacks and Hispanics cannot live what we call a "decent life." For the homeless the 80s were a decade of despair. In front of San Francisco's City Hall a second city has arisen, cardboard condos that draw busloads of photo-snapping foreign tourists. At this moment of our joy our sisters and brothers are dying in our streets.

Take this precious love you have for each other today, bring it together not to some faraway mission but to the dear Christs you pass each day. Do this and, I promise you, not only will you help shape this country into a genuine "land of the free"; not only will you hear from the lips of our Lord, "Come, blessed of my Father" (Mt 25:34); your very love for each other will deepen beyond human telling.

Good friends all: a final word. You have gathered in this lovely house of God not as spectators, observers, lookers-on, as you might crowd Shea Stadium for your beloved Mets or Jets. You are here because each of you has played a part, large or medium or small, in the love that reaches so prominent a peak today. But your task is not done. If the love of Kathy and Tim is to endure, to grow, to reap its rich promise, they need not only the help *God* pledges them this day. They need *you*. And even more than Wedgwood china or Waterford glass, they need your example. I mean especially the example of husbands and wives who for one year or 50 have lived the poet, the lunatic, the lover. Men and women of profound *faith* who see God and themselves, the world and others, with ever-fresh eyes. Men and women of unconquerable *hope* who have exchanged all else for God and each other. Men and women with a *love* that mirrors the love of Christ, that extends their crucified arms to their sisters and brothers.

And so, to symbolize your share in the future of Kathy and Tim, I offer an unusual suggestion. As Kathy and Tim give themselves to each other, to the other outside, and to God, I ask the wedded among you to join your own hands and murmur with new meaning enriched by experience: "My dearest, I take you for better for worse, for richer for poorer, in sickness and in health, as long as life shall last."

Here, dear friends, is one wedding gift that need never grow old, never wear out. It is more enduring than "diamonds for ever." For the gift you are giving is the gift of yourself. Your gift to Kathy and Tim is . . . you.

Saint Ignatius Martyr Church
Long Beach, New York
February 15, 1992

27

ROOTED AND GROUNDED IN LOVE
Wedding Homily 2

- Deuteronomy 10:12–22
- Ephesians 3:14–21
- John 6:41–51

You have just heard an unusual word: Jews and Christians call it the Word of *God*. Stacy and John selected three passages from that Word—passages that suggest how they see their life together. It is summed up in a phrase from St. Paul: "rooted and grounded in love" (Eph 3:17). But the love in question has three facets. The love of John and Stacy must (1) be directed to each other, (2) be rooted in God, (3) go out to others. A word on each.

I

First, the love of Stacy and John for each other. Obviously, this is basic; without it, we may have a contract, but not much else. Unfortunately, in our culture the word "love" is tossed about with reckless abandon. Love is a one-night stand that blossomed in a singles' bar; a cruise on TV's "Love Boat"; a summer romance on Fire Island; delight in a Bud Lite or Chanel Number Five. A macho way of saying "Good-bye" is . . . "Love ya."

All such usage trivializes a sacred word, makes it petty, paltry, of small account. The love we celebrate today is a remarkable wedding of so much that makes for genuinely human living. For Stacy and John, love is a gift—not of some thing but of their total selves. For them, love is profound friendship—what two other dear friends of mine inscribed on their wedding invitation: "This day I will marry my best friend, the one I laugh with, live for, love." For John and Stacy, love is a commitment, a pledge: "I promise to be true to you, not through '92 but as long as life shall last." For them, love is ceaseless wonder—all lost in wonder at the miracle of the other, in good times and bad, in sickness and in health, in poverty and wealth. For them, love is a wedding of magic and routine, of high points and low. For them, to love is to care, to feel deeply, to be sensitive to the other's hurt. For them, love is something that grows, that matures, that is never so perfect they can take it for granted. For them, love is inseparable from stress, from anxiety, from disagreement, from crucifixion; for, as the incomparable lover that was Jesus declared, "Greater love than this no one has, to lay down one's life for one's friends" (Jn 15:13).

That is why it is so difficult to reduce love to a definition. Lovers like Stacy and John know love by living it, know love by loving, know love from a touch more surely than from words. It is indeed a blessing, a grace, for us to see the face of love on the faces of two we love so dearly.

II

Second, the love of Stacy and John for each other must be rooted in God. Oh yes, there is human love that has little obvious relationship to God. I remember Elizabeth Barrett Browning's touching sonnet,

> If thou must love me, let it be for naught
> Except for love's sake only. . . .[1]

Such love is good. But that love deepens immeasurably when the two who love are aware that their love was born of God. I mean the God who knew them before He shaped them; who shaped them from the excess of God's love; who with divine imagination shaped them not one but two, similar but not the same; who shaped them not only *from* love but *for* love; who made it possible for them to "be fruitful and multiply" (Gen 1:28). It is this God who, at a wedding in Chicago, against all the odds brought Waterloo and Philadelphia together, Mizzou[2] and Notre Dame, biology and law. It is this God whose grace touched each to the other when so much might have kept them apart.

It is this God who deepened their natural love through Christ, accomplished in them the prayer they have lifted from Paul's letter to the Christians of Ephesus: "I pray that . . . Christ may dwell in your hearts through faith, . . . that you may have the power to comprehend, with all the saints, what is the breadth and length and height and depth, and to know the love of Christ that surpasses knowledge, so that you may be filled with the fulness of God" (Eph 3:16–19).

It is in this Eucharist, the endless memorial of history's most incredible love, that they will receive, for the first time as man and wife, the Christ who promised, "I am the living bread that came down from heaven. Whoever eats of this bread will live for ever; and the bread that I will give for the life of the world is my flesh" (Jn 6:51).

It is this God who made the marriage of Christians a breath-taking symbol. You see, for St. Paul and Catholic theology, the union of Stacy and John expresses, more powerfully perhaps than any other symbol, the incredible oneness that links the bridegroom Christ to his bride the Church. Yes, Paul proclaims, "This [Christian marriage] is a great mystery, and I am applying it to Christ and the Church" (Eph 5:32).

III

This slides nicely into my third movement. The reading from Deuteronomy asks a direct question: "So now, O Israel, what does the Lord your God require of you?" (Deut 10:12). The reply is so sweeping that it takes your breath away: "Fear God and love God, walk in all God's ways and keep God's commandments, serve God with all your heart and soul" (v. 12). The commands are clear and I commend them to all of you, married and unmarried, men and women. But as the passage moves on, God says something that is thrillingly concrete, that spells out in one specific direction what it means to love God, fear God, walk in God's ways, keep God's commandments, serve God the way God wants. "The Lord your God . . . executes justice for the orphan and the widow, loves the strangers, providing them food and clothing. You shall also love the stranger, for you were strangers in the land of Egypt" (vv. 17–19).

I focus on this because it touches on a biblical imperative of supreme importance for genuine Judeo-Christian living, for the religious life of a man and woman who want very much to love not only each other but each other in God. You see, for the Israelites, justice was not simply ethics or law: Give to others what they deserve, what they can claim from philosophy or in a courtroom. Justice was a set of relationships that stemmed from a covenant with God. The Jews were to give to others what they had been given by God, and precisely because God had so given. This was what the prophet Micah meant when he confronted his people: "What does the Lord require of you? Act justly, love steadfastly, and walk humbly with your God" (Mic 6:8). Not to do justice was not to worship God.

If the love story of Stacy and John is to have its full realization, then the love that began with God, the love they focus on each other, must move out to a wider world. They do not, will not, live on a fantasy island. All around them are images of the crucified Christ: the children never to be born and the aged discarded as useless, teenagers prostituted and teenagers pregnant, shivering men huddling on warm grates and hungry women scraping for food in garbage cans, white and black in a tenuous truce, untold millions on hospital beds in helpless pain. And the Lord who in love shaped one human family, the Christ who shed his blood for each one of these, sighs whenever we, like the priest in the Gospel parable, pass by "on the other side" (Lk 10:31).

Fortunately, in John and Stacy God's justice and God's mercy meet. He the president of Lawyers for Life, linking love for law with the law of love, she about to move from biology, the science of life, to nursing, the art of healing—how graciously, how gracefully, God is working in these two so human to mimic divine justice, divine mercy, to love as Jesus loved, to "walk humbly with [their] God." Today they link not only their hearts but their heads and their hands, place those hands in the pierced hands of the Jesus who took our flesh, the flesh of each human, to save it, to free it, to see that it is loved.

That is why the recessional, their exit from this house of God, will be more than the end of a lovely service. It is highly symbolic; for it symbolizes the movement of Stacy and John from church to world, from God to people, from two-in-one to two-for-all.

A final word. Each time I preach for dear friends about to wed, I end with a special word for the dear ones in the pews. You see, a wedding is not a spectator sport. You have come together not to "ooh" and "ah," but because each of you has played a role—feature or supporting—in the love story that reaches a certain high point today. Indeed take pride in that! But the good news gets better: Your part in the love story has a long way to go. If, as St. Paul put it, Stacy and John are to be "rooted and grounded in love" increasingly as the years move on, they need you. Not simply the chinaware and the crystal. Even more importantly, the realization that you are always there for them—when the sun is shining and when the dark clouds gather. Above all, the example of so many of you who, for one year or for 50, have been "rooted and grounded in love," know from experience the delights and the depressions of wedded existence, have proven that what is impossible for men and women left to themselves is possible indeed when God is there—God and dear ones.

So then, a few moments from now, when Stacy and John join their hands with God's hands, I would ask the wedded among you to link your own hands and murmur with them, quietly or in the silence of your hearts, the words that ground your nuptial love: "I take you . . . for better for worse, for richer for poorer, in sickness and in health, till death do us part." No gift more substantial can you give to Stacy and John; for that gift to each other is your gift to them . . . the gift of your very selves, your promise to be with them, for them, as long as life shall last.

St. Patrick's Church
Cleveland, Ohio
April 24, 1992

28
ON EAGLE'S WINGS
Wedding Homily 3

- Genesis 2:18–24
- Philippians 2:1–4
- Matthew 7:24–27

Good friends: A wedding liturgy like ours has an in-built problem. There is so much joy in the event, so many friends meeting once again, so much interest in what Kate looks like and Joe—Kate never before so lovely, Joe more than a bit dazed by the wonder of it all—that the readings you just heard from God's own Book can pass over you lightly. Nice indeed to have something from Scripture, but easily forgotten. And that would be a shame. For the three passages read to you were chosen by Joe and Kate—chosen with extraordinary care. Why? Because these readings sum up what their life together means to them, sum it up in the singular way God speaks to them in the Scriptures. So then, to recapture what speaks so significantly to them but may have slipped by you, let me develop briefly three facets of their love relationship that emerge from the three passages. These facets have to do with the relationship of Joe and Kate (1) with God, (2) with each other, (3) with the world outside of them.

I

First, God. Wise people, the Gospel declares, build their house not on sand but on rock. Think of houses on Malibu or the shores of Lake Michigan. Torrential rains fall, floods rage, winds beat against lovely houses, yet this particular house does not fall. Why not? Because its foundation is rock. This parable of Jesus in today's Gospel raises a question for every man and woman, especially for men and women linking their lives for life: What is your rock? What gives you the surest guarantee that your life will stand up, will withstand what Shake-speare's tortured Hamlet called "the slings and arrows of outrageous fortune, the heart-ache and the thousand natural shocks that flesh is heir to"?[1]

For some, the rock is obvious; it hits you literally in the eyes every day from your TV screen. The rock is . . . Prudential. Build your future on that rock, on an insurance as impregnable as Gibraltar, and you have nothing to worry about. I'm afraid it will not wash. Prudential can indeed be an act of prudence, but "the shocks that flesh is heir to" are more than financial. They go to the very heart of human living—to the discouragement and despair that can plague us, the hostility and hate than tear humans apart, the illnesses mental and physical that change our personalities.

In a moving letter Joe wrote me in May about today's Gospel, he said: "Our partnership is built on a foundation of trust and com-munication." He was speaking explicitly of trust and communication between Kate and himself. But behind that letter, hidden in every line, was a sentence in Kate's letter the same day: "We feel that, rooted in family and faith, we can withstand the storms that are destined to try the walls." The only Rock that is really impregnable, utterly trustworthy, incapable of change is the One of whom our soloist sang so thrillingly in the Responsorial Psalm, "On Eagle's Wings":

> You who dwell in the shelter of the Lord,
>   who abide in His shadow for life,
> say to the Lord: "My refuge, my Rock
>   in whom I trust."
> And He will raise you up on eagle's wings,
>   bear you on the breath of dawn,
> make you to shine like the sun,
>   and hold you in the palm of His hand.[2]

"You who dwell in the shelter of the Lord." As Kate wrote to me, "good foreshadowing for the Gospel, huh?" Yes, Kate, yes indeed!

II

This moves us to my second point, a pointed question: Why ought husband and wife put their trust in the Lord? One good reason emerges from the first reading, the moving story from the second chapter of Genesis. It tells us much about God's mind-set in fashioning us, in shaping Kate and Joe.

Let your imaginations loose on that story. See the first human in Eden, glorying indeed in his masculinity, but feeling a strange sense of inadequacy, of being alone. God senses that. "It is not good that the man is alone; I will make him a helpmate like himself—a helper corresponding to him, a helper as his partner" (Gen 2:18). What does God do? Like a skillful designer, God first shapes the beasts of the field and the birds of the air, brings them to the man "to see what he would call them" (2:19). He "calls" them by name— that is, he recognizes them for what they are. And he sees that no one of them—however swift or strong or supple—can possibly be his helpmate, a genuine partner, a suitable companion. They are all so different from him. So God shapes another human—a second image of God, similar to the man but not the same—brings her to Adam: "What think you now, my good fellow?" And the man bursts out in a lyrical cry, an incomparable exclamation of gratitude and love: "This, this, this at last is bone of my bones and flesh of my flesh. . . . For this reason a man leaves his father and his mother and clings to his wife, and they become one flesh" (2:23–24).

In a word, the Lord God made marriage a significant part of God's creation. God made man and woman for each other. Why place your trust in God? Because it is God who made you for each other. Not only is there a chemistry that attracts you to each other. Over and above that, God made you in such fashion that each of you can recognize, appreciate, marvel at the wonder, the miracle of the other.

More than that—think of the plans laid in heaven for these two. How God must have smiled when Joe and Kate first met in 1990— on Pearl Harbor Day no less, just as she was leaving a Happy Hour; how God must have frowned when Kate left for ten months in Japan, with Joe a fond memory; how God's smile returned when Joe flew to Japan weeks later; how God burst into delighted laughter when Joe proposed to Kate—in Hong Kong, of course! Love literally on clouds; all this obviously "On Eagle's Wings."

Little wonder that Kate and Joe resonate to St. Paul's encouraging words: "Make my joy complete." How? "Be like-minded, share the same love, . . . do nothing from selfish ambition, but in humility regard the other as better than yourself" (Phil 2:2–3).

III

Trust in God . . . love each other. What is left? What Kate and Joe plucked from St. Paul's exhortation to the Christians of his time: "Let each of you look not only to your own interests, but also to the interests of others" (Phil 2:4). Sounds dreadfully abstract, doesn't it? But the principle conceals and reveals a remarkable realization about Christians in general and the wedded in particular. Your love for each other, Kate and Joe, dare not remain a *pas de deux*, a dance for two. A penetrating woman psychologist put it splendidly:

> A love that is not for more than itself will die—the wisdom of Christian tradition and the best we know from psychology both assure us of this truth. It is often very appropriate at the early stages of a relationship that the energy of romance and infatuation exclude the larger world from our vision. But over the long haul an intimate relationship . . . which doesn't reach outward will stagnate.[3]

A warning to be scotch-taped to your refrigerator door: "Over the long haul an intimate relationship which doesn't reach outward will stagnate." The recessional—Kate and Joe bouncing down the aisle arm in arm, man and wife—is not simply or primarily the first steps to the reception. Here are the first steps from church to world, from altar to people, from Christ crucified on Calvary to Christ crucified again and again.

You know far better than I, Kate and Joe, how richly God has blessed you. Individually and together. These gifts of mind and heart are not yours to clutch in hot little hands. They are given you to be given away. Lavishly. The needs outside these sacred walls have rarely been so desperate. Take only our children, our future, our tomorrow. In the richest nation on earth, 1.6 million little ones each year never see the light of day; 67 newborn babies die each day; one out of every five children grows up hungry, ill-clad, illiterate; two and a half million children are physically, emotionally, or sexually abused or neglected each year; 25 percent of our teenagers drop out of school; untold thousands are hooked on crack or coke; more teenage boys die of gunshot wounds than from all natural causes combined; eight million children live in families without health insurance.

These are not cold statistics, to be shrugged off with a cynical "That's life." Each of these children is a despairing plea to you, to share your life, your love. This is not a foreign note, an inappropriate digression, in today's nuptial joy. I promise you, your love for each other will grow, will deepen immeasurably, each time you reach out to one small image of God, each time you see hope lighting a child's eyes from your love.

In sum, dear Kate and Joe, I have focused on three facets of your love: God, each other, and the others. (1) Put your trust without reservation in the hands of a loving Lord who shaped you for this day and as long as you two shall live. (2) Never take each other for granted; be ceaselessly amazed at the wonder of the other; recapture time and again that singular day in Hong Kong. (3) Leave this church together to reach out to the crucified images of Jesus, perhaps to walk every so often in the shoes of the unfortunate.

If there is a more noble, more necessary vocation on earth than yours, I have not heard of it. As you live this vocation together, allow me to pray for you the lovely Irish Blessing for Weddings:

> May the road rise to meet you.
> May the wind be always at your back.
> May the sun shine warm upon your face,
> The rains fall soft upon your fields.
> May the light of friendship guide your paths together.
> May the laughter of children grace the halls of your home.
> May the joy of living for one another
>   trip a smile from your lips,
> A twinkle from your eye.
> And when eternity beckons,
>   at the end of a life heaped high with love,
> May the good Lord embrace you
>   with the arms that have nurtured you
>   the whole length of your joy-filled days.
> May the gracious God hold you both
>   in the palm of His hands.

Mother of God Church
Mooseheart, Illinois
August 11, 1992

29

LOVE AMID THE RUINS
Wedding Homily 4

- 1 Corinthians 12:27—13:13
- Matthew 5:1–16
- Luke 10:25–37

I wonder if you realize the significance of the Scriptures that have just been read to you? These are not just lovely passages included in the wedding Mass because Rome has commanded it. Here Annie and Michael tell you and me how they see married life in the light of God's revealing Word. From these readings I extract three profound ideas, three ideas centering on love, three ideas I link today to the love of man and wife. To focus the three ideas, let me ask three questions: (1) What is real love like? (2) What does this mean for the relationship of Annie and Michael to each other? (3) How does the parable of the Good Samaritan fit into their married life?

I

First, what is real love like? Recently I discovered a fascinating fact. It has to do with words.

The Inuit people of Canada have at least twenty-four words for snow. Each word refines the overall concept of snow in some way. There will be a term for snow before a storm, another for snow after a storm, another for snow lying in a certain direction, another for snow at a certain season of the year. The reason for this absolute precision of language about snow is obvious; they live, eat, sleep, work, play and survive in snow.[1]

Twenty-four words for snow. Below the Canadian border we have reversed the process. For something that covers our entire lives, we have one word with at least 24 different meanings. If ever a four-letter word could cry out against its abuse, that word is "love." Make love is the total self-giving of a man and a woman, *and* make love is a one-night stand after a casual meeting in a singles' bar. Love is a growing experience that never ends, *and* love blossoms after an earth-shaking experience like Doublemint gum, a Bud Light at the beach, Cologne for Men, a dash of Right Guard. Love is patient day-by-day togetherness, *and* love is diamonds that are for ever. Love is a thoughtful, difficult, selfless, agonizing life-experience of one man and one woman, *and* love is what a movie star discovers after six marriages. Love is two and only two special persons, *and* love is the unbuttoned promiscuity of Fire Island, prime-time sex, what Woody Allen discovers by "making love" to roommate Mia Farrow's adopted daughter. Love is a family, *and* love is a secret love nest. You love your cat, your car; your teenager loves MTV; I love preaching at weddings; we love mustard on our hot dogs, pepperoni in our pizzas. Love is obsession, desire, addiction, lust, affection. Love is whatever you want to make of it.

Believe it or not, God's Book is much more realistic—even more romantic. True love never had a beginning; for love began with God: three memorable monosyllables, "God is love" (1 Jn 4:8). God not only loves; God *is* love. And God showed us what true love is like by sharing it. I mean, by shaping male and female like God, with an inborn capacity for loving. God showed love when God's Son took our flesh, was born as we are born, died an incredibly cruel death— all for love of us. God showed love, as St. Paul put it, by pouring "God's love into our hearts through the Holy Spirit who has been given to us" (Rom 5:5). God showed love by fashioning you and me without any deserving on our part—simply because God loved us from eternity.

Do you want to know what genuine love is? The love God's own Son brought down from heaven and lived on the soil of Palestine? Take St. Paul's paean to love and think of our Lord Jesus Christ. "Love is patient, is kind. Love is not envious, boastful, arrogant, rude. Love does not insist on its own way, is not irritable or resentful, takes joy not in wrongdoing but only in the truth. Love bears all things, believes all things, hopes all things, endures all things" (1 Cor 13:4–7). In a nutshell, love is my very self . . . given.

Such, Michael and Annie, is the love our Lord expects of you.

II

Second question: Concretely, what does this mean for your relationship to each other? If your very human love is to reflect divine love, if it is to respond to St. Paul's paean to love, love lays several heavy demands on you.

The first is . . . wonder. I don't mean curiosity, perplexity, doubt: "I wonder whether the Israelis and the Palestinians will ever make peace together." I mean surprise, amazement, awe, delight. Wonder at what? At being alive. Not only that you can watch stars at night, drink in Handel's *Water Music,* smell a rose, ingest an Imperial Crab, stroke your Labrador. More importantly, alive to each other, to the wonder of the other. Ceaselessly amazed by the wonder that is Annie, the wonder that is Michael. Amazed at the miracle that is your love. Surprised that, among the millions who occupy your world, your eyes should ever have met and, having met, should have locked together in love. Delighted that you respond to each other's voice as to no other in this world. Awed that your touch sends signals that thrill through the other's whole being.

A second demand? Worship. Yes, worship. You see, worship is not some weekly obligation you should not omit, like taking a shower or working out on the Nautilus. Worship is the way you relate to what life is ultimately all about, what meaning life has, how you relate to the God who made you, who loves you, who expects love in return but never compels it. The unique love you have for each other has only one love more important—what Jesus called "the greatest and first commandment" (Mt 22:38): "You must love the Lord your God with all your heart, with all your soul, with all your might, with all your mind" (Lk 10:27; Mt 22:37). Today is a turning point: From now on, as long as life lasts, you love your God *together.*

A third demand? Jesus expressed it succinctly: "Greater love than this no one has: to lay down life itself" for the one you love (Jn 15:13). It is summed up in a touching story related recently by a Dominican Sister:

Five year old Johnny Quinn loved his big brother, Tommy. The doctor told Johnny that his brother was very sick and needed a blood transfusion, and the doctor asked: "Johnny, would you be willing to give some of your blood to your brother?" Johnny gulped hard, his eyes got big, but after only a moment's hesitation he said: "Sure, doctor." The doctor took the blood and Johnny was resting quietly on the table. A few minutes later, Johnny looked up at the doctor and said: "When do I die, doctor?" It was only then that the doctor fully appreciated the extent of this little boy's love.[2]

Wonder at each other, worship of the Other, self-giving even unto crucifixion—what else remains? My third point, the parable of the Good Samaritan.

III

The parable is another Jesus gem. A Jewish gentleman is traveling from Jerusalem to Jericho—about 18 miles, through "desert and rocky" country.[3] He is set upon by highway robbers, beaten half to death. Two Temple ministers—a priest and a levite—come upon him; each passes him by on the other side—perhaps afraid of ritual defilement. A Samaritan, despised by the Jerusalem Jews, has compassion on the poor fellow, bandages his wounds, provides for his recovery at a public inn.

The point of the parable for Annie and Michael? They discovered it at the beginning of the Gospel: "You must love your neighbor [at least as much] as you love yourself" (v. 27). The neighbor? Not just the neighbor in the adjoining apartment; not only those I like, the beautiful people, "cool" folk who will return my Six Pack. My neighbor is anyone in need whose path I cross and to whom I can be kind, show compassion. One of those insightful rabbinical stories puts it pungently. An old rabbi asked his students: "How can you recognize when night ends and day begins?" One student suggested: "Is it when from a great distance you can tell a dog from a sheep?" "No," said the rabbi. Another student asked: "Is it when from a great distance you can tell a date palm from a fig tree?" "No," said the rabbi. "Then when is it?" the students asked. Responded the rabbi: "It is when you look into the face of any human creature and see there your brother or your sister. Until then, night is still with us."

My point? The love Annie and Michael shower on each other cannot be a selfish love. It must turn outward; they must turn together to the world where they live and eat, sleep and work, play and survive. Symbolic of this will be the recessional—when they traipse down the aisle after the final blessing. Not a swift exit to the reception. Rather, their movement from church to world, from altar to people, from Christ crucified outside Jerusalem to Christ crucified in our own country. In point of fact, they are already into that movement. For their heads and their hearts are given to the most vulnerable, the most defenseless, of this earth's humans. In New York's Bellevue and D.C.'s Children's Hospital, they minister to our little ones. Minister not only medicines but hugs and love—often to tots and teenagers who have rarely heard anyone say "I love you." To 14-year-old mothers, "babies having babies." In the emergency room, where death never takes a holiday.

Michael and Annie, love can flicker and die—but all too frequently because the love is smothered within four walls, is not allowed to flame, to spread like wildfire, to touch the loveless, the unloved. Not such is your love. When I see how endearingly you look at each other in love, when I see how you turn together in love and, like Jesus, take into your arms our crucified children, when I see you linking your lives in a liturgy that celebrates Jesus' own crucifixion for love of all God's children, my hopes for you are deliriously high. For, as Jesus promised in a passage of your own choosing, "Blessed are the merciful [men and women who show compassion], for they will receive mercy [God will show them compassion]" (Mt 5:7). And genuine compassion, you know, is another word for . . . love.

St. Ignatius Church
Baltimore, Maryland
September 12, 1992

30
MALE AND FEMALE GOD CREATED THEM
Wedding Homily 5

- Genesis 1:26–28, 31
- Romans 12:1–2, 9–18
- John 15:12–16

Some years ago I had a devastating experience. I was addressing a Jesuit honor society, Alpha Sigma Nu, in Milwaukee. In the course of my address I had what I considered a rather insightful sentence. I was comparing a famous French existentialist and an equally famous Swedish film producer. I said: "For Sartre, hell is other people; for Bergman, hell is being alone." I felt quite good over that sentence . . . till I picked up the diocesan newspaper the next week. The reporter was much taken by my sentence, decided to quote it, but felt he should add one word on his own, a first name, to make sure his readers recognized one of the parties I was talking about. He wrote: "As Father Burghardt said, 'For Sartre, hell is other people; for Ingrid Bergman, hell is being alone.' "

I

Today, good friends, the Genesis story of creation moves me from film creator Bergman to a God of even more incredible creativity. Theologians may argue whether "hell is" actually "being alone," and you yourselves may challenge whether being alone is hell; but the Lord God told us something undeniable in declaring, "It is not good that the man should be alone" (Gen 2:18), not good that only a male should occupy the earth. If I had to fasten one item on Lisa and Justin's refrigerator door, it would be the passage they have plucked from the first chapter of the Bible: "God created humankind in God's image. . . . Male and female God created them" (Gen 1:27).

It's wild, off the wall. That single sentence conceals a creative artistry we could never have imagined unless God had revealed it to us. It grows on you, gets richer and richer. Let your imaginations loose on it.

Imagine the Trinity that is God—Father, Son, and Spirit—-utterly and eternally happy in their own existence, needing no one else, needing nothing save their own perfect love. Freely, they decide to do what genuine love always wants to do: share itself, give of itself. And so, billions of years back, about the time when time began, God shaped not only the heavens and the earth, not only sun and moon and stars, not only fish to plow the waters, birds to trill the sky with music, beasts to roam the forests. God went one divine step further: God shaped a creature very much like God. In fact, two like God: male and female. Similar, but not the same. Similar indeed, for each would image God. Each would share God's precious prerogatives; for each would be intelligent, each would have the power to love, each would be free.[1] Not the same, for each would mirror God's mind and heart in a distinctive way—he his way, she her way.

And all this why? So that down the ages, till time is no more, male and female would be drawn to each other by attractions chemical and spiritual, would react to each other in a godlike response called love, would live a life where there is always "I and thou" but never "mine and thine." Similar but not the same, they would have the awesome power to fashion of their flesh and spirit images of themselves, images of God. Awesome because, as an inspired unknown thinker put it, "The great events of this world are not battles and elections and earthquakes and thunderbolts. The great events are babies, for each child comes with the message that God is not yet discouraged with humanity, but is still expecting goodwill to become incarnate in each human life."[2]

From such God-given beginnings, through two and a half million years of loving and shaping, after unnumbered unrecorded ancestors and events, two images of God called Lisa and Justin have come together to continue God's dream for our human story. Very much like the billions who have preceded them; unlike because they are unique, unrepeatable, one only Lisa and one only Justin. They have come together not forced by some divine decree, compelled only by what St. Augustine called the cords of love. Freely indeed, yet under God's gracious smiling—not utterly by chance. Even Jimmy the Greek would hardly have wagered that these two would not only enter Harvard Business School the same year, but out of 900 they would be assigned to the same Section C, he would sit behind her, he would quickly sense she was not your standard HBS "quant jock." Surely one of Harvard's swiftest and most creative business deals.

Justin and Lisa: When clouds gather, when storms rage, when the earth shakes beneath your feet, if ever you are tempted to feel that no one loves you, that no one cares, remember this: From all eternity God knew you; before time began, God held you two lovingly in the palm of God's hand; never did God *not* know that this day would be thrillingly yours together.[3] For your response to such love, I recommend the ancient prayer brought down to millions through the musical *Godspell:* "These three I ask, dear Lord: to see you more clearly, love you more dearly, follow you more nearly."

II

From God's love for you we move to your love for each other. Here another Scripture text dear to Lisa and Justin holds center stage. It's a challenging command flung out to us by Jesus the night before he died for us. Not an invitation. "This is my commandment, that you love one another as I have loved you" (Jn 15:12). And how did Jesus love? Listen to one who experienced it, the evangelist John: "Having loved his own who were in the world, [Jesus] loved them to the end, to the uttermost" (Jn 13:1): totally, with all his heart and mind and strength, even unto crucifixion. Such is the burden and the privilege God's vision of marriage and Jesus' insight into love lay on the wedded. Two profound expressions: without reservation, without end.

Without reservation. Your gift to each other is total. Not indeed open to inhuman demands. Marriage is not the story of a caveman and his woman. Marriage is total in its gift not of slavery but of love. A unique love. Here is communication at its most perfect, where you share with only one other all that is most precious to you, what makes you who you are—mind and body, heart and soul. Here there is indeed "I and thou," two persons who never cease to be themselves, never become the other; but there is no "mine and thine," no dividing line where self-giving stops and self-interest takes over. Yes, as Gibran put it, there should be "spaces in your togetherness."[4] But not to separate you; only to prevent a deadly mistake: trying to "possess" the object of your delight. Here a paragraph from author/critic Walter Kerr is indelibly imprinted in my memory:

> To regain some delight in ourselves and in our world, we are forced to abandon, or rather to reverse, an adage. A bird in the hand is

not worth two in the bush—unless one is an ornithologist, the curator of the Museum of Natural History, or one of those Italian vendors who supply restaurants with larks. A bird in the hand is no longer a bird at all: it is a specimen; it may be dinner. Birds are birds only when they are in the bush or on the wing; their worth as birds can be known only at a discreet and generous distance.[5]

It is not birds alone that "can be known only at a discreet and generous distance." Lovers too. The more generously you allow the other to grow, to be genuinely free, to develop rich relationships, the more total is your self-giving. Paradoxically, the more generous your space, the more likely is a lifetime of togetherness.

Without end. Think of it. In our culture, apparently nothing lasts for ever: your health or your hair, a star quarterback or a CEO, Republican administrations. Contracts are made to be canceled, rules to be broken, promises to be fractured. In this context you two dare to do with conviction what an older marriage ceremony declared: "Not knowing what lies before you, you take each other as long as you both shall live." Not "As long as it works," not "Till we tire of each other." Till death do you part. Not knowing what lies before you: a remarkable act of faith—in each other and in God. Not knowing what lies before you: only that the Holy Spirit will ceaselessly surprise you, but that whatever happens, God will be there.

You have good reason for confidence. For this is not puppy love, not infatuation. Between you, you have experienced a good deal of human living: much of the world and something of war, Southern California and South Africa, London and Exeter, Boston and D.C., the world that is Morgan Stanley and the world that is NBC. All this you bring to this day, all this you delight to share. To share. For I suspect you are aware of an old truism: The opposite of love is not hate; the opposite of love is indifference.

III

God's love for you; your love for each other. One last love remains: The love that turns you to each other must turn you together to "the others." You see, the recessional that will close this nuptial Mass is not primarily a swift move to the reception before the congregation gets to the cocktails. The recessional is highly symbolic. It is your movement from church to world, from altar to people, from the broken body of Christ to the broken bodies of Christ's images.

The broad insight is captivatingly captured in a single sentence by Marian Williamson in her book *Return to Love:* "We do not marry each other to escape the world; we marry each other to heal it together."[6]

Farfetched? Florence Nightingale and Ralph Nader? No. Simply your God-given vocation: to help heal the acres of God's world in which you work, on which you dance. For our world is wounded— woefully wounded when wars kill two million children in 15 years, when seven million children are growing up in refugee camps, when 40,000 children die every day from malnutrition and related diseases, when AIDS may produce ten million orphans this decade in Africa alone. Our own "land of the free" is dreadfully enslaved when 43% of African American children grow up in poverty, 32% of Hispanic children; when we can win a war in the Persian Gulf but lose it in our streets; when 37 million Americans are without health insurance; when heroin and ice, coke and crack blunt the minds and savage the spirits of our youth.

This is hardly news to either of you; some of it you have touched and smelled. Not mine to spell out your vocation; let the Lord speak to you as you speak to each other. I simply say this—to you two and to all before me. I make bold to suggest that in our time and culture the endangered species called "man and wife" can entertain hopes for a remarkable revival. But only with a large "if." If man and wife see their union not simply as a vocation to their biological family but as a call from God to help build up the whole human family. If the love that in its days of wine and roses is so intense and passionate is made to focus intensely and passionately on the less fortunate images of Christ. If the children of a man and wife are not only those born of their physical oneness but "children of a lesser god," for whom there is "no room, no place in [our world's] inn" (Lk 2:7), children who can be redeemed only by others' love. If their extended family extends not only to biological grandparents but to the elderly bereft of love, rummaging in garbage cans for the crumbs from top-heavy tables. If, in short, man and wife are man and wife "for others."

Lisa and Justin: A wise aphorism has come down to us from the Pennsylvania Dutch: "We get too soon old, and too late smart." Much too late smart, let me suggest strongly to you young lovers that your wedded love is less likely to grow cold if you see your love lighting hope in the staring eyes of a battered child; if you help one black or white teenager get off the drug corner and through high school; if you limit by one the number of "babies having babies"; if your graciousness to a down-and-outer lends an hour of dignity to his existence; if you fill a hungry belly, take in a stranger, hug an AIDS-infected, shatter the bars that separate you from the imprisoned. Do this together, and love that may have cooled between you will glow again.

Good friends all: You have come together impressively from near and far not to ooh-aah at a splendid spectacle, to applaud a picture performance. You are here because each of you has played a role, feature or supporting, in the love story that scales new heights today. But here a bit of NBC News Update: Your task is not done. If Lisa and Justin are to live the kind of love I have portrayed, they need more than high IQs, pleasing personalities, green eyes and blue. They need God and they need you. God's gracious giving they are guaranteed. But they need more. They need the example of men and women who, for one year or 50, in agony and in ecstasy, in warmth and in chill, all through the bittersweet of human living, have turned their hearts again and again to God, to each other, to their sisters and brothers. *Your* example.

For this reason, when Justin and Lisa join hands and hearts for ever, I would ask the wedded among you to join your own hands, recapture swiftly your own love story, and murmur softly or in the silence of your soul that awesome original self-giving: "I take you . . . for better for worse, for richer for poorer, in sickness and in health, till death do us part. I will love you and honor you all the days of my life."

It is a unique gift to Lisa and Justin; for you are promising them . . . yourselves.

St. Brendan's Church
San Francisco, California
December 12, 1992

31

LOVE, COMMUNICATION, HOSPITALITY
Wedding Homily 6

- Romans 12:1–2, 9–13
- Colossians 3:12–17
- John 15:9–12

From the three passages Kathy and Sean have plucked from God's own Book three ideas emerge that are particularly pertinent to this celebration: (1) love, (2) communication, (3) hospitality.

I

We begin with the very heartbeat of Christianity. For in the Christian vision the focal point of religion is love. And the height of love? The breath-taking demand of Jesus in the Gospel of John, "This is my commandment, that you love one another as I have loved you" (Jn 15:12). Not a request: If you don't mind, you might try to love as I loved; if you have the time; if it doesn't inconvenience you. No, "This is my commandment."

A difficult word to define, this word "love." And a homily is not a class in philosophy. But this much must be said. The word "love" expresses two things: an experience and a mystery. An experience many humans share and a mystery no human can fully understand.[1] Rather than bore you with the mystery, let me share with you the experience.

We use the word "love" of so much in our experience. I shall not bother today with the misuse of the word, where it takes in everything from a one-night stand after a singles'-bar pickup to the "love" we have for peanuts and ice cream, jogging or disco, a McDonald's 99-cent burger. You may still feel quite justified in saying "I love my country," "I love New York." Here there is a very personal

157

dimension: It involves me as a person, has to do with other persons, demands a certain surrender to what I love.

It is this personal facet of genuine love that is most important in our setting here. For here we do well to recall a God who not only loves but *is* Love, a love that means total self-giving of Father to Son, Son to Father; a self-giving that, mystery of mysteries, is itself a Person whom Scripture reveals as the Holy Spirit. Today we do well to recall a Trinity that, out of sheer love, has shaped uncounted billions of humans, like Kathy and Sean, into two images of God, male and female. Today we do well to recall the love that led God's only Son to take our flesh, wear it as his own, pin it to a bloody cross to destroy the Sin that severs us from God. Today we do well to recall the love that led God's Son to leave with us, when he left us, not only his Holy Spirit as our Gift of love, but the very flesh and blood of the God-man to rest on our fingers, on our tongues, within our flesh. Today we do well to recall that Christ our Lord raised the wedded love of Christians to the dignity of a sacrament, made it the special symbol of the love that links Christ to his people, to his Body the Church.

We do well to recall all this, not simply because it stems from God's own Book, but because God's love for us calls for a response of love. What response? What Jesus himself demanded: to love God with all our heart and soul, mind and strength, and to love our sisters and brothers at least as much as we love ourselves—in fact, to love them as Jesus loves us. Today that response of love focuses on two persons, two products of God's love, two images of God, similar but not the same. The vows they will exchange bind them to an experience of love that resembles the love God revealed in creating us and redeeming us, in fashioning us and refashioning us. What sort of love is that?

1) God's love is *open-ended:* It has no limits save what we in our stubbornness and sinfulness put upon it, what God cannot give only because we refuse it. So too, Sean and Kathy, so too with you, with your love for each other. You give yourself without reserve—mind and heart, flesh and spirit. Not how much you must give; not punishing the other by holding back. The marvel lies in the result: Love generates love. As with God, so with you: The more you love, the more you enable the other to love.

2) God's love is *sacrificial:* It involved the life, the death, of God's only Son. "He loved me," St. Paul proclaims so simply, "and gave himself for me" (Gal 2:20). So too, Kathy and Sean, so too with you. Your wedded love will not be a perpetual honeymoon. Wedded love is a tough love, bittersweet, a wedding of ecstasy and anguish, of

likes and dislikes, of forgetfulness and forgiveness, of smallness and greatness, of hurt feelings and laughter together, of neurosis and normalness, of physical strength and fleshly decline. Living with another for life can be dreadfully difficult. I am reminded of a quick interchange after a heated argument between a man and his wife:

> He: Why can't we live peacefully like our two dogs that never fight?
> She: That's right, they don't fight. But tie them together and see what happens![2]

I have experienced perhaps the only thing more difficult: *not* living with another.

3) God's love has a tremendous potential for *healing*—healing the wounds of our humanness. Think only of Calvary; think of the strength God's gracious loving brings to our everyday weakness. So too, Sean and Kathy, so too with you. No medicine will ever match the miracle of your touch, no placebo replace the power of your tenderness. Love may not conquer all, but it sure deflects many of the slings and arrows that lay siege to life together.

II

A second pertinent idea is closely tied to love. It surges up from the passage our dear couple has lifted from St. Paul's letter to the Christians of a little town called Colossae in Asia Minor. Paul simply says: "Bear with one another; forgive one another; clothe yourselves with love; let the peace of Christ rule in your hearts; teach and admonish one another in all wisdom; sing psalms, hymns, and spiritual songs to God" (Col 3:13–16). Behind all these examples is a contemporary catchword: communication.

Communication here is more than passing on information: I read to you the headlines in the *Washington Post*, because there is only one copy and of course I have it. Communication is a mutual sharing; something passes between people. It happens in genuine conversation—conversation in its original Latin sense, "living together and talking together."

Communication traces back to God. For in the Trinity there is a perfect sharing. There is indeed "I and thou" but never "mine and thine"—what St. Augustine called "those ice-cold words." No Person in the Trinity has anything which the other two do not have. If that item from Trinitarian theology doesn't impact you, recall the striking sentence that opens the New Testament Letter to the Hebrews: "Long ago God spoke to our ancestors in many and various ways by the prophets, but in these last days [God] has spoken to us through a Son" (Heb 1:1–2). Remember how God walked and talked with the first man and woman in the cool of Eden's evening? That "conversation" was harshly interrupted by sin—sin that put distance between humans and their God; they no longer walked and talked in intimacy. Men and women even tried to "build a tower with its top in the heavens" (Gen 11:4), but it resulted only in something called Babel, a confusion of language: Humans could not communicate among themselves, much less with God.

Communication was re-established when, as John's Gospel puts it, God spoke to us through God's Word, God's Son. "The Word became flesh and lived among us" (Jn 1:14). God spoke to us through the mouth and lips of Jesus, restored our "conversation" with God, made it possible for us to address our God.

Such is the model for our own conversation, our living and talking together, especially the conversation between husband and wife, the conversation which, St. Paul says, symbolizes the conversation between Christ and his bride the Church. In God's intent, wedded life is a lifelong conversation. Not always a diarrhea of words; that can destroy communication, especially if it is joined to a constipation of thought. Rather, a living together where words are indeed important but not always necessary; what two people share is their life; it becomes one life. Not that one becomes the other. Sean remains always Sean, Kathy never ceases to be Kathy. Still, something is ceaselessly passing from one to the other, insensibly affecting the other, changing the other. Not absorbing, only helping to shape, to complete, the other. Through Kathy, Sean images Christ more and more the way God wants him to; through Sean, Kathy gradually realizes in herself the full humanness of Christ.

Without this kind of close encounter, this kind of conversation, marriage is not only the usual risk; it courts disaster from the first words of the vows. My experience of marital breakups? One cause over any other: little or no communication. In two forms: (1) silence that is more destructive than words; (2) words that are more destructive than silence.

III

My third point is suggested by the reading Sean and Kathy have drawn from St. Paul's letter to the Christians of Rome. It has a four-word phrase that in its brevity and simplicity may have slipped by you: "Extend hospitality to strangers" (Rom 12:13). It's not an open-ended cocktail party for the neighborhood, a get-to-know-your-neighbors open house. It's broader than that. Behind it is the primitive Christian insistence on the second great commandment of the Christian gospel: Love your sisters and brothers at least as much as you love yourself (cf. Mt 22:39).

And who is your sister, who your brother? Jesus answered that question in the parable of the Good Samaritan, the man who took care of a Jew who had been beaten half to death by robbers, took care of a man who was his traditional enemy. My brother, my sister, is in a special way every man or woman in need—each of God's unfortunates pleading for bread, for justice, for love.

Kathy and Sean, when you exit this sacred spot to the strains of Beethoven's "Ode to Joy," that recessional is not primarily a swift movement to the Bolling Officers' Club, a privileged route to the reception. The Eucharistic recessional has a symbolism all its own. It is a movement from church to world, from altar to people, from the wounded Christ of Calvary to the wounded images of Christ who will haunt your life wherever you settle.

I commend to your Christian "hospitality" especially the children who will intersect your life. Children born with AIDS; children with one parent or none; children with bellies swollen from hunger; children gunned down on our streets; children coming to school with deadly weapons; children giving birth to children; children sleeping on our streets; children maiming their minds and debasing their bodies with coke; children utterly without hope. Small wonder that in 1991 the National Commission on Children declared that addressing the needs of America's children is no longer a matter of choice. "It is a national imperative as compelling as an armed attack or a natural disaster."[3]

I have no wish to restrain your ode to joy. I simply submit that your wedding in Christ lays a burden on you that is also a privilege. For if the land we love is to survive as a "land of the free," if the children who are our future are to grow up human, it is in large measure couples such as you that can effect it. You are young and still restless; you are highly intelligent and impressively vigorous; you are gifted with imagination and compassion; you are committed to sharing what you have and who you are; you have God's grace coursing through you like another bloodstream. One day, God willing, you will be blessed with children of your own. I know no better preparation for the fruitful days ahead than your care for those crucified images of the Christ Child who seem to be "children of a lesser god."

A final suggestion. In an adventure as demanding as marriage, Kathy and Sean dare not go it alone. God's support they will surely have; what they need as well is your own. I mean in particular the example of husbands and wives who for one year or 50 have struggled (1) to model their lives on the open-ended, sacrificial, healing love of God; (2) to make of their wedded life a continuous "conversation," living and talking together; and (3) to share their love and their conversation not only with those who can return it, but also with those whose lives are so often faithless, hopeless, loveless. And so, when Sean and Kathy join their hands once for all, I would ask the wedded among you to link your own hands and murmur again, "I take you to have and to hold, for better or worse, for richer or poorer, in sickness and in health, as long as we both shall live."

No more precious wedding gift can you give to Kathy and Sean; for in this gift you are giving them . . . yourselves.

St. Michael Archangel Chapel
Bolling Air Force Base
District of Columbia
May 15, 1993

MEDLEY

32
CHRIST, CROSS, PRIEST
Feast of St. Ignatius Loyola

- Ephesians 3:14–21
- Luke 9:18–26

The saint our liturgy celebrates today was something of a paradox. He was a mystic yet an organizing genius, dearly devoted to the Church yet imprisoned by the Church's men, a man of tradition who adapted his Company to a world in transition. Much could be said of him this day, but I suggest an approach that may say much to you and me as priests.[1] Three facets to my development: (1) Christ, (2) the cross, (3) you and I.

I

First, Christ. Jesus Christ was Ignatius' center: center of his theology, of his spirituality, of his mysticism. That Christ is the Christian center Ignatius knew from his theology in Paris and Venice; but more importantly, he had already experienced it. His program of Spiritual Exercises could have for preface the words of Paul to the Christians of Corinth: "No one can lay any foundation other than the one that has been laid; that foundation is Jesus Christ" (1 Cor 3:11). Since a homily is not a history, I shall not prove that statement. Let me focus on one aspect of that Christic center, an aspect that speaks loudly to me, should appeal to all Christians, is a must for priests. I mean the final contemplation in Ignatius' Spiritual Exercises. Traditionally it has been titled "Contemplation for Obtaining Divine Love." More recently a fresh translation of the title has been gaining currency: "Contemplation for Learning To Love Like God." In the third point of that contemplation Ignatius asks us to consider how God [that is, Christ[2]] works and labors for me in all creatures upon the face of the earth, that is, he conducts himself as one who labors. Thus, in the heavens, the elements, the plants, the fruits, the cattle, etc., he gives being, conserves them, confers life and sensation, etc.[3]

Dreadfully philosophical? Only if you focus on technical terms like creation and conservation; only if you glide swiftly over Christ the laborer, Christ imitating a laboring man, a woman at work. Ignatius insists that we see Christ not only seated at the right hand of his Father, not only present body and blood, soul and divinity in the Eucharist. The risen Christ is incredibly active in simply everything that is.

Let your Christian imaginations loose. How is it that 200 billion billion (yes, billion billion) stars can roam the skies day and night, Pikes Peak tower 14,000 feet above the soil of Colorado, water cover over 70 percent of the earth's surface? Because Christ gives them *being*. Not now and again, but ceaselessly, continually. How is it that the water lily can float lazily on ponds and streams, a magnificent redwood grow to 368 feet, vegetables provide us with life-giving vitamins and minerals? Because Christ gives them *life*. How is it that the lordly lion can stalk the grasslands, geese fly over the Himalayas at 29,000 feet, arctic terns migrate 22,000 miles, golden eagles dive at 180 miles an hour, sparrows sing 20 variations of the same song? Because Christ gives them *sensation*, sense life. How is it that you and I can shape an ethical argument, program a word processor, recapture Bethlehem and Calvary, see in another human being an image of God, love another human person as Jesus has loved us? Because Christ is constantly giving us *intelligence and love*.

Ignatius' insight can transform our human, our priestly existence. Whatever or whomever we see or hear, touch or taste or smell—however dull or insipid, however prosaic or unattractive—is instinct with Christ—Christ like a laborer working to shape, to preserve, to transform. Yes indeed, as poet Gerard Manley Hopkins sang, "The world is charged with the grandeur of God,"[4] charged with the activity of Christ.

II

Second, the cross. Here I go back to a critical journey Ignatius made to Rome in 1537, before he actually founded his Company of Jesus. On the way he stopped at a small town called La Storta, about ten miles to the north of Rome, entered an abandoned chapel to pray. Here, we are told by a reliable contemporary,

> [Ignatius'] heart was completely transformed. Such a bright light illuminated the eyes of his soul that he perceived how God the Father commended him and his companions to the divine Son, who bore his cross, and entrusted him to the victorious hand and protection of the Son. The meek Jesus took him under his protection. Still bearing his cross, he turned to Ignatius and with smiling face and kind expression said to him, "I will show you my favor in Rome."[5]

Ignatius admitted later that he did not know what God's "favor in Rome" meant. He used to say, "I do not know what is in store for us; perhaps we may be crucified in Rome." It seemed to him, he said, "that Christ stood by him with the cross on his shoulders, and the Eternal Father by his side, and the Father said to His Son, 'Will you take this man for your servant?' " And Jesus took Ignatius saying, "I want you to serve us."[6]

The La Storta experience is the critical source of Ignatius' mysticism of the cross.[7] In his spirituality the one only way by which Jesus leads to the Father is the cross. His meditation on the kingdom includes Christ's call: "It is my will to conquer the whole world.... Whoever wishes to join me in this enterprise must be willing to labor with me, that by following me in suffering he may follow me in glory."[8] This is not a newfangled Christianity; it repeats Christ's fundamental requirement for discipleship: "If any want to become my followers, let them deny themselves and take up their cross daily and follow me" (Lk 9:23). And in the Spiritual Exercises it is with my gaze on Jesus dying for me on the cross that I must ask myself three crucial questions: "What have I done for Christ? What am I doing for Christ? What ought I to do for Christ?"[9]

III

Those three questions lead to my third point: What of you and me? You may wonder why I focus on such obvious facets of priestly spirituality. Of course Christ is the center of my existence; of course Christ's cross is critical to Christian living. Were that not so, none of us would have signed up for a life that mirrors the poverty of Christ in Palestine, the celibacy of Christ in a hostile culture, the obedience of Christ to his Father. My concern is, how real are Christ and the cross to us? I don't mean, do we *believe* in the God-man, in the centrality of the cross for salvation? Of course we do! My problem is, how do I concretely see Christ? How closely linked are Christ's cross and my cross?

There is a twin peril here. First peril: I can limit my experience of Christ to his glorious presence in heaven, to the abiding presence of Christ in my soul through grace, and to his Eucharistic presence beneath the appearances of bread and wine. Remarkable realities indeed. But then Christ can be left on the periphery, the edge, of so much that makes the world go round, everyday living. It seems to say so little to economics and ecology, to sexual abuse and child neglect, to politics and the social order, to the whole world of Islam that looks so far removed from Christ.

No. If our work of evangelization is to catch fire in ourselves and in our world, if we are to redeem this earth that God once saw "was very good" (Gen 1:31), we must see Christ as incredibly active in whatever is, in whoever is. The environment is not only a life support for us humans; it is instinct with the power of Christ, charged with the grandeur of the God-man. Children at risk—from hunger to AIDS—are not only objects of compassion; Christ is touching to them the wounds of his passion. What we call "grace"—the presence and action of the divine in men and women of flesh and blood redeemed by the priceless blood of Christ—is not limited to card-carrying Christians. Christ is like a laborer touching everyone who is, everything that is. Grasp this vision, and you will see your ministry catch fire. You never go out to a Christless world; your every activity for others, for the world, goes out to someone, to something, where Christ already is. You do not bring Christ there; you collaborate, co-labor, with Christ to expand his presence.

Turn now to the cross of Christ. If we see the cross as a sheerly historical fact, an event that took place on a hill outside Jerusalem two millennia ago, if the cross only did something *then,* redeemed the world *then,* we misunderstand its power, it dynamism. The cross of Christ is now. It is St. Paul's startling declaration to the Christians of Colossae: "I am now rejoicing in my sufferings for your sake, and in my flesh I am completing what is lacking in Christ's afflictions, for the sake of his body, the Church" (Col 1:24). Calvary is now.

There precisely is the heart of our priesthood in the nineties. We are hurting as rarely before—a period of priestly peril without parallel perhaps since the Reformation. The elements that have fueled our contemporary crisis are many: celibacy complexified by homosexuality; crossfire from liberal and conservative, Vatican and laity, bishop and parish; a sense of ineffectiveness; closures of parishes and schools dear to our hearts; an inadequate theology of priesthood; burnout; fear of the future; the aging process.

Such is our Calvary. Our response? Not primarily resignation: I can do naught else, so I lay my burdens at the foot of the cross— "Thy will be done." That much of course. But even more critically, a realization that it is in our very brokenness that we preach Christ most effectively. It is Paul appealing to the Lord to take away the thorn in his flesh; Paul hearing from the Lord, "My grace is sufficient for you, for [my] power is made perfect [becomes effectively present] in weakness"; Paul declaring "whenever I am weak, then I am strong" (2 Cor 12:7–10). Not that weakness is power, rather that Paul's weaknesses reveal the power given him by Christ for his ministry.[10] Very simply, "I can do all things through him who strengthens me" (Phil 4:13).

My brothers in the priesthood of Christ: I pray for you, as I pray for myself, the grace for which Ignatius ceaselessly asks retreatants to pray. It is a striking triad. "Dear Lord Jesus, let me see you more clearly, let me love you more dearly, let me follow you more nearly." Murmur it in the context of the cross, of your cross, of Christ's cross: "Those who would save their life will lose it; those who lose their life for [Christ's] sake will save it" (Lk 9:24). So be it. . . .

Seton Hall University
South Orange, N.J.
July 31, 1992

33

CHRIST, EUCHARIST, COMMUNITY
Feast of St. Ignatius of Antioch

- Ephesians 1:15–23
- Luke 12:8–12

About the year 110, in Antioch of Syria, persecution racked the Christian Church. The bishop himself, Ignatius, was cast in chains, dragged over land and sea to Rome, to be savaged by wild beasts in the Colosseum. Much ink has been spilled on Ignatius the martyr: "God's wheat I am, and by the teeth of wild beasts I am to be ground that I may prove Christ's pure bread."[1] So high-wrought was his passion for death that unsympathetic critics have uncritically called him a fanatic, neurotic, unnatural, a weakling fleeing reality; one prolific biographer has claimed that "All the wilder elements [in Christianity] descend from him, from the terrible look in his eyes."[2] In our context here,[3] let me focus not so much on his bloody death, rather on the Christian realities for which he was willing to die, yearned so intensely to shed his blood. Three foci: Christ, Eucharist, the Christian community. A word on each in Ignatius, then a word on each in you and me.

I

First, Ignatius, Here is a man flanked by ten soldiers whom he compares to "ten leopards" for their malevolence.[4] During that painful journey to Rome, Ignatius somehow manages to write seven letters—letters to six communities and a young bishop—letters which have been termed the most beautiful pearls of ancient Christian literature. What grips Ignatius is a passionate love for his crucified Lord and for that Lord's communities, a love so overpowering that it breaks through grammar. Language is inadequate, and his ideas tumble headlong one upon another.

His center? Christ. One Christ—a unique wedding of heaven and earth. "There is only one physician, both carnal and spiritual, begotten and unbegotten, God become man, true life in death, sprung both from Mary and from God, first subject to suffering and then incapable of it—Jesus Christ our Lord."[5] His target? Docetism—the affirmation that the human in Christ—birth, death, resurrection—was unreal; he only seemed to be born, to die, to rise. No, he responds; this is raw reality. "He was really born of a virgin, was really nailed to the cross in the flesh for our sake, really raised himself from the dead."[6] Those who "maintain that his suffering was a make-believe," why "it is they that are make-believes."[7] Unless Christ was really born, really suffered, really rose, "then I in my chains, too, am a make-believe. Why did I surrender myself to death, to fire, to the sword, to wild beasts?"[8]

In sum, Christ is Ignatius' life, his radical reason for living. That is why he can beg the Christians of Rome not to use their influence to have him spared. That would be to show him "unseasonable kindness."[9] "Fire, cross, struggles with wild beasts, wrenching of bones, mangling of limbs, cruel tortures inflicted by the devil—let them come upon me, provided only I make my way to Jesus Christ."[10]

Linked intimately to Ignatius' consuming love for Christ is his profound reverence for the Eucharist. Here is St. Paul's insight to the Christians of Corinth: "Because there is one bread, we who are many are one body, for we all partake of the one bread" (1 Cor 10:17). That is why Ignatius can exhort the Christians of another Philadelphia, "Take care . . . to partake of one Eucharist; for, one is the flesh of our Lord Jesus Christ, and one the cup to unite us with his blood, and one altar . . . ."[11] That is why he can urge the Christians of Ephesus, ". . . break the same Bread, which is the medicine of immortality, the antidote against death, and everlasting life in Jesus Christ."[12]

But the dying/rising Christ, the Christ of the Eucharist, finds his deepest meaning in the community. Each letter of Ignatius begins not with a petition for prayer for this martyr-to-be, but with a warm, respectful, congratulatory greeting to a community in Asia Minor. It is *their* problems, *their* needs he discusses: how to preserve "the faith" in its pristine purity; how to keep *their* faith from faltering; how to "stand firm" against strange doctrines, "like an anvil under the hammer";[13] how to praise Christ "in the symphony of [their] concord and love";[14] how to prove themselves brothers and sisters of unbelievers "through courtesy";[15] how to deepen their oneness with bishop, presbyters, and deacons; how to help the community in Syria now deprived of their bishop; how to serve the needy. Ignatius reminds the community in Smyrna that what distinguishes them from the enemies of Christ is that these unbelievers "concern themselves with neither works of charity, nor widows, nor orphans, nor the distressed, nor those in prison or out of it, nor the hungry or thirsty."[16] And infallibly Ignatius closes with gracious greetings, affectionate farewells. "Greetings . . . to the whole community, individually and collectively. . . ."[17]

II

And now Ignatius of Antioch leads me to the sons of Ignatius Loyola and our colaborers. I suspect you know that the Spanish Ignatius had a remarkable devotion to the Syrian. In honor of the martyr, he changed his name from Iñigo to Ignatius. The first of his maxims was a phrase from the first Ignatius: "My Love has been crucified."[18] He made the motto of his Jesuit order the first three letters (IHS) of the name of Jesus in Greek, because he had read in *The Golden Legend* that when the Romans tore out the heart of the martyred Ignatius, they found those letters graven on his heart in gold. Together they suggest three facets of Ignatian spirituality that must lie at the heart of our social, pastoral, and international ministries.

The center is Christ—the Christ of the Spiritual Exercises. I mean the Christ we pray to see more clearly, love more dearly, follow more nearly.[19] The Christ who co-opts us for his standard by attracting us to a tough imitation: "the highest spiritual poverty and, should it please the Divine Majesty, even actual poverty."[20] The crucified Christ who from his cross compels three questions: What have I done for him? What am I doing for him? What ought I do for him? The risen Christ who invites us to share his joy even from our cross. The Christ who brings our discipleship to a thrilling peak with a contemplation not so much "for obtaining divine love" as rather "for learning to love like God," to love like Christ.

Now in our Father Ignatius this Christocentrism "developed almost exclusively in the atmosphere of the Mass."[21] His entire day had the Eucharist for focus. The Eucharist was the milieu in which he made significant decisions for himself and his Society. The Eucharist was where he developed his mysticism of loving reverence. The Eucharist was where God favored him with extraordinary mystical graces. Paradoxically, as time went on, Ignatius had to give up celebrating the Eucharist. Why? Because the mystical graces he received were so powerful that they left him weak or ill for long periods of time.

It is only in this context—the centrality of Christ and the grace of the Eucharist—that our spirituality of service makes sense, that our social, pastoral, and international ministries are effective, that we can help fashion communities of faith, hope, and love. When the Woodstock Theological Center was struggling to give concreteness to my dream *Preaching the Just Word,* the most penetrating, significant suggestion stemmed from New York's Father Philip Murnion. He insisted that, if the project was to succeed, it could not be exclusively or even primarily a communication of ideas, of information, of skills; it had to operate in the context of a spirituality, a conversion process that turns the preacher inside out, puts "fire in the belly." On this the Syrian Ignatius and the Spanish Ignatius join hands and hearts. Only if we learn to love like Christ, only if in our Eucharist we can murmur to our world each day "This is my body, and it is given for you," only then can we expect to experience what they experienced: hearts and minds changed, the poor rejoicing over the gospel preached to them, a joy in our own flesh and spirit that no human being can take from us. Only thus can we help create what St. Paul called "one new humanity" in Christ (Eph 2:15), put to death through the cross the deadly hostilities that divide and crucify the family of man and woman.

Through the intercession of Ignatius of Antioch and Ignatius of Loyola, may our dear Christ expand in us his Gospel promise: his Holy Spirit teaching us at every hour not only "what [we] ought to say" (Lk 12:12) but how we ought to live.

Jesuit Center for Spiritual Growth
Wernersville, Pa.
October 17, 1992

34

PAUL CONVERTED,
PREACHER CONVERTED
Feast of the Conversion of St. Paul the Apostle

- Acts 22:3–16
- Mark 16:15–18

Conversion. . . . A theme that dominates the Prior Testament and the New. Understandably, for the experience that is conversion is ever so often a radical change in a man or woman's existence.[1] The prophets called Israel to turn away from idolatry, from immorality, from injustice. Jesus' first challenge to the Jews in his public ministry was a striking imperative, "Be converted, and believe in the good news!" (Mt 4:17, Mk 1:15). Today's feast[2] summons us to reflect on two conversions: (1) the conversion that was Paul's and (2) the conversion of today's Christian preacher.

I

We begin with the convert that was Paul. The accounts of his conversion in Acts[3] reveal four pertinent facets of conversion.[4] First, it was God who took the initiative. Paul did not decide on his own native smarts to follow the Lord; the Lord chose him. It was the God-man who hurled from his horse the Saul who was "still breathing threats and murder against the disciples of the Lord" (Acts 9:1): "I am Jesus, whom you are persecuting" (Acts 9:5, 22:8, 26:15). Saul experienced what St. Augustine was to phrase so pithily several centuries later: If we but turn to God, that itself is a gift of God. God takes the first step. Sometimes simply by God's loving presence within us; at times by offering a specific divine assistance for a particular saving action on our part.[5] If there is to be a radical reform in who we are and what we do, it will not be because we have raised ourselves by our Pelagian bootstraps. No, the very freedom I exercise in saying yes to God is itself a gift, a grace. Briefly, where my Christian activity is concerned, I have to grant with Augustine, "Christ did not say, 'Without me it will be hard.' He said, 'Without me you can do *nothing*' " (Jn 15:5).

Second, there is Saul's response when he discovered it was Jesus who was speaking: "What am I to do, Lord?" (22:10). Jesus did not disclose the Pauline mission right off the bat; he told Saul to go into the city, into Damascus; "there you will be told everything that has been assigned to you to do" (22:10; 9:6). And even that was not a bill of particulars. Like Mary before Gabriel, Saul did not know all that the Lord's call would ask of him; he knew only that it was the Lord who was calling. God rarely supplies a detailed scenario—certainly not when we enter the ministry. What *do* we know? That it is God who is calling.

Third, the basic call, as Ananias told it to Saul: "You will be [God's] witness to all the world of what you have seen and heard" (22:15; cf. 22:16). Saul did not know it then, but the reality was there. An apostle is a witness, and the essential task of a witness—John, Magdalene, Paul—is to testify to what he or she has seen or heard. Such is the burden and the privilege of an apostle: like John the Baptist, to point to Christ: "Look! Here is the Lamb of God" (Jn 1:29).

Fourth, a fact of Christian life inseparable from the apostolate. The Lord said to Ananias: "He is an instrument whom I have chosen to bring my name before Gentiles and kings and before the children of Israel; I myself will show him how much he must suffer for the sake of my name" (9:15–16). To turn to Jesus was to turn to a crucified Master who still insisted that to follow him his disciple had to carry his cross every day, that to save his life Saul had to lose it. It goes back to Jesus' own question to two discouraged disciples after his rising from the rock: "Was it not necessary that the Christ should suffer these things and [then] enter into his glory?" (Lk 24:26). It goes back to a startling sentence in the Letter to the Hebrews: "Although he was a Son, [Jesus] learned obedience through what he suffered; and having been made perfect, he became the source of eternal salvation for all who obey him" (Heb 5:8–9). And so Paul would later confess about himself: "often near death, five times 40 lashes minus one, thrice beaten with rods, once stoned, three times shipwrecked, in danger from rivers, bandits, my own people, Gentiles; danger in the city, in the wilderness, at sea, from false brothers and sisters; many a sleepless night, often without food, cold and naked, . . .

under daily pressure from my anxiety for all the churches" (2 Cor
11:23–28).

II

Now what of us? In the early days of this dream of mine, *Preaching
the Just Word,* New York's Father Philip Murnion made a salutary,
saving suggestion. He insisted that the project would fail of its purpose
if its primary focus were to be information, factual data, strategies.
Important as these are, priority must still be given to spirituality, a
fresh turning to Christ, an experience that turns the preacher inside
out, puts fresh fire in the belly. In short, a conversion, seeing with 20-
20 vision, hearing with newly opened ears, feeling with fresh passion.
Hence this retreat/workshop.

Not every conversion is as dramatic as Paul's gallop to Damascus
or Augustine's experience in the Milanese garden. Not every conversion is a once-for-all event; indeed, conversion is a constant movement, a development. Not every single one of us has to be persuaded
that the just Word must be proclaimed in season and out. Still, Paul's
four facets should be a constant in our conversion, in our homiletic
turning to Christ, whether radical or not: (1) God calling: "I am
Jesus." (2) A total yes to whatever the Lord might be asking: "What
am I to do, Lord?" (3) A basic mission: "You will be [God's] witness."
(4) Inevitable crucifixion: "I will show him how much he must suffer." A word on each at it touches us.

First, it is God who has called us together. Back in 1990, who
but God could have plucked this man of 75 with his head and heart
for half a century in theology, filled his mind with a dream for a
society no longer ravished and an earth no longer raped, torn his
heart over the poverty-stricken and the sexually abused, and flung all
this into the Catholic pulpits and congregations of the country? Who
but God could have stolen Raymond Kemp from a vibrant black
parish he loved in D.C., planted him behind a Jesuit desk and phone
at Georgetown University, fired him up to plant the just Word in
the marrow of every Catholic preacher? Who but God could have
generated such enthusiasm among the laity everywhere, the feeling
and conviction that here is an idea whose time has come? Who but
God (and Ray Kemp) could have called you together in community
from California and Colorado and Connecticut, from Florida and
Georgia, Kansas and Louisiana, from Massachusetts and Minnesota
and Michigan, Missouri and Mississippi, from New York and North

Carolina, Ohio and Oklahoma, from Pennsylvania and South Dakota, Virginia and Wisconsin? Believe it, and do not fear: God is here.

Second, your response: "What am I to do, Lord?" This is the ceaseless question that enables radical conversion, the question that puts flesh daily on your turning to the Lord. This is the question you must put to the Lord with quiet urgency these five days. I dare not predict what each one of you will be told to do. So much depends on who you are and where you are, the stage of your preaching, the state of your people. This I do know: If, like Saul, you are thrown from your parochial horse, you still will not receive a crystal ball, a script, a scenario detailing the way to go. You will have to listen, agonizingly, not so much to a voice from heaven as to the haunting cries of the destitute, the disadvantaged, the derelict.

Third, despite the uncertainty on details, there is your basic call: to bear witness. Each of you is called not only to preach, but to preach the just Word. Your task is bear witness not only to the Jesus who dwells one-on-one in the hearts of your parishioners, of your coworkers, of your dear ones, but to the Jesus who proclaimed in Nazareth's synagogue, "The Spirit of the Lord has anointed me to bring good news to the poor, to proclaim release to captives and sight to the blind, to let the oppressed go free" (Lk 4:18). If all goes well, if the Spirit of the Lord fills "the entire house" (Acts 2:2) where you, like the original apostles, are sitting, you will be told to go back to your city, discover increasingly how to witness afresh, to point to Christ, to preach the just Word with passion. I expect it; for to preach the just Word is simply to preach the second great commandment of the law and the gospel: Love your sisters and brothers at least as much as you love yourself; love them as Jesus has loved you.

Fourth, inevitable for such as preach the just Word is . . . suffering. For the preacher, suffering can come in different forms, various ways: from my own rhetorical deficiencies, from the reaction of Catholics to what they hear as politics in the pulpit, from Catholics who come to weekend liturgy as a vacation from the workaday world of sin and war, from the hostility of many to a macho male priesthood, from my reluctance to share my people's uncertainties and agonies, to experience something of what they experience. The dangers in preaching the just Word may not be as melodramatic as Paul's; they may well be just as intense.

A final word for your strength and consolation: You need never again be alone, a lonely convert. The word has gone out across the land. The just Word must be preached; the just Word can be preached; the just Word will be preached. As with the apostles before the Pharisee Gamaliel in the council, so with you before your people: Preaching God's justice is an undertaking that is of God. Since it is of God, God's enemies are not likely to overthrow it. Paradoxically, only the preachers of the gospel, only you and I, can slow its progress. So then, God lead you; God feed you; God speed you.

San Pedro Center
Winter Park, Florida
January 25, 1993

35

ANOINTED TO BRING GOOD NEWS
Homily for Four Dominican Preachers

- Romans 10:13–17
- Luke 4:16–21

Back in 1838, at the Harvard Divinity School, Ralph Waldo Emerson gave vent to a harsh homiletic frustration:

> I once heard a preacher who sorely tempted me to say, I would go to church no more. . . . He had lived in vain. He had no one word intimating that he had laughed or wept, was married or in love, had been commended, or cheated, or chagrined. If he had ever lived and acted, we were none the wiser for it. The capital secret of his profession, namely, to convert life into truth, he had not learned. Not one fact in all his experience, had he yet imported into his doctrine. This man had ploughed, and planted, and talked, and bought, and sold; he had read books; he had eaten and drunken; his head aches; his heart throbs; he smiles and suffers; yet was there not a surmise, a hint, in all the discourse, that he had ever lived at all. Not a line did he draw out of real history. The true preacher can always be known by this, that he deals out to his people his life,—life passed through the fire of thought. . . .[1]

For me, that final sentence sounds the keynote of our celebration, its motivating force. Tonight we celebrate four preachers who through half a century have dealt out to living men and women what St. Dominic would have applauded: life passed through the fire of thought, life converted into truth—their thought-fired life into God's transforming truth. Still, a golden jubilee is not an obituary. Unlike Shakespeare's Mark Antony over the corpse of Caesar, we do not come to bury our four preachers but to praise them. Yet not in isolation. Rather, in the company of their brothers and sisters, and in the context of the Dominican mission yesterday, today, and tomorrow. So then, three movements to my song. (1) A swift look into the past, to see where our jubilarians have come from. (2) A critical glance at the present, to see where we Catholic preachers are. (3) A peek into the future, to suggest where Dominican preaching might fruitfully go.

I

First, where have these devotees of Dominic come from? From John the Baptist, who came preaching in the wilderness, preaching repentance because the kingdom of God was in Israel's midst. From Jesus spelling out his mission in Nazareth's synagogue: "The Spirit of the Lord is upon me, because He has anointed me to bring good news to the poor. He has sent me to proclaim release to the captives and recovery of sight to the blind, to let the oppressed go free" (Lk 4:18). From St. Paul asking how anyone can call on the name of the Lord "without someone to proclaim him" (Rom 10:13–14).

They come from Dominic founding a community specifically of preachers, a ministry of salvation by the word of God,[2] "a new *order of preachers* side by side with that of the bishops."[3] From master general Humbert of Romans, with his masterly manual for the preachers of his day. From Thomas Aquinas, prince of theologians, not only preaching in Lent on love and the Decalogue but extolling to the skies "that form of active life in which by preaching and teaching [you deliver] to others the fruits of [your] contemplation."[4] From Vincent Ferrer, commissioned in a vision "to go through the world preaching Christ,"[5] setting forth from Avignon of the Western Schism, for 20 years preaching repentance and judgment in Switzerland and Spain, in Lombardy and the Low Countries. From reformer Savonarola, castigator of vice, political nuisance, fearless in the face of Pope Alexander and the Medici, tortured with papal permission, perhaps a martyr to God's word.[6] From Bartolomé de las Casas, indefatigable advocate of the Indians, sworn enemy of inhuman colonization. From liberty-loving Lacordaire and his Lenten conferences in the pulpit of Notre Dame during his order's second spring.

Our jubilarian preachers come from the Preaching Apostolate that began in this very city in 1866, down on Mott Street, the parish missions that flourished for a hundred years. From Ignatius Smith at Catholic University, with his Preachers' Institute in the midst of philosophical preoccupations. From your Wilsons and Whelans, your

McKennas and Nagles, your Hills and Higginses, your Slavins and Burkes. From the unnumbered Dominicans who preached devotion to the Holy Name of Jesus and made the rosary the most popular nonliturgical devotion in the Western Church.[7] From the unnumbered thousands of Dominicans whose names rarely if ever hit the headlines, yet whose zest for God's word changed the Catholic face of America and beyond.

You have reason to rejoice in your philosophers and theologians from the 13th century down, in your colleges and universities from Paris to the Philippines, in the mystical life of Eckhart and Suso and Tauler, in the monasteries of your second and third orders. But I do them no dishonor when I suggest that Dominic's lasting gift to the Church and the world lies in the priority he gave to the spoken word—the word of God on human lips. I believe Aquinas would agree—the Aquinas whose theology led him to the pulpit and drove him to his knees in the *Adoro te* (I borrow the masterly version of Jesuit Gerard Manley Hopkins):

> Godhead here in hiding, whom I do adore
> Masked by these bare shadows, shape and nothing more,
> See, Lord, at thy service low lies here a heart
> Lost, all lost in wonder at the God thou art.[8]

II

Move now from the past to the present, from yesterday to today. Here two realities stand in striking contradiction: theory and practice. Over two decades ago, my favorite Dominican, the remarkable Frenchman Yves Congar, penned a startling sentence: "I could quote a whole series of ancient texts, all saying more or less that if in one country Mass was celebrated for thirty years without preaching and in another there was preaching for thirty years without the Mass, people would be more Christian in the country where there was preaching."[9]

That observation should be scotch-taped to every rectory refrigerator. For, despite Vatican II's insistence that "priests . . . have as their *primary duty* the proclamation of the gospel of God to all,"[10] despite the flat confirmatory assertion of the U.S. Bishops' Committee on Priestly Life and Ministry, "The other duties of the priest are to be considered properly presbyteral to the degree that they support the proclamation of the Gospel,"[11] the view from the pew is discouragingly critical. All too consistently, our people are not confronted with a word that nourishes while it challenges, heals while it bruises. The criticism is further fueled by an increasingly educated populace no longer silent before homiletic pap and bromides, and by articulate Catholic women who are even more thoroughly convinced of their calling to the pulpit when they must submit to our contemporary constipation of thought and diarrhea of words. And all the more eloquent is the mute witness of untold thousands of "ordinary folk" forsaking our liturgy for the impassioned preaching of the Pentecostals. I much fear that today, a century and a half later, Emerson might well rephrase his tormented cry: "*Each day* I hear preachers who sorely tempt me to say, I shall go to church no more."

Is this true of Dominican preaching? My limited personal experience cries a resounding no. For I follow with delight your men of the word, dear friends like Val LaFrance, Hugh Burns, and John Burke. I toast you for your vision—as belated as my own—in shaping women of the word, your Cannons and Hilkerts and Delaplanes. And yet I dare not disregard the sobering statement of your 1989 General Chapter of Oakland:

> Inquiries and reports by superiors and commissions stated in general a steady decrease in the numbers of brethren engaged in active preaching and a weakening in the quality of preaching. . . . Let us admit we are in need of a profound conversion if we want to discover the truthfulness of our life, the strength and full meaning of our vocation as preachers.[12]

For a smidgen of consolation, know that Ignatius joins Dominic in mourning within his own ranks the decline of a charism essential to evangelization.

Like the Cynic Diogenes cruising about at midday with a lighted lantern in search of an honest man, I roam our country in search of men and women yearning to proclaim the gospel with "fire in the belly." Six decades ago I laughed when our retreat preacher thundered to us Jesuit scholastics, "If you can't resist the bubble in the glass, the tinkle of the silver coin, or the smile on a woman's lips, tear that habit off and get out!" I no longer laugh; the man had imagination. Young priests tend to scoff at dear old Bishop Sheen, the dated rhetoric. What they never experienced was Tuesday evening in the States, Protestants and Catholics glued to the tube as Fulton Sheen outdrew comedian Milton Berle; what they never experienced was St. Patrick's Cathedral in New York City with SRO crowds hanging on every minute of his Three Hours. The preacher had fire in the belly.

Are there persuasive, passionate preachers around? Yes indeed; your jubilarians bear living, vibrant testimony. But not enough by half. I weep when priests tell me they have no time to prepare, weep when their homilies begin, "As I was walking over from the rectory, the thought struck me. . . ." I weep because so few preach with the passion of Paul, so few make preaching their priority, so few realize that a dull, dreary, dismal homily makes uncounted Catholics resolve that they will go to church no more—no more to *our* church.

III

This leads naturally into my third point: a peek into the future. Where is your preaching to go from here? There is no single response, no easy "way to go." Once again Dominic comes riding to your rescue. What, he asked, are the needs of the Church at a given moment in history?[13] Given the signs of *our* times, one way you must go, a path that can rekindle fire in the belly, is the path of social justice, "option for the poor." I mean specifically "the least" in our society. I mean the homeless and the hopeless, the child abused and the aged confused. I mean the teenage mother hooked on coke and the teenage schoolboy toting his gun to class. I mean the refugee watering the earth with his tears, the black and the brown and the red despised for their color. I mean "God's lost children," the 28,000 runaways who pass through Covenant House each year—tired and hungry, lonely and scared, abused at home and pimped on the streets.[14] I mean the nine million who look for work but cannot find it, the six million who cannot find full-time jobs, the million too discouraged to look for work.[15] I mean the unnumbered hearts that harbor hate, eyes empty of hope, stomachs bloated with hunger. To preach not only a gospel of hope *to* them, but a gospel of love *about* them.

Here in our time must be the heart of our homilies. Not only because we cannot escape the calvaries that dot our earth. Equally important, the unique word we call God's is social through and through, from the shaping of the first man and woman to Christ's return to gather his body into one. By God's design, by God's initiative, human existence is fundamentally social: We are "we" before we are "I" and "thou." Through Isaiah and Hosea, through Amos and Micah and Jeremiah, Yahweh ceaselessly told Israel: I reject just those things you think will make me happy. I am weary of burnt offerings, delight not in the blood of bulls or lambs. Incense is an abomination to me. Your feasts my soul hates. I will not listen to your prayers, do not want rivers of oil, thousands of rams, even your first-born. Then what was left? What could God possibly want? Two things: Act justly and love steadfastly.[16]

It is simply to recognize that there are *two* great commandments of the law and the gospel: We must indeed love God above all else, but we must also love our sisters and brothers at least as much as we love ourselves. Better still, love them as Jesus has loved us. But to preach this effectively, to raise the consciousness of our people, to incite our hearers not only to agonize but to organize, there are several tough conditions.

First condition: a neuralgic question from your General Council. "Have we really discovered that the preaching of the gospel and the promotion of justice cannot be separated?"[17] This is not a liberal Dominican fad; it is church doctrine, as valid and forceful as the ban on contraception. This is the vision that emerged from the 1971 Synod of Bishops: The vindication of justice is "a constitutive element of the preaching of the gospel."[18] This is the vision of the 1974 Synod: The Church "believes firmly that the promotion of human rights is required by the gospel and is central to her ministry."[19] For the Jews of old, not to execute justice was not to worship God. For the Dominicans of today, not to preach justice is not to preach the gospel.

Second condition: fire in the belly. Like the Hebrew prophets, we preachers have to feel fiercely, be stunned by human greed, see our preaching as the voice God has lent to the silent agony of the plundered poor. In our voice our very God must rage.[20] How achieve this? We must mirror the prophets' incredible intimacy with their Lord and their passionate concern for a chosen people. To hear the word, we must love the Lord who speaks it. And to speak the word ourselves, to inflame the hearts of the faithful, we must love this paradoxical people—this struggling, sinning, saintly people—love them with a crucifying passion. Love especially those who experience more of Christ's crucifixion than of his resurrection.

Third condition: some experience of injustice. Many of us preachers have lost, or have never had, the sharp sensitivity to evil that should mark every prophet. Some surely share that sensitivity; but it is usually those who have experienced firsthand the sorry exis-tence of the poor and the imprisoned, the hungry and the downtrod-den. More of us simply deplore injustice; we are against sin; we take up collections for Catholic Charities. It compels me to ask myself a troubling question: Does my life enter the pulpit with me? What does my life say to my people, say to the poor? Am I the priest in the Gospel who always passes by "on the other side" (Lk 10:31)?

Fourth condition: an acute awareness that social preaching is not class struggle. *All* to whom we preach are "poor," the haves as well as the have-nots, we preachers ourselves. All need the gospel preached to them—and that gospel is a gospel of Christian hope, of Christian love. Not ours to savage the rich, the well-fed, those who laugh, as if "the good life" is an evil in itself. Ours to help rich and poor, sleek and starving, joyful and sad to love one another as Jesus has loved us, and to express that love by sharing the gifts God has given to each—to those privileged with this world's goods as well as those privileged to be crucified.

Good friends: I am reminded of an unforgettable phrase in Lincoln's Gettysburg Address. "The world will little note, nor long remember what we say here, but it can never forget what they did here."[21] For to forget, as Jewish storyteller Elie Wiesel reminds us, is a crime against justice *and* memory; if you forget, you become the executioner's accomplice. For the sake of God's people, and literally "for Christ's sake," I hope and pray that the Dominican family will never forget what preachers like Harold Regis Barron and Francis Leo Regan, John J. Sullivan and Patrick Walsh have done for God's children, even at times unto crucifixion. Why remember? Not to imitate them slavishly, but to be touched by the same Spirit who put fire in their bellies, to read the signs of *your* times, to preach passionately to all of God's people the words of the Lord on the lips of Micah: "What does the Lord require of you? Act justly, love steadfastly, and walk humbly before your God" (Mic 6:8).

St. Catherine of Siena Church
New York, N.Y.
March 24, 1992

36

YOU ARE PRECIOUS IN MY SIGHT AND I LOVE YOU
Baccalaureate Homily for a University

- Isaiah 43:1–4
- Colossians 3:12–17
- John 10:27–30

Ten days ago I had a homily all set for you. It was based on the first reading you selected for your exodus liturgy, your exit from Gonzaga. I had the Lord saying to you what the Lord said to the Israelites in exile:

> Thus says the Lord who created you, who formed you:
> "Do not fear, for I have redeemed you;
>   I have called you by name, you are mine.
> When you pass through the waters, I will be with you;
>   and through the rivers, they shall not overwhelm you;
> when you walk through fire you shall not be burned,
>   and the flame shall not consume you. . . .
> You are precious in my sight . . . and I love you."
>
> (Isa 43:1–4)

Ten days ago all hell broke loose in L.A.: looting, arson, shootouts; 58 dead, 2000 injured, 120 critically; a billion dollars in damage; an area larger than the District of Columbia in flames. And into the flames went a homily too Pollyannish, too unreal, for your exodus, your movement from campus to concrete, from church to world, from the life of the mind to death on the streets. Two stages to my movement: one downward, the other upward.

I

First, the downward movement. Not long before his death, Martin Luther King Jr. wrote to his mother to share with her the title of his next sermon. The title? "Why America May Go to Hell." I don't know what America's black martyr intended to say. But after seven decades of America-watching, as a priest now totally involved in justice issues, let me suggest to you why America may go to hell. Briefly and pungently, because of what sociologists like Robert Bellah see as a frightening phenomenon dominating our times: the resurgence of late-19th-century rugged individualism, a horrifying emphasis on "me" and "mine." What is of supreme importance is for me to get to the well first before it dries up. The race is to the swift, the shrewd, the savage, and the devil take the hindmost. And the resurgence is most evident, they tell us, in the younger generations.

The data, the facts? We trumpet America's love for its children, yet we let one of every five little ones grow up hungry. Fifteen countries are ahead of us in life expectancy; 40,000 each year do not reach birthday number one. 1.6 million each year are kept from seeing life outside the womb. We proclaim our young as the flower of the future, yet every 26 seconds a child runs away from home, every 47 seconds a child is abused or neglected, every 67 seconds a teenager has a baby, every 7 minutes a boy or girl is arrested for drug abuse, every 36 minutes a child is injured or killed by a gun.[1] In 30 years the rate of teenage suicide has tripled.[2] We have stopped saying women have no souls, yet we pay them less for comparable work, 43 percent of single mothers are poor, and in 1990 683,000 women were raped, 29% younger than eleven.[3] We are hipped on health, wear out the Nautilus and the Reebok, yet 37 million Americans have no access to health care, and we face "a calamity that will not only fill the corridors of our hospitals but will soon cripple our economic engine."[4]

We have literally "out-lawed" racism, yet one black child out of three is poor; a black male in Harlem has a life expectancy of 46 years, less than males in Sudan or Cambodia;[5] there are more blacks in jail than in college. Twenty-seven years after Watts, South Central Los Angeles has lost about 70,000 industrial jobs. An African-American scholar and activist tells us, "Black male unemployment is a devastating blow to the men themselves and heaps a crushing burden on the women they might otherwise marry. It sears the children they father and destroys the families they might otherwise strengthen. It poisons the physical and psychological environment in which they are confined."[6] Is it any wonder that, when a black man is savagely clubbed and kicked by four white policemen and a jury with 10 whites virtually absolves them from guilt, the pent-up passions of a race still enslaved burst violently upon the City of Angels? Remember, it was a court of law that conferred civil rights on blacks, not our Christian

Sermon on the Mount. They look back in anger; they look forward to . . . nothing.

What has all this to do with Martin Luther King's phrase, "Why America May Go to Hell"? It goes back to a declaration from Dostoevsky, "Hell is not to love any more." Can we honestly say to these sisters and brothers of ours, the children and the teenagers, the women and the blacks, "Do not fear. When you walk through fire, you shall not be burned. God calls you by name. You are precious to God. God loves you"? Which leads naturally into my second point, my upward movement.

II

Yes, God loves them; God's Son died for each one of them. The sobering question is: How genuinely do you and I love them? The same Bellah who insists that the dominant characteristic in young economic man and young economic woman is autonomy, personal fulfilment, told us Catholic theologians at an annual convention that Catholics come up little different from the rest of the American population.

I am not claiming that love has left America. Across this rich land of ours millions of Americans live the second great commandment of the law and the gospel; they love others, the less fortunate, at least as much as they love themselves. In my own Maryland the Catholic Church operates the largest private, nonprofit social-service system you can find in the state: shelters for the homeless, soup kitchens and food pantries for the hungry, adoption services for children unwanted, programs for youth, residences for the handicapped, counseling for the troubled, homes for the ill and aging, migration and refugee assistance, services for crisis pregnancies, hospitals, AIDS ministries.[7] And such love dots our land, from rock-ribbed Maine to your Evergreen State of Washington.

And still it is not enough. Every major city in this "land of the free" continues to cry out to us in black accents, "Let my people go!" The most vulnerable of humans, our children, still beg mutely for scraps from our rich tables. The elderly are now economic problems, a threat to the very children to whom they gave life.

What does this say to you as you take your diploma into the streets of your city? What is foremost in your mind? Is it simply TGIO, "Thank God it's over"? Is it fear, apprehension: It's a scary world out there, jobs at a premium, death around every corner? Is it one of the three goals that preoccupy so many graduates: money, power, prestige? Or is it what you heard St. Paul tell the Christians of Colossae: Above everything else that you put on, "put on love, which binds everything together in perfect harmony" (Col 3:14)?

Graduates of '92: You are incredibly gifted, by nature and grace. However limited you see yourself, you share two of God's precious possessions: You have the leisure to think, and you are free to love. These gifts, honed here in Spokane, make it possible for you, incumbent on you, to realize in your lives what Jesuit education has a high mandate to fashion: "young people and adults able and willing to build a more just social order, . . . men and women for others." [8]

This kind of love is hardly romantic; it's a tough love. It combines compassion and courage; it involves initiative and imagination; it will sear your mind and tear your heart. For you will confront not just hungry bellies but a system that exploits them; not a few "skinheads" but racism in American bones; not abstract poverty but an unjust world order. And the people you are asked to love, commanded by Jesus to love, are not always easy to love: the drug-addicted and the AIDS-afflicted, the homeless and the hopeless, the Qaddafis and the Saddam Husseins, those who hate you because you have so much, the frustrated who know only to cry "Burn, baby, burn." You confront a country that, as a *Time* columnist wrote this week, "each day reveals itself as two nations, where almost everyone sees race first and the individual second, where there still exist children of a lesser god." [9]

Can you love such as these, live for them, give them reason to hope? Not if you rely on your Brite smile, your Type-A personality, your native ability to persuade. Only if you take seriously St. Paul's declaration to the Christians of Rome: "hope does not disappoint us, because God's love has been poured into our hearts through the Holy Spirit who has been given to us" (Rom 5:5). God's love for each one of you—the love that "calls you by name," that *makes* you "precious in [God's] sight"—is incredibly realistic. It means that within you is a living Power, the Holy Spirit, the "dynamite" [10] in your life, the divine Force that turned fearful men like Peter and most of the original Twelve into apostles who changed their world. It means that in the power of the Spirit you can love as Jesus loved, love without discrimination, love even unto crucifixion. In the power of the Spirit you can say to your crucified sisters and brothers what Yahweh said to Israel, "You are precious in my sight . . . and I love you." Love like this, and the less fortunate who surround you may listen to you—listen as the thousands in Calcutta listen to Mother Teresa when she carries them from the gutter to her home, to die with dignity.

A homily is not a strategy for a successful revolution. Still, no strategy will succeed, this "home of the brave" will not turn into a "land of the free," unless millions such as you become "all that you can be." Not by joining the Army. Only by realizing how powerful you are with the Power inside you, realizing with St. Paul that you "can do all things in [the Lord] who strengthens" you (Phil 4:13).

So then, go from Gonzaga as women and men for others—but also as women and men of Power. Dynamize your acre of God's world, even if it only means that you touch one crucified child of God with your love. Live like this, and you will never be bored. Live like this, and you will experience the joy that Jesus promised, "no human being will take from you" (Jn 16:22).

God lead you, God feed you, God speed you.

Gonzaga University
Spokane, Washington
May 9, 1992

37

PHYSICIAN, HEAL YOUR NATION!
Homily for a Medical School Graduation

- 1 Corinthians 12:4–13
- 1 John 4:7–12
- John 15:1–5, 7

Good colleagues in the art of healing: You lay on me a heavy burden. Several weeks ago I had a fair homily outlined for you. It was to be constructed largely on a level of hope. It would have played up the glories of a vocation I prize highly, one which you heard me extol almost three years ago, on the feast of St. Luke.[1] I was going to ring the changes on a paragraph from a prominent member of your profession, a physician with a touch of the poet:

> I must confess that the priestliness of my profession has ever been impressed on me. In the beginning there are vows, taken with all solemnity. Then there is the endless harsh novitiate of training, much fatigue, much sacrifice. At last one emerges as celebrant, standing close to the truth lying curtained in the Ark of the body. Not surplice and cassock but mask and gown are your regalia. You hold no chalice, but a knife. There is no wine, no wafer. There are only the facts of blood and flesh.[2]

But since that first outline, the nation we love has been devastated by a disaster difficult to digest. We have been brought face to face, as rarely before, with the color line, the two nations, in our country. The pent-up frustrations, the hatreds that bubble beneath the surface of our living, burst into flame in L.A.[3] It is a context I find impossible to avoid as you move out from classroom to country, from church to world, from the Bread of Life to the streets of death. Three short acts to my play: (1) national crisis, (2) gospel reaction, (3) personal challenge.

I

First, a national crisis. It is a crisis of health. Physical health indeed, but broader than that. You see, the country we love, the country that will engage most of you, is a living paradox. We can free far-away Kuwait from a madman, yet our own people lie enslaved at home. What do I mean? TV trumpets our love for children, yet one of every five little ones grows up hungry in the richest nation on earth; each year 40,000 do not live to see their first birthday. We proclaim our young as the flower of the future, yet every 26 seconds a child runs away from home, every 47 seconds a child is abused or seriously neglected, every 67 seconds a teenager has a baby, every 7 minutes a boy or girl is arrested for drug abuse, every 36 minutes a youngster is killed or injured by a gun. We piously dedicate this decade to unparalleled American education, second to none in science, yet Johnny still can't read, 25% of our teenagers drop out of school, and every day 135,000 children go to class with a deadly weapon. We claim to be people of compassion, yet with between 390,000 and 480,000 cases of AIDS projected by the end of 1993, uncounted Americans see in AIDS God's Black Death on the promiscuous. We disown revenge as a pre-Christian relic, yet most Americans clamor for the gas chamber, an eye for an eye.

We have literally "out-lawed" racism, yet one out of every three black children grows up in poverty, and there are more blacks in jail than in college. We have stopped saying women have no souls, yet we pay them less than men for comparable work, and it took us longer to legislate against sexual abuse than to condemn black slavery. We honor the elderly, till they become an economic liability meriting a merciful hemlock. We want more prisons for the criminal, more hospitals for the unbalanced, but NIMBY, "Not in my back yard." We are hipped on healthy bodies, wear out the Nautilus and the Reebok, yet 37 million Americans have no access to health care— eight million children and 430,000 pregnant women.

If none of this chokes your Bud Light, get this: Across the world, do you know how many children will die this decade alone, the 90s, most from diseases we know how to prevent? One hundred and fifty million! Almost as staggering as the national debt and the scandal of Savings & Loan. More staggering because here are the most vulnerable of humans, as defenseless as the child in the womb.

This world of ours, this country of ours, needs healing on a massive scale.

II

All of which raises my second point: a gospel response. Now Scripture, Old Testament or New, is not a set of prescriptions for malnutrition or AIDS, for lead poisoning or crack-cocaine addiction. It is not a desk manual for doctors. But the religious man or woman of medicine will find, in the very liturgical readings you have chosen, the indispensable basis for a more rounded ministry of healing than sheer competence or brilliance can supply. Take each text swiftly.

First, Jesus insists that, if you are to bear the fruit you should, you must be alive in him. "I am the vine, you are the branches. If [you] abide in me, and I in [you], [you will bear] much fruit; for apart from me you can do nothing" (Jn 15:5). Oh yes, you can be a sparkling surgeon apart from Christ, a distinguished diagnostician, but the richer fruits of your vocation will not be there. One example: one of the dying derelicts Mother Teresa carried to her hospice in Calcutta. He was so filthy, so covered with maggots, as to be physically repulsive. The sisters cleaned him up, and Mother Teresa held him in her arms. He looked into her eyes and said: "All my life I've lived like an animal; but today I'm going to die like an angel." Only if you are alive in Christ can you have that effect on the crucified images of God you will serve.

Second, St. Paul reminds us, in vivid language, that the Son of God took our flesh to transform the sinful, sickly humanity of Adam and Eve into a single body, wherein all—"Jews or Greeks, slaves or free" (1 Cor 12:13)—would be so wonderfully one that no one could say to anyone else, "I have no need of you" (v. 21). A splendid Presbyterian novelist/preacher, Frederick Buechner, once compared humanity to an enormous spider web:

> if you touch it anywhere, you set the whole thing trembling. As we move around this world and as we act with kindness, perhaps, or with indifference, or with hostility, toward the people we meet, we too are setting the great spider web a-tremble. The life that I touch for good or ill will touch another life, and that in turn another, until who knows where the trembling stops or in what far place and time my touch will be felt. Our lives are linked. No man [no woman] is an island. . . .[4]

Are you aware that in the breath-taking Christian vision of redemption not only does your patient need you—you need him, you need her?

Third, the First Letter of John is uncompromising: "Beloved, let us love one another; for love is of God, and whoever loves is born of God and knows God. Whoever does not love does not know God; for God is love. . . . If God so loved us [as to give God's only Son to die for us], we also ought to love one another" (1 Jn 4:7–8, 11). The point is this: If you want to set the spider web that is humanity a-tremble with love, you must yourself love—and love like Christ, perhaps unto crucifixion.

III

This brings me to my third point: a personal challenge. The challenge leaps from the national crisis and the gospel response. I don't know if you've see the book recently edited by Dr. Kevin Cahill, *Imminent Peril: Public Health in a Declining Economy.*[5] Cahill claims that, unless we Americans can recapture "the vision that the good health and welfare of the public is the very foundation of our society," "we shall fall victim to a calamity that will not only fill the corridors of our hospitals but will soon cripple the economic engine. . . ."[6] He points out that

> The "public" served by the public health system is increasingly the disenfranchised, the uninsured, the impoverished, the homeless, the aged, the addicted. Failing their needs is more than morally indefensible in our "new world order"; it threatens the health of all. For as surely as an untreated tuberculosis lesion will cavitate the lungs of a homeless vagrant, so too will the deadly mist of his infection disseminate through every social and economic class, among innocent fellow riders in the subway, or passengers in an elevator and, inevitably, from child to child in the classrooms of our city.[7]

In that context Mario Cuomo reminded us recently of a truth long recognized in public health: "that illness does not occur in a vacuum, that the roots of illness are usually deeply implanted in homelessness, in poverty, in other persistent social ills"[8]—joblessness, substandard housing, illicit drugs.

What am I asking of you? I realize that this weekend will put distance between you, sever you one from another. Not only your home bases: Arlington and Augusta, Charlotte and Chevy Chase, Old Greenwich and Guaynabo, Hoboken and Honolulu, Jamestown and

Youngstown, New London and L.A., Oakland and Olyphant, Tecumseh and Tucson. Your placements for graduate training: Ann Arbor and Atlanta, Bethesda and Buffalo, Detroit and Durham, Portland and Portsmouth, San Diego and St. Louis. Even your specialties, from anesthesiology to urology. What do I suggest that will unite you as never before? I hope and pray that, when you return for alumni weekends, you will have more to share than job descriptions, balding pates, and pictures of your children. I am asking that your profession as healers, as servants of life, involve you in more than your direct relationship with patients. Not only or primarily for the health of our economy. Literally "for Christ's sake," out of a burning love for the crucified images of Christ, to fashion a nation where none are "children of a lesser god."

Yours is a powerful profession—for more than one reason. As individuals the touch of your compassionate hand is often more powerful than my own, the assurance that a gifted man or woman cares. In small cohesive groups you can work miracles in an operating room, raise the near-dead to new life. But over and above that, as a well-knit profession you can extract miracles from state legislatures, from the federal government, from foundations; you have powerful voices that can reach all of America. If American taxpayers can be compelled to pay 33.7 million dollars *an hour* to bail out the Savings & Loan industry,[9] why can we not willingly pool our wealth for the health of our nation, for a country in "imminent peril"?

Is this politics from the pulpit? No. I am asking you to live *to the full* the second great commandment of the law and the gospel: You shall love your sisters and brothers at least as much as you love yourself. This commandment, Jesus said, "is like" the first (Mt 22:39): Loving your sisters and brothers is like loving God.

To heal a nation, you must think big, work together, pool your profound resources. But above all, you must look into the staring eyes of an abused child, or the drug-dazed eyes of a teenager, or the angry eyes of an African-American, or the hopeless eyes of the elderly, and see the crucifixion of a nation, see the crucified Christ. Are you ready for that?

Holy Trinity Church
Washington, D.C.
May 23, 1992

38

DAY BY DAY THE LORD ADDED TO THEIR NUMBER
150th Anniversary of a Parish Church

- Acts 2:42–47
- 1 Peter 1:3–9
- John 20:19–31

How does one capture 150 years in a homily? It's like the problem of Maria in *The Sound of Music:* "How do you catch a wave upon the sand? How do you hold a moonbeam in your hand?" I suspect you don't. Let me simply peer swiftly into your past, then spend some time on your present, and finally focus on your future.

I

First, I am intrigued by your past,[1] a past you know more intimately than I. My interest is in part selfish: because Jesuits ministered to your milltown before St. Mary's Chapel was built, offered Mass in the mill's assembly room; because the Jesuit president of Georgetown College, James Ryder, celebrated the first Mass in that chapel; because Georgetown Jesuits served the people of St. Mary's continuously for 23 years. And somehow the parish survived!

It is amazing to read how much your pioneering ancestors accomplished, under such difficult circumstances. Stones for the church carried by oxcart, a few at a time, from a nearby quarry. No resident pastor till 1888. A parish school that started with 40 students, many of whom missed classes because they had to work at the mill—a school to which students walked miles on lonely country roads each day. Only 300 parishioners at the turn of the century. The engaging period of 32 years when Father Joe Myer shaped church and rectory furniture from trees he himself had felled; moved the rectory downhill on greased skids; built a new rectory "just to have something to do"; built a model railroad for the children in the rectory cellar; organized and equipped Laurel's first baseball team; sped to blaze after blaze as chaplain of the Fire Department; allegedly took most corners on two wheels of his Stutz Bearcat. A new school in 1953 that now serves 260 children. Debts that were paid through painful parish generosity. A $300,000 addition to the church in 1959.

And now, by God's grace and the devotion of dedicated priests and unsung parishioners, six Masses on weekends, a parish of 2000 families . . . and still growing. The secret? Your first reading, from the Acts of the Apostles: "[The first Christians] devoted themselves to the apostles' teaching and fellowship, to the breaking of bread and the prayers. And day by day the Lord added to their number those who were being saved" (Acts 2:42, 47).

II

And what of your present? Again I am amazed. I see in place the pastoral council that has for function what Vatican II wanted in the laity: "to collaborate energetically in every apostolic and missionary activity sponsored by their local parish." [2] I see an up-to-date elementary school that has a profoundly Catholic vision: "educate its students to promote effectively the welfare of the earthly city, and prepare them for service in extending the reign of God." [3] I see programs in religious instruction that touch Catholic faith to child and adult, touch sacraments to each age and need. I sense a liturgy that finds Christ effectively present in the gathering of God's people, in the proclamation of God's Word, in the transformation of bread and wine into our Lord's body and blood, in the rich moment when God-in-flesh rests in your hands or on your tongue.

I see an outreach to the third millennium: I mean the young, the teenagers, who are our future, who will decide what our country is like, our Church, our family life. I see special ministries to the hospitalized and the housebound, to the hungry and the homeless, to the bereaved and the bewildered. I see an organized effort to call a halt not only to the war on our streets, the drugs and the guns, but to the war on the womb, the destruction of 1.6 million holy innocents each year in our country alone. I see an impressive dedication to the aging, those wrinkled images of Christ whom our society finds useless, a burden, a drain on our economy. I see barriers of race, sex, and creed slowly coming down, as you sweat to promote human understanding, opportunities for home ownership, improved public schools. I see you laboring to assist the poor and the vulnerable by influencing legislation. I note even a keen interest in sports—poetry in motion.

In all this, and so much more, you are a church for *this* season, remarkably suited to challenge a culture that some sociologists characterize as a resurgence of late-19th-century rugged individualism, where what ultimately matters is the almighty dollar and the mighty I. No. Your focus is on community, on family: the domestic family that is your home, the religious family that is your church, the human family that is every man, woman, and child shaped in the likeness of a loving God.

Your risen life today reflects the spirited prayer read to you from the First Epistle of Peter:

> Blessed be the God and Father of our Lord Jesus Christ! By His great mercy He has given [you] a new birth into a living hope through the resurrection of Jesus Christ from the dead, and into an inheritance that is imperishable, undefiled, and unfading, kept in heaven for you, who are being protected by the power of God through faith for a salvation ready to be revealed in the last time. In this you rejoice, even if now for a little while you have had to suffer various trials, so that the genuineness of your faith . . . may be found to result in praise and glory and honor when Jesus Christ is revealed. Although you have not seen him, you love him; and even though you do not see him now, you believe in him and rejoice with an indescribable and glorious joy, for you are receiving the outcome of your faith, the salvation of your souls.
>
> (1 Pet 1:3–9)

III

All of this leads into my third point: your future. I am not a psychic, not competent to predict what your parish holds for you. Let me try only to organize the many and diverse facets of your parish life under a single heading, make it easier for you to see your community life—thought, word, and action—as part of a basic, gigantic project that engages the Catholic Church today, will challenge your Catholic faith, hope, and love into the next millennium. The single heading is a big, six-syllable word. The big word is . . . evangelization.

What is evangelization? More than a quarter century ago Pope

Paul VI sounded it loud and clear: To evangelize is to proclaim "that in Jesus Christ . . . salvation is offered to every man [and woman] as a gracious gift." [4] This is basic; for there is no evangelization if Jesus Christ is not preached. But there is more to preaching Christ than talking about him. Evangelization, Paul VI insisted, "must be a message, especially strong and pointed today, of liberation." [5] Liberation from what? From "hunger, chronic illnesses, illiteracy, penury, injustice at the international level and especially in commercial relations, and economic and cultural neocolonialism." [6] Very simply, each Christian is called to a faith that does justice.

But what does "justice" mean here—justice as it comes to us through God's own Book? When the Hebrew prophet Micah declared to Israel, "What does the Lord require of you but to do justice?" (Mic 6:8), he was not saying simply: Give to each person what is due to each, what each person has a strict right to demand, because he or she is a human being, has rights that can be proven from ethics or have been written into law. Biblical justice was a whole web of relationships that stemmed from Israel's covenant with God. The Israelites were to father the fatherless and feed the famished, cover the naked and bring the homeless poor into their houses, not because these unfortunate folk deserved it, but because this was what Israel's covenant with God demanded; this was the way God had acted toward Israel. The practice of justice was an expression not simply of fairness but of love. At bottom, not to execute justice was not to worship God.

It is this background that sparked the ministry of Jesus. He summed it up in the synagogue of his native Nazareth: "The Spirit of the Lord is upon me. He has anointed me to preach good news to the poor, has sent me to proclaim release for prisoners and sight for the blind, to let the oppressed go free" (Lk 4:18).

The early Christians grasped that. If *anyone* is hungry or athirst, naked or a stranger, sick or in prison, it is always Christ who clamors for bread or water, Christ who cries to be clothed or welcomed, Christ whom you visit on a bed of pain or behind bars (cf. Mt 25:31–36). And the First Letter of John is frightening: "If anyone has the world's goods and sees his brother [or sister] in need, yet closes his heart against him [or her], how does God's love abide in him?" (1 Jn 3:17).

The underlying theology is God's basic revelation. There are *two* great commandments of the law and the gospel. (1) You must love the Lord your God with all your heart and soul and mind. (2) You must love your sisters and brothers at least as much as you love yourself. This second commandment, Jesus declared, "is like" the first: Loving your brothers and sisters is like loving God (Mt 22:37–39).

Such is the justice to which St. Mary's is called in the years that lie ahead. The justice to which you are already committed, the justice that engages you in your many activities, demands even greater involvement, demands that every parishioner get involved. Not only individually but in community. Lone Rangers will not change the controlling culture—the emphasis on possessions and power, on me and my wants, on getting to the well first, on a struggle where the race is to the swift, the shrewd, the savage. The culture will change only if Christians organize—organize to feed the hungry and clothe the naked, organize to cherish our children and protect the powerless, organize to offer a sense of dignity to the millions who feel unloved, unwanted. The culture will change only if Christians in massive numbers carry their Christianity into marketplace and counting house, into law court and genetics lab, into every area where you live and move and have your being, conscious of your solidarity not only with your own kind but with every man, woman, and child "redeemed not with silver or gold but with the precious blood of Christ" (1 Pet 1:18–19).

I know, uncounted Catholics call this politics, economics, social work; they claim that the task of Christians is to save souls, their own and others', not change the social structure. I am afraid they do not understand what the Hebrew prophets and the prophet Christ have stressed: The task of God's people is to transform our earth into a realm of justice, of peace, of love. And Vatican II made it limpidly clear that this is specifically the task of the laity.[7] You are not substitutes for a declining priesthood, to be relegated to the sidelines if and when vocations to ordination blossom again. This is your God-given turf. Take hold of it—with all due modesty if you can, aggressively if you must.

Here I dare two recommendations. First, get the children involved even more than they already are. In their hands lies the future: our nation and government, our politics and economics, our social structure and religious reality. It is they who will decide what economic man/woman look like in the decades that lie ahead. But they are unlikely to change the culture if what they see in parents and teachers, in priests and religious, in you and me is what sociologist Robert Bellah called the amoral majority,[8] if our legacy to our children is the survival of the fittest, if the controlling American symbol continues to be the Dow and not the cross. Should they complain that they were made Christians without their own say-so, retort with Jesuit Father William O'Malley, "To complain that they baptized me without my approval is as foolish as complaining that they toilet-trained me without my approval. . . ." [9]

Second recommendation: Stay close to the gracious Lady who overshadows all that St. Mary's is and does. In the turbulent 60s, trying desperately to put our Lady "in her place," we often left her no place. We forgot, if we ever knew, that our Lady is the perfect disciple, for she more than any sheerly human figure heard God's word and treasured it in her heart.[10] We forgot, if we ever knew, what splendid Scripture scholars tell us: Beneath Calvary's cross, Jesus' words to Mary and John, "Here is your son," "Here is your mother" (Jn 19:26–28), show us Mary as the New Eve, figure of the Church that ceaselessly brings forth new children modeled after Jesus.[11] If you want to evangelize effectively, stay close to her who first gave us Jesus and still holds him out to us with the words from the Transfiguration's bright cloud, "This is my beloved Son; listen to him" (Mt 17:5).

Let me close with a stunning paragraph from the bishops of Latin America as they ended a crucial meeting last October to chart the course of their churches—churches that comprise 43 percent of the world's Catholics. Their "cry of the poor" and vulnerable is not limited to Latin America; much of it you can link to Laurel.

> To see the face of Jesus in the suffering faces of the poor is something which challenges all Christians to a profound personal and ecclesial conversion. In faith we find the faces disfigured by the hunger which results from inflation, foreign debt, and social injustices; the faces of those disillusioned by politicians who make promises but don't keep them; the faces of those humiliated because of their own culture, which is not respected and is even deprecated; the faces of those terrorized by daily and indiscriminate violence; the anguished faces of abandoned young people who walk our streets and sleep under our bridges; the suffering faces of humiliated women. . . ; the weary faces of migrants who aren't given a dignified reception; the faces, aged by work and time, of those who don't have the minimum needed to survive with dignity. . . .[12]

A question for each and all of us: In the suffering faces of our own unfortunates, do I see the suffering face of Jesus? If, like Thomas, I want to put my finger in the mark of Jesus' nails, let me touch with love the crucified flesh of those who carry his Calvary image. It is then that the risen Christian becomes the risen Christ.

St. Mary of the Mills Church
Laurel, Maryland
April 18, 1993

39

LET THE LITTLE CHILDREN COME TO ME
150th Anniversary of Holy Childhood Assn.

- 2 John 4–6
- Luke 18:15–17

In your Association[1] we celebrate something quite singular in the Catholic Church. You see, the Church has always been remarkable for new men, new women, new institutions to confront new crises. There was Francis of Assisi, combating a new worldliness by literally imitating Christ and courting Lady Poverty. There was Ignatius Loyola, countering the Reformation with an order of priests bound indeed by monastic vows but incredibly free to roam the world. There is Mother Teresa, founding an order of women to care for a whole fresh world of unfortunates, including a new black plague called AIDS.

What amazes me this evening is a project that is far from new, that is 150 years old, and yet is made to order for a new crisis that threatens our civilization. Bear with me then, good friends, as I (1) sketch what I see as today's major crisis across the world, (2) summarize what strikes me as a God-given counteragent to this crisis, and (3) suggest how this counteragent can be given even fuller life in our time.

I

Today's crisis? Children. Not indeed the only crisis; simply the one that spans the world and transcends cultures; is most cruelly affected by drugs and drought, by economics and ecology; is threatened ceaselessly by war on the womb, war on our streets, war in Bosnia and Northern Ireland; touches the most vulnerable and defenseless of humans.

Lay hold of some sheer facts. In our land alone one out of every five children is growing up hungry—one out of every three black children. Teen suicides have doubled since 1970. Every 8 seconds of every school day a child drops out of school. Every 26 seconds a child runs away from home. Every 67 seconds a teenager has a baby. Every 7 minutes a child is arrested for drug abuse. Every 36 minutes a child is killed or injured by a gun. Every day 135,000 American children go to school with a deadly weapon. Says a Special Report in *Fortune:* "AIDS has turned youthful experimentation with sex into Russian roulette." [2] A book on America's homeless kids by the president of Covenant House is "dedicated to the 1,000,000 homeless children who slept on America's streets last year [1990], scared, cold, hungry, alone, and most of all, desperate to find someone who cares." [3]

As for our well-fed, well-educated, more normal young, we are losing all too many to a resurgence of late-19th-century rugged individualism, to the stress on the almighty "I," to the contemporary lust for power, for possessions, for applause. Most are terribly ignorant of Christ and his Church—what it means to believe, to hope, to love as Jesus did. When only 40% of our Catholic people share regularly in the central act of our worship, is it any wonder that many of our teenagers have little relationship with the living Christ of Catholicism, find our sexual morality ridiculously outdated, have no basic spirituality on which to hang their daily living? When half of America's marriages fall apart, the primary victims are our children—dreadfully confused, sexually abused, with no models save the Rambos and Madonnas of our age.

And this touches simply our "land of the free." Across the world, do you know how many children will die in this decade alone, in the 90s, most from illnesses we have learned to cure? One hundred and fifty million. A quarter of a million young children die every week; millions more suffer from malnutrition. More than a million girls die each year simply because they are born female. In the developing world, only about 12% of government spending is devoted to basics like primary healthcare and primary education for the poor majority. Far more goes into the nations' debt and the military; for the poor world transfers $50 billion a year to the rich nations, and the amount spent on the world's military exceeds the combined annual incomes of the poorest half of humanity.[4]

But statistics are dreadfully cold. Read the daily newspapers, see the pictures on TV—refugee children watering the world's ways with their tears, hungry children with bellies bloated, abused children with eyes staring blankly into a hopeless future. Read, see, and weep for God's lost children.

II

So much for the crisis; now for its counteragent. It's true, hundreds of organizations exist to confront the crisis, aware that the proper measure of a civilization's health is the well-being of its children. And so we have the United Nations Children's Fund (UNICEF). We have the Children's Defense Fund here in Washington. We have some 2000 residences and group homes like Boys Town where some 200,000 boys and girls live, at an average annual cost of $30,000 per youngster. We have Catholic Charities spread across the country. We have St. Hope Academy in Sacramento founded by Phoenix Suns' star guard Kevin Johnson: HOPE, acronym for "Helping Our People Excel." And so on, far into the night.

And yet, the counteragent that can proudly claim to be singular is the Holy Childhood Association. Isn't it remarkable how contemporary this counteragent is? Pauline Jaricot's suggestion to Bishop Charles de Forbin-Janson a century and a half ago ranks among ideas that change the world: To help the children of the world, appeal to the children of the world. Children helping children.

It is HCA's children who enable a Salvadoran mother and father to accept work, because their two children now spend the day in Our Lady Day Care Center. It is U.S. kids who enable a little girl to attend pre-school in the Philippines. It is children who enable children in the Sudan to have food and uniforms, books and medicine. Uncounted children in one hundred countries are alive and well today because young Catholics far away have learned to respect their cultures, to love children who look different, talk different, smell different. And all this started in 1843 with a penny from each child each month . . . and a prayer.

A prayer. Don't discount it, don't undervalue it. The prayer is as important as the penny. For the prayer underscores the Catholic dynamism, the Catholic force, the Catholic power that propels the penny. Not discrimination. To qualify for HCA's love, all you need is . . . need. I mean hunger—for milk or a cereal, for a warm coat or a warm home, for medicine or a leg brace, for justice or freedom— whatever. And yet, behind it all is Christ's commandment of love: Love not only God but every sister and brother shaped in God's

likeness. Love them all at least as much as you love yourself; in fact,
love them the way Jesus loves you. Loving like this is, in Jesus' own
words, "like" loving God (Mt 22:39).

Such love underscores the sense of mission within your Association, within the children who serve. HCA is not just a neat idea; it is
your involvement in a Church whose essence is mission, whose essence is literally to be "sent." Sent where? To the whole wide world,
wherever humans yearn for a more Christian existence, yearn simply
for a life that is more human. There is no one of you—adult or
child—who is not a missionary; for by your baptism you were commissioned to bring the gospel to some acre of God's world. And the
gospel is not just the Trinity and the sacraments, important as they
surely are. You preach the gospel if you live what you discover in the
Letter of James:

> What good is it, my brothers and sisters, if you say you have faith
> but do not have works? Can faith save you? If a brother or sister
> is naked and lacks daily food, and one of you says to them, "Go
> in peace; keep warm and eat your fill," and yet you do not supply
> their bodily needs, what is the good of that? So faith by itself, if it
> has no works, is dead.
>
> (James 2:14–17)

A remarkable by-product of such missionary activity? The children who give, who respond to the urging of Jesus, "Let the little
children come to me, for it is to such as these that the kingdom of
God belongs" (Lk 18:16), the children who give are themselves given.
In giving, they themselves come to Jesus.

III

My third point: How can this admirable counteragent, your Association, be given even fuller life in our time? I say "fuller" life because
life is already there, has been richly there for a century and a half.
Still, every organization, even within the Body of Christ, requires an
occasional injection, an infusion of fresh blood. For to stand still is
to risk a slow, painful dying.

But what precisely? Let me speak simply from my own limited
experience. The problem? For all your exposure, much, perhaps
most, of Catholic America does not know you. Understandable; for
schools have been closed, Sisters who propagated your apostolate are

decimated, ignorance of things Catholic is rampant, families are not notable for a broad and deep Catholic culture. Take a sampling, unscientific but not negligible, of a cross section of your Catholic friends. Toss at them "Holy Childhood Association." Blank stares. Do the same with the young. More expressive looks, like "Holy Childhood! You off your rocker?"

And yet, here is youthful Catholicism at its best, at its most challenging, its most satisfying, its most efficient, its most missionary. Not just catechism, but a faith that does justice, that lives the second great commandment of the law and the gospel. What we need here is what we need in so much else: in our teaching and preaching, in pastoral documents and parish life. I mean . . . imagination. I want to see the children with my own eyes, those who receive and those who give, in North America and South Africa, in Zaire and the Sudan, not only in a brochure but on the TV screen. Get the Christophers to do a documentary for you. Challenge Ted Koppel and Mike Wallace, Barbara Walters and Maria Shriver, to extend their Catholic coverage beyond the scandals of priestly perversion to the scandal of the cross erected over history, beyond the admirable adults to the thousands of children who help millions of children to live more humanly. Let's stop complaining that the airwaves and boob tubes are owned by the ethnic sons of Abraham, and provide them with examples of the greatest story ever *un*told.

Where are our songwriters? What Amy Grant did for Jesus in "Love of Another Kind," is this out of the question for American Catholics? Is rock-and-roll the preserve of unbelievers? What Whoopi Goldberg did in *Sister Act,* could she not do for our children's act? Can't any Catholics sing?

Let me turn uncommonly honest. Before Father Wright asked me to preach to you, I knew nothing about Holy Childhood save for its name. Now I'm delighted, I'm amazed, I'm in awe. But I'm also fearful. HCA can die, you know. Projects do each day. But if HCA were to die, it would not only be an organization, a structure, that died. Countless children would die as well. Not matter for confession, but indeed for copious tears. The solution? A gigantic effort of imagination linked to prayer, with profound hope in the risen Christ— the Christ who rebuked his own apostles for keeping the children from him. The Christ who wanted those children in his arms, wants today's children in his arms. Not later, in heaven. Now.

Dupont Plaza Hotel
Washington, D.C.
April 27, 1993

40
AGING, CHANGING, GIVING
Homily for a Seniors Clubs Celebration

- Revelation 12:1–12
- Luke 1:26–38

Your celebration[1] centers on a significant monosyllable: change. Change can be frightening: I've lost my job. Change can be welcome: My hiatus hernia has stopped mimicking a heart attack. Change can be challenging: I have a chance to contribute something new to society. In the context of this Eucharistic gathering, let me focus on change in our Catholic existence. Three stages to my development: (1) change in the Church; (2) our Lady's response to change; (3) change as it touches you and me.

I

First, change in the Church. It happens, you know. The Church changes—in the way it thinks, in the way it worships, in the way it lives. I don't mean that the Church ceases to be what Christ intended it to be. I do mean that the Church—the pope included—grows in understanding. Understanding what God has revealed to us in Christ; understanding how our sacraments can better serve our people; understanding what it means to live morally in a whole new technological age.

Several concrete examples. Vatican II startled many a Catholic when it declared that the grace of Christ is at work, richly and incessantly, not only within individual Protestants but with the community called Protestant, suggested strongly that the bonds that unite us (for example, living faith, fruitful baptism) link us not only as individuals but more importantly as communities.[2] Rome surprised many a Cath-

208

olic when it turned our altars around, changed a centuries-old Latin into our native tongues, allowed us to enfold the body of Christ within our hands. Not only don't we encourage any longer the burning of heretics; not only has the Church moved forward on organ transplantation.[3] The Church and its theologians are newly struggling to decide if and when we may withhold nutrition from a patient in a permanently vegetative state.

The point of these examples? The Church of Christ does change, has to change. Why? Because to stand still is to die; because Christ wants the Church to grow, as he grew, not only in age but in wisdom. But, not to worry! Led by the Spirit through trial and error, through fortune and misfortune, the Church retains its identity, remains the Church of Christ.

II

Second, our Lady's response to change. As I grew up early in our century, many of us had a childlike conception of Jesus' mother: a sweet teenager surprised by joy in Nazareth; a young mother cradling her infant in a stable warmed by friendly animals; a dutiful wife to Joseph in Nazareth; a somewhat worried mother searching for her 12-year-old in Jerusalem; a sorrowful mother standing silently beneath the cross of her only child.

Nothing false about those pictures. Still, they do not represent the reality that gives them her profound life. What is that reality? Change—radical change. This girl was to change in a moment from a Jewish teenager indistinguishable from her playmates to a unique young lady pregnant with God's only Son, in danger of being stoned to death in accordance with Jewish law. This young lady changed into an unusual mother; for while pregnant she had to leave her native Nazareth for Bethlehem 85 miles away, could find no decent room there, gave birth where only brute animals gave birth. This mother had to live with agony when she lost her teenage boy in Jerusalem: "Child, why have you treated us like this? Look, your father and I have been terribly worried and have been searching for you" (Lk 2:48). And she "did not understand" his explanation (v. 50). This mother experienced change when her fellow Nazarenes, who "spoke well of [Jesus] and were amazed at the gracious words that came from his mouth" (Lk 4:22), suddenly turned on him and tried to "hurl him off [a] cliff" (v. 29). This mother had to cope with change when Jesus' own relatives "went out to restrain him, for people were saying, 'He has gone out of his mind' " (Mk 3:21). This mother had to watch helplessly while soldiers stripped him, pinned him to a cross between two robbers, and gambled for his garments, while the people he loved jeered at him, taunted him to come down from the cross. This mother had to cradle her lifeless Son in her arms, place his cold flesh in a tomb, and hope that his Father would raise him from the dead.

Yes, hope. Always hope, rooted in faith. For no angel gave our Lady a script for Jesus' life, a scenario for his dying. No angel told this Jewish girl about the Trinity, about a Son who was equal in every respect to the Father of us all. No angel explained his leaving her from a criminal's cross. No angel told her, "Not to worry, Mary! Come around Sunday and you'll find an empty tomb."

The point of all this? For our Lady, too, to change was to grow, to become more and more like her Son. Our Lady could live with change, with radical change, with deathly change, because she lived to perfection the response to God she first spoke to Gabriel: "Let it be with me as you say" (Lk 1:38). She was Jesus' first and perfect disciple; for she it was who lived more remarkably than any other sheerly human person Jesus' definition of disciples: "those who hear the word of God and do it" (Lk 8:21).

III

This brings me to my third point: change as it touches you and me. Most of us here have passed from adolescence, from young adulthood, from middle age to a generation for which America has a frightening term: old age. We inhabit a culture that canonizes youth and beauty, activity and productivity, power and sexual prowess. If you are eternally young and ceaselessly attractive, if after 60 or 65 you continue your career with little letdown and still make an impact on an acre of God's world, if you can jog or play squash or straddle a Honda, if you can still satisfy a man or woman sexually, then your aging is ideal. In fact, you're not growing old at all! The ideal is a compound of Churchill and John XXIII, Picasso and Susan B. Anthony, Maurice Chevalier and Marlene Dietrich, George Meany and Mae West, George Burns and Lauren Bacall, Clark Gable and Grandma Moses. The only ideal of senior citizen we accept in America is an aging without change or limits or loss.

Not so the Christian vision. Here you and I are as important as Michael Jordan and Bill Clinton, as Madonna and Barbra Streisand, as Joe Montana and Princess Diana. For our ideal is the resounding call of St. Paul to the Christians of Philippi in Macedonia:

> I regard everything as loss because of the surpassing worth of knowing Christ Jesus my Lord. For his sake I have suffered the loss of all things, in order that I may gain Christ and be found in him. . . . I want to know Christ and the power of his resurrection and the sharing of his sufferings. . . . This one thing I do: Forgetting what lies behind and straining forward to what lies ahead, I press on toward the goal. . . .
>
> (Phil 3:8–14)

"Forgetting what lies behind." You and I are not doomed to live in the past. We are to live today and tomorrow. For our task is to grow—grow into what Paul called "full-grown adulthood." And what is that? "The fulness of Christ" (Eph 4:13). "Speaking the truth in love, we are to grow up in every way . . . into Christ" (v. 10).

So then, our maturity, our fulness, lies ahead of us. That maturing process can hardly be spelled out in a homily. Let me focus on one area where you and I can, perhaps must, grow into Christ, an area that is increasingly critical in our society, is intimately linked to Catholic Charities and our Offices of Justice and Peace. Paul has suggested it: "speaking the truth in love." Better still, living the truth in love. It is a vivid way of saying that your Catholicism and mine should be a faith that does justice. Here justice turns into love. For the justice that the Old Testament prophets proclaimed, the justice that Jesus preached as his own reason for taking our flesh, is not simply an ethical concept: giving to others what they deserve, because they are human persons, because they have rights that can be proven from philosophy or have been written into law. Biblical justice is treating our sisters and brothers as our covenant with God demands. We are to father the fatherless and mother the motherless, feed the famished and shelter the homeless, clothed the naked and visit the housebound and imprisoned, because this implements the second great commandment of the law and the gospel: We are to love our sisters and brothers at least as much as we love ourselves. In fact, we are to love them as Jesus loves us.

Our times demand it. For we live in an age that some sociologists describe as a resurgence of late-19th-century rugged individualism, where what ultimately matters is the one-and-only I, where there is only so much water in the well and I had better get there first, where the race is to the swift, the shrewd, the savage, and the devil take the hindmost. A paradoxical country where one out of every five children grows up hungry, crack and coke ravage the flesh and savage the minds of our teens, a million youngsters sleep on our streets each night, racial hatred bubbles beneath the surface of our cities, elderly men and women rummage in garbage cans for the food we discard so lightly, 37 million Americans have no realistic access to healthcare.

In our stress on youth and strength, on computers and dollars, we have neglected an incredibly rich resource. These tortured sisters and brothers of yours need *you*, need your love, need to hear your warm voice, see the compassion in your eyes, profit from your experience of joy and sorrow, of love exchanged and love amid the ruins. You need not walk alone; the organizations exist, are there, within walking distance. If we Catholics were to mobilize our "third age" men and women, organize them to confront the ills of our country, send them out in pairs like the original disciples, we could change the face of this land.

Not all of you can walk the streets, raise up the fallen, speak the truth in love. And yet, no one of you is powerless. Listen to inspired St. Paul: "[The Lord] said to me, 'My grace is sufficient for you, for my power is made perfect in weakness.' So, I will boast all the more gladly of my weaknesses, so that the power of Christ may dwell in me. Therefore I am content with weaknesses . . . for the sake of Christ; for whenever I am weak, then I am strong" (2 Cor 12:9–10). "I can do all things through him who strengthens me" (Phil 4:13). The power behind those who walk and talk is the hidden army that suffers and prays. Never underestimate that power. It brought an angel from heaven to strengthen Jesus in the hour when he was sweating blood, afraid to die.

Good friends in Christ: I who share your years and tears can promise you one gift with supreme confidence. Get involved with even one person who experiences more of Christ's crucifixion than of his resurrection, and the change in your own life will amaze you. Many of you have already experienced it. I can only hope and pray that every single one of you will. For your own sake, for the sake of your bleeding Church, for the sake of your tortured land. In your "third age" apostolate, God lead you, God feed you, God speed you.

St. Frances de Chantal Church
Wantagh, New York
April 22, 1993

NOTES

Homily 1

1. *Washington Post,* Dec. 5, 1992, A 16.
2. The occasion for this sermon was an annual Advent Chorale by the Georgetown Community Chorale, directed by Dr. Elaine Rendler, that involved Christian and Jewish believers.
3. In the original, to "love *hesed,*" "which implies fidelity, goodness, or kindness: an expression of love on their part in response to God's love" (Léo Laberge, O.M.I., "Micah," in *The New Jerome Biblical Dictionary,* ed. Raymond E. Brown, S.S., Joseph A. Fitzmyer, S.J., and Roland E. Murphy, O.Carm. [Englewood Cliffs, N.J.: Prentice Hall, 1990] 16:31, p. 254).
4. John R. Donahue, S.J., "Biblical Perspectives on Justice," in *The Faith That Does Justice,* ed. John C. Haughey, S.J. (Woodstock Studies 2; New York: Paulist, 1977) 68–112, at 69.
5. Statistics in this sentence from Sr. Mary Rose McGeady, *God's Lost Children: Letters from Covenant House* (New York: Covenant House, 1991) 31.
6. Ibid. 51.
7. Ibid. 48.
8. John Paul II, *Familiaris consortio.*

Homily 2

1. Ignatius Loyola, Spiritual Exercises, no. 65.
2. Graham Greene, *Monsignor Quixote* (New York: Simon and Schuster, 1982) 206–7. I have compressed the dialogue.
3. William J. Bausch, *More Telling Stories, Compelling Stories* (Mystic, Conn.: Twenty-third Publications, 1992) 120.

Homily 3

1. Lance Morrow, "Voters Are Mad as Hell," *Time* 139, no. 9 (March 2, 1992) 16–20.
2. Ibid. 20.
3. See Joseph Blenkinsopp, "Deuteronomy," *New Jerome Biblical Commentary* (Englewood Cliffs, N.J.: Prentice Hall, 1990) 6:42, p. 106.
4. I was moved to ask this question by a one-page article by the remarkable Presbyterian novelist/preacher Frederick Buechner, "Preaching on Hope," *The Living Pulpit* 1, no. 1 (January-March 1992) 5, particularly: "The trouble with many sermons is not so much that the preachers are out of touch with what is going on in the world of books or in theology but that they are out of touch with what is going on in their own lives and in the lives of the people they are preaching to." He urges preachers to talk as honestly as did St. Paul about the darkness and pitiableness in their own condition, "into which hope brings a glimmer of light," about "their own reasons for hoping—not just the official, doctrinal, biblical reasons but the reasons rooted deep in their own day by day experience."
5. From the live recording "I Have a Dream" produced by Twentieth Century Fox and distributed by ABC Records, TFS 3201 (no date).
6. See *The Long Loneliness: The Autobiography of Dorothy Day* (New York: Harper & Brothers, 1952) 149–50; William D. Miller, *Dorothy Day: A Biography* (San Francisco: Harper & Row, 1982) 341, 343–44.
7. See Morrow (n. 1 above) 17.

Homily 4

1. C. S. Lewis, *The Last Battle* (New York: Collier Books, 1971) 169–70.
2. See Frederick Buechner, *Telling the Truth: The Gospel as Tragedy, Comedy, and Fairy Tale* (San Francisco: Harper & Row, 1977) 49–50.

Homily 5

1. The occasion was the third retreat/workshop in my project *Preaching the Just Word*, a national effort, under the auspices of the Woodstock Theological Center, to move the preaching of social-justice issues more effectively into the pulpits and parishes of the country.
2. See Joseph A. Fitzmyer, S.J., *Paul and His Theology: A Brief Sketch* (2nd ed.; Englewood Cliffs, N.J.: Prentice Hall, 1989) 56–58, esp. no. 64.
3. See Augustine, *Sermon 153* 1; also F. Van der Meer, *Augustine the Bishop:*

The Life and Work of a Father of the Church (London and New York: Sheed and Ward, 1961) 450–51.

4. David H. C. Read, *This Grace Given* (Grand Rapids: Eerdmans, 1984) 129.

Homily 6

1. On the absence of a suffering Messiah in the Old Testament and in pre-Christian Judaism, see Joseph A. Fitzmyer, S.J., *The Gospel according to Luke (X–XXIV)* (Garden City, N.Y.: Doubleday, 1985) 1565–66.
2. See ibid. 1559. On whether Jesus celebrated the Eucharist before these disciples, see ibid. 1560.
3. Constitution on the Sacred Liturgy, no. 7.
4. *The Faces of Jesus,* text by Frederick Buechner, photography by Leo Boltin (New York: Stearn/San Francisco: Harper & Row, 1989).
5. Ibid. 14.
6. Ibid. 240.
7. From an unsigned obituary in *Time* 141, no. 16 (April 19, 1993) 24. The information in these paragraphs stems from this notice.

Homily 7

1. From excerpts in *Catholic Health World* 4, no. 13 (July 1, 1988) 1 and 12, with corrections from a text graciously supplied by the editor of that journal.
2. See Raymond E. Brown, S.S., *The Gospel according to John (xiii–xxi)* (Garden City, N.Y.: Doubleday, 1970) 612–14. Brown stresses that "the 'love of one another' of which Jesus speaks is love *between Christians.* In our own times a frequent ideal is the love of all men, enunciated in terms of the fatherhood of God and the brotherhood of man. Such a maxim has some biblical base in the creation of all men by God (see Matt v 44), but the idea is not Johannine. For John, God is a Father only to those who believe in His Son and who are begotten as God's children by the Spirit in Baptism" (613).
3. See Jean Giblet and Pierre Grelot, "Covenant," in Xavier Léon-Dufour, ed., *Dictionary of Biblical Theology* (2nd ed. rev.; New York: Seabury, 1973) 93–98; A. Yonick, "Covenant (in the Bible)," *New Catholic Encyclopedia* 4 (1967) 401–5.
4. Note that Brown (n. 2 above) finds "dubious the suggestion that the newness consists in the fact that Jesus commands the Christian to love 'as I have loved you,' while the OT commands the Israelite to love his neighbor *as himself*" (613).
5. So Patrick J. Ryan, " 'All You Need Is Love,' " *America* 166, no. 16 (May 9, 1992) 419.

6. From a letter of Fr. Angelo D'Agostino in the May 1992 issue of *Offerings*, a newsletter published by the Social, Pastoral & International Ministries of the Maryland Province Jesuits.
7. The title is "Love Don't Need a Reason"; words and music by Peter Allen, Michael Callen, and Marsha Malamet.
8. A reference to a widespread outbreak of violence in Los Angeles consequent on a jury's virtual dismissal of charges against four white policemen who had brutally assaulted a black man they were arresting.

Homily 8

1. This brief homily was given at the Eucharistic liturgy that concluded the fourth retreat/workshop of my project *Preaching the Just Word*, an effort to move the preaching of social-justice issues more effectively into all the Catholic pulpits and congregations of the United States.
2. A reference to the engaging motion picture *Arthur*, with Dudley Moore playing the title role.

Homily 9

1. Here I am persuaded by what St. Ignatius Loyola in his Spiritual Exercises (no. 299) calls "the first apparition" of the risen Jesus: "He appeared to the Virgin Mary. Though this is not mentioned explicitly in the Scripture, it must be considered as stated when Scripture says that he appeared to many others. For Scripture supposes that we have understanding. . . ." (Louis J. Puhl, S.J., *The Spiritual Exercises of St. Ignatius* [Chicago: Loyola University, 1952] 132).
2. See Joseph A. Fitzmyer, S.J., "The Letter to the Romans," in *The New Jerome Biblical Commentary*, ed. Raymond E. Brown, S.S., Joseph A. Fitzmyer, S.J., and Roland E. Murphy, O.Carm. (Englewood Cliffs, N.J.: Prentice Hall, 1990) 51:77–78, pp. 851–52.
3. For justification of this translation, see Raymond E. Brown, S.S., *The Gospel according to John (xiii–xxi)* (Garden City, N.Y.: Doubleday, 1970) 640.

Homily 10

1. I see no point in distinguishing, within a homily, between the several authors of "Isaiah." The author of chapters 40–55 is ordinarily designated Deutero-Isaiah; reasons for separate authorship (historical, literary, and thematic) are succinctly provided by Carroll Stuhlmueller, C.P., "Deutero-Isaiah and Trito-Isaiah," in *The New Jerome Biblical Commentary*,

ed. Raymond E. Brown, S.S., Joseph A. Fitzmyer, S.J., and Roland E. Murphy, O.Carm. (Englewood Cliffs, N.J.: Prentice Hall, 1990) 21:2–3, pp. 329–30.

2. Ibid. 21:3, p. 330.
3. See ibid. 21:35, p. 339.
4. See ibid. 21:20, p. 335.
5. From Poem 57, beginning "As kingfishers catch fire," in W. H. Gardner and N. H. MacKenzie, eds., *The Poems of Gerard Manley Hopkins* (4th ed.; New York: Oxford University, 1970) 90.

Homily 11

1. This homily was delivered at the final liturgy in a week-long institute for priests, "Rekindling the Gift of God That Is the Ongoing Activity of Holy Orders Within," sponsored by the National Institute for Clergy Formation (centered at Seton Hall University, South Orange, New Jersey) and held at Our Lady of Florida Spiritual Center, North Palm Beach, Florida, January 17–22, 1993.
2. Decree on the Ministry and Life of Priests, no. 4.
3. I realize that proclaiming the gospel is not limited to formal preaching; but surely liturgical homilies day after day and week after week are for the majority of the clergy their most significant form of proclamation.
4. Boston: Beacon, 1986, at 121.

Homily 12

1. This homily was preached at the final liturgy for my *Preaching the Just Word* project held at San Pedro Center, Winter Park, Florida, January 24–29, 1993, for 25 ordained priests, four laypersons (two women, two men), and three permanent deacons.
2. *Coresponsibility in the Church* (New York: Herder and Herder, 1968) 31.
3. William J. O'Malley, S.J., "Ten Commandments for Homilists," *America* 149, no. 3 (July 23–30, 1983).
4. I borrow this understanding of the Greek *automatē* (Mk 4:28) from Daniel J. Harrington, S.J., "The Gospel according to Mark," *The New Jerome Biblical Commentary*. ed. Raymond E. Brown, S.J., Joseph A. Fitzmyer, S.J., and Roland E. Murphy, O.Carm. (Englewood Cliffs, N.J.: Prentice Hall, 1990) 41:30, p. 606.
5. A reference to Ms. Eileen Danis, one of the retreatants, who works as a volunteer in the District of Columbia Jail, mostly with psychiatric residents.

Homily 13

1. Three years ago I preached on these texts to the Holy Trinity congregation; see my homily "Choose Life . . . in Christ," in my collection *Dare To Be Christ: Homilies for the Nineties* (New York/Mahwah: Paulist, 1991) 71–76. The present approach is similar but not the same.
2. André-Alphonse Viard and Jacques Guillet, "Life," *Dictionary of Biblical Theology,* ed. Xavier-Léon Dufour (2nd ed.; New York: Seabury, 1973) 313–16, at 314.
3. *Time* 69 (June 10, 1957) 104.
4. St. Augustine of Hippo, *Confessions* 3.1.
5. I used the shorter form, Mt 5:20–22, 27–28, 33–34, 37.
6. In my 1990 homily (note 1 above) I noted that Jesus does not distinguish a righteous anger such as he himself experienced, does not discuss dangerous repressions of anger, does not put a time limit on parents' anger when their daughter is gang-raped. He is simply trying to lift his followers from a narrow legalism to a new integrity, a gospel wholeness. He wants us to be aware how dangerous anger can be, justified or not.
7. See the review by Richard Corliss in *Time* 141, no. 5 (Feb. 1, 1993) 68, 70.

Homily 14

1. For an earlier effort, on Feb. 17, 1980, to deal with the Lucan beatitudes and woes, see my homily "Blessed Are You?" in my *Sir, We Would Like To See Jesus: Homilies from a Hilltop* (New York/Ramsey: Paulist, 1982) 93–98. I am also borrowing from my homily "Easier for a Camel" in my *Still Proclaiming Your Wonders: Homilies for the Eighties* (New York/Ramsey: Paulist, 1984) 134–38.
2. Inevitably, I shall make use of material in the 1980 homily (n. 1 above), while availing myself of more recent research into Luke, especially Joseph A. Fitzmyer, S.J., *The Gospel according to Luke (I–IX)* (Garden City, N.Y.: Doubleday, 1981), and *The Gospel according to Luke (X–XXIV)* (Garden City: N.Y.: Doubleday, 1985), as well as his *Luke the Theologian: Aspects of His Teaching* (New York/Mahwah: Paulist, 1989).
3. From a commentary on this Sunday's liturgical readings by Joseph A. Tetlow, S.J., "A Prickly Pair," *America* 142, no. 5 (Feb. 9, 1980) iii.
4. On the meaning of "blessed" (Greek *makarios*), see Fitzmyer, *Luke (I–IX)* (n. 2 above) 632–33.

Homily 15

1. See my article "Unity through Ecstasy: A Tribute to John Courtney Murray," *Dominicana* 53, no. 1 (spring 1968) 3–5.
2. See Leonard S. Kravitz, "A Martyr for Love," *The Living Pulpit* 1, no. 3 (July–September 1992) 18–19, at 18.

3. See William Klassen, *Love of Enemies: The Way to Peace* (Philadelphia: Fortress, 1984) 28: "The commandment, 'love your enemy,' occurs nowhere in the Old Testament. The concept, however, cannot be confined to the words themselves. When enemies are fed and cared for, rather than killed or mistreated, then in effect love for the enemy is being practiced."

4. I am aware of the thesis denying that Jesus taught love of enemies in reference to Romans and their puppets, reserved this love for fellow peasants in the local community; so Richard Horsley, as noted by Walter Wink, "Counterresponse to Richard Horsley," in *The Love of Enemy and Nonretaliation in the New Testament*, ed. Willard M. Swartley (Louisville: Westminster/John Knox, 1992) 133–36, at 134. But I agree with Wink that "there is nothing noteworthy in such a teaching. Even the tax collectors do the same" (ibid.).

5. Paul Gray, "What Is Love?" *Time* 141, no. 7 (Feb. 15, 1993) 47–49; Anastasia Toufexis, "The Right Chemistry," ibid. 49–51.

6. Toufexis, ibid. 51.

7. St. Augustine of Hippo, *Confessions* 4.6.11.

8. See my homily "Let Compassion Take Wing," in my collection *When Christ Meets Christ: Homilies on the Just Word* (New York/Mahwah: Paulist, 1993) 208–12.

9. Klassen, *Love of Enemies* 6–7.

10. St. Augustine of Hippo, *The First Catechetical Instruction* [*De catechizandis rudibus*] 1.4.7 (tr. Joseph P. Christopher, in Ancient Christian Writers 2 [New York/Ramsey: Newman reprint 1978] 21).

Homily 16

1. The occasion was the opening of the annual Assembly of the Catholic Health Association of the United States and Canada, held in Anaheim, California, June 14–17, 1992. Three more homilies relating to healthcare followed on successive days and are included in this volume immediately following the present homily.

2. Here I am indebted to Jean Giblet and Pierre Grelot, "Sickness/Healing," in Xavier Léon Dufour, *Dictionary of Biblical Theology* (2nd ed.; New York: Seabury, 1973) 543–45.

3. A reference to riots, looting, and burning in Los Angeles consequent on the acquittal of four white policemen accused of brutality in the arrest of a black—a beating caught on video and transmitted to much of the world.

4. Frederick Buechner, *The Hungering Dark* (New York: Seabury, 1969) 45–46.

5. Here I relate to a conviction of St. Irenaeus, bishop of Lyons in the second century, that in the beginning God fashioned the first man and

220 SPEAK THE WORD WITH BOLDNESS

woman in the image of Christ to come, that this was precisely the image
that was lost or defaced, this the image the Son of God came personally
to restore in its original fulness.

Homily 17

1. See Jerome T. Walsh, "1 Kings," in *The New Jerome Biblical Commentary*,
   ed. Raymond E. Brown, S.S., Joseph A. Fitzmyer, S.J., and Roland E.
   Murphy, O.Carm. (Englewood Cliffs, N.J.: Prentice Hall, 1990) 10:37,
   pp. 173–74.
2. John Paul II, Encyclical *Sollicitudo rei socialis*, Dec. 30, 1987, no. 28 (tr.
   USCC, publication no. 205–5 [n.d.], p. 49).
3. Quoted from Thomas B. Edsall, "GOP Battler Atwater Dies at 40," *Washington Post*, March 30, 1991, 1 and 7, at 1.

Homily 18

1. Julia Preston, "The Man with the Rio Plan," *Washington Post*, June 3,
   1992, B1.

Homily 19

1. The Hebrew word here, often translated "piety," is a thematic word in
   the Gospels and has all the complex meanings of "justice" and "righteousness." See Benedict T. Viviano, O.P., "The Gospel according to
   Matthew," in *The New Jerome Biblical Commentary*, ed. Raymond E. Brown,
   S.S., Joseph A. Fitzmyer, S.J., and Roland E. Murphy, O.Carm. (Englewood Cliffs, N.J.: Prentice Hall, 1990) 42:37–38, 40, pp. 644–45.
2. See St. Athanasius' *Life of St. Antony* 4 (tr. Robert T. Meyer, Ancient
   Christian Writers 10 [New York/Ramsey, N.J.: Paulist, 1978] 21).
3. *Time* 134, no. 23 (Dec. 4, 1989) 11.

Homily 20

1. This homily was preached at the Wednesday liturgy during the fifth
   retreat/workshop in my project *Preaching the Just Word*, a continuing effort
   to move the preaching of social-justice issues more effectively into all the
   Roman Catholic pulpits and congregations of the United States.
2. On Amos, I have learned much from Michael L. Barré, "Amos," in *The
   New Jerome Biblical Commentary*, ed. Raymond E. Brown, S.S., Joseph A.

Fitzmyer, S.J., and Roland E. Murphy, O.Carm. (Englewood Cliffs, N.J.: Prentice Hall, 1990) 13:1–3, pp. 209–10, and 13:15–17, pp. 213–14.

3. Abraham Joshua Heschel, "No Religion Is an Island," *Union Seminary Quarterly Review* 21 (1965–66) 121.

Homily 21

1. The reference to "Thunderbird" was introduced because the occasion was a Mass at Manresa for a former leader of the Thunderbirds and his wife, together with a daughter and her fiancé.
2. See Robert J. Karris, O.F.M., "The Gospel according to Luke," in *The New Jerome Biblical Commentary*, ed. Raymond E. Brown, S.S., Joseph A. Fitzmyer, S.J., and Roland E. Murphy, O.Carm. (Englewood Cliffs, N.J.: Prentice Hall, 1990) 43:127, p. 702.
3. Joseph A. Fitzmyer, S.J., *The Gospel according to Luke (X–XXIV)* (Garden City, N.Y.: Doubleday, 1985) 892. My homily owes much to his exegesis (891–95).

Homily 22

1. Here I am indebted to John R. Donahue, S.J., *The Gospel in Parable: Metaphor, Narrative, and Theology in the Synoptic Gospels* (Philadelphia: Fortress, 1988) 175.
2. See ibid. 171.
3. I have dealt with this idea in greater detail in "Stewards of God's Dappled Grace," published in my collection *Tell the Next Generation: Homilies and Near Homilies* (New York/Ramsey: Paulist, 1980) 186–93.
4. Frederick Buechner, *The Hungering Dark* (New York: Seabury, 1969) 45–46.
5. Richard Selzer, *Mortal Lessons: Notes on the Art of Surgery* (New York: Simon and Schuster, 1976) 106.
6. See the dedication in Kevin Casey, *Children of Eve* (New York: Covenant House, 1991).

Homily 23

1. This homily was addressed to the (permanent) Diaconate Community of Western Washington within the Archdiocese of Seattle.
2. On this text and other faith-texts, I have learned much from Joseph A. Fitzmyer, S.J., *The Gospel according to Luke (I–IX)* and *The Gospel according to Luke (X–XXIV)* (Garden City, N.Y.: Doubleday, 1981, 1985).

3. See Fitzmyer, *Luke I–IX* 235–37.

4. See also Mt 21:21; Mk 11:22–24.

5. See Fitzmyer, *Luke X–XXIV* 1142.

6. The verse is open to several different translations. The version I give is based on a pious note in the margin of the manuscripts. The context, with its defiant mood, seems to demand a negative, "I have no hope."

7. *Time* 134, no. 23 (Dec. 4, 1989) 11.

8. Karl Rahner, "Following the Crucified," *Theological Investigations* 18: *God and Revelation* (New York: Crossroad, 1983) 157–70, at 165–66.

9. Specifically, it is part of Catholic doctrine (though not defined) that from the moment of his conception Jesus enjoyed the beatific vision; see, e.g., the 1943 encyclical of Pius XII *Mystici corporis* (Denzinger-Schönmetzer [ed. 32, 1963] 3812 [2289]; AAS 35 [1943] 230).

10. James A. Coriden, *The Code of Canon Law: A Text and Commentary*, ed. James A. Coriden, Thomas J. Green, and Donald E. Heintschel (New York/Mahwah: Paulist, 1985) 551.

11. Yves Congar, O.P., "Sacramental Worship and Preaching," in *The Renewal of Preaching: Theory and Practice* (Concilium 33; New York: Paulist, 1968) 62.

Homily 24

1. See Patrick J. Ryan, "Double Outcast," *America* 167, no. 9 (Oct. 3, 1992) 231.

2. John R. Donahue, *The Gospel in Parable: Metaphor, Narrative and Theology in the Synoptic Gospels* (Philadelphia: Fortress, 1988) 189.

3. Thomas Merton, *Conjectures of a Guilty Bystander* (Garden City. N.Y.: Doubleday, 1966) 140–41.

4. John Donne, *Holy Sonnets*, no. 15.

5. Samuel H. Dresner, "Remembering Abraham Heschel," *America* 146, no. 21 (May 29, 1982) 414.

6. Paul J. Wadell, C.P., "A God Who Suffers," *Emmanuel* 97, no. 2 (March 1991) 75–81, at 80.

7. See Joseph A. Fitzmyer, S.J., *The Gospel according to Luke (X–XXIV)* (Garden City, N.Y.: Doubleday, 1985) 1155: Re the emphasis on the participle "seeing" in v. 15: "In the Lucan story this is an awakening; his eyes of faith were opened. The implication is that as a result of this awakening he no longer follows Jesus' injunction to show himself to the priest, but returns spontaneously."

8. The homily was followed by the baptism of Elizabeth Juliet Angel and Lara Duncan Tito.

Homily 25

1. Joseph A. Fitzmyer, S.J., *The Gospel according to Luke (X–XXIV)* (Garden City, N.Y.: Doubleday, 1985) 1323.
2. In today's segment from Jesus' discourse, he is not talking about the end of the world; that comes later (see v. 26). He is talking about the fate of Jerusalem and its temple.
3. See Josephus, *Jewish Wars* 1.21,1 #401.
4. So Reginald H. Fuller, *Preaching the Lectionary: The Word of God for the Church Today* (rev. ed.; Collegeville, Minn.: Liturgical, 1984) 528.
5. Karl Rahner, "The Spirituality of the Priest in the Light of His Office," *Theological Investigations* 19: *Faith and Ministry* (New York: Crossroad, 1983) 117–38, at 134.
6. Constitution on the Sacred Liturgy, no. 7.

Homily 26

1. Frederick Buechner, *The Magnificent Defeat* (New York: Seabury, 1966) 23.
2. Elizabeth Barrett Browning, *Sonnets from the Portuguese* 43.
3. Gerard Manley Hopkins, "The Blessed Virgin Compared to the Air We Breathe," in *The Poems of Gerard Manley Hopkins,* ed. W. H. Gardner and N. H. MacKenzie (New York: Oxford University, 1970) 93–97, at 95.
4. Julian of Norwich, *Revelations of Divine Love,* chap. 5 (*The Revelations of Divine Love of Julian of Norwich,* tr. James Walsh, S.J. [St. Meinrad, Ind.: Abbey, 1974] 53).
5. On this lavishness see Raymond E. Brown, S.S., *The Gospel according to John (i–xii)* (Garden City, N.Y.: Doubleday, 1966) 104–5.

Homily 27

1. Elizabeth Barrett Browning, *Sonnets from the Portuguese* 4.
2. A popular name for the University of Missouri.

Homily 28

1. William Shakespeare, *Hamlet, Prince of Denmark,* Act 3, Scene 1.
2. Based on Psalm 91; arranged by Michael Joncas; copyright by North American Liturgy Resources, Phoenix, Arizona, 85029.
3. See Evelyn Whitehead and James D. Whitehead, "Christian Marriage," *U.S. Catholic* 47, no. 6 (June 1982) 9.

Homily 29

1. Herbert O'Driscoll, "The Source," *The Living Pulpit* 1, no. 3 (July–September 1992) 4.
2. Joan Delaplane, O.P., "That Two Lettered Word," ibid. 12. The two-lettered word is the "as" in our Lord's "As the Father has loved me, so I have loved you" (Jn 15:9).
3. Josephus, *The Jewish War* 4.8,3 #474.

Homily 30

1. I am not suggesting that these facets of divine imaging were what the author(s) of Genesis intended; here I am borrowing from the Christian tradition.
2. Quoted in the Final Report of the National Commission on Children, *Beyond Rhetoric: A New American Agenda for Children and Families* (Washington, D.C.: National Commission on Children, 1991) [xv].
3. In this section I have tried to steer a middle (if vague) course between a God who moves humans like pawns on a chess board, and a God who has no influence whatsoever on what happens to people.
4. Kahlil Gibran, *The Prophet* (New York: Knopf, 1961) 15.
5. Walter Kerr, *The Decline of Pleasure* (New York: Simon & Schuster, 1962) 245.
6. Marian Williamson, *Return to Love* (New York: HarperCollins, 1992).

Homily 31

1. On this and much else on this subject in summary fashion, see Enda McDonagh, "Love," *The New Dictionary of Theology,* ed. Joseph A. Komonchak, Mary Collins, and Dermot A. Lane (Wilmington, Del.: Glazier, 1987) 602–16.
2. From Anthony de Mello, S.J., *Taking Flight: A Book of Story Meditations* (New York: Doubleday, 1988) 154 (with a few word changes).
3. Final Report of the National Commission on Children, *Beyond Rhetoric: A New American Agenda for Children and Families* (Washington, D.C.: National Commission on Children, 1991) 12.

Homily 32

1. This homily was preached at the closing liturgy of the annual Institute for Priests shaped by Msgr. Andrew Cusack, director of the National Institute for Clergy Formation located at Seton Hall University, South Orange, New Jersey.

2. Cf. Hugo Rahner, S.J., *Ignatius the Theologian* (New York: Herder and Herder, 1968): "In full accordance with Ignatian theology, the 'creator and Lord' of this contemplation is Christ, the incarnate Word, who in virtue both of what he is and of what he does, dwells in all creatures and 'behaves as one who works'. . . ."

3. Text from Louis J. Puhl, S.J., *The Spiritual Exercises of St. Ignatius* (Chicago: Loyola University, c1951) 103 (no. 236).

4. Gerard Manley Hopkins, "God's Grandeur," in *The Poems of Gerard Manley Hopkins,* ed. W. H. Gardner and N. H. MacKenzie (New York: Oxford University, 1970) 66.

5. The incident was related by Fr, Pedro Ribadeneira in the second volume of his classical life of Ignatius, *Vida de San Ignacio* 2:11 (*Fontes narrativi de s. Ignatio* 4, 268 f.).

6. Related by one of Ignatius' first companions, Fr. Diego Laínez, in a sermon given in Rome three years after Ignatius' death. See Mary Purcell, *The First Jesuit: St. Ignatius Loyola (1491–1556)* (Chicago: Loyola University, 1981) 195–96.

7. So Harvey D. Egan, S.J., *Ignatius Loyola the Mystic* (Wilmington, Del.: Glazier, 1987) 133.

8. Spiritual Exercises, no. 95 (tr. Puhl [no. 3 above] 44).

9. Ibid., no. 53 (tr. Puhl 28).

10. See Jerome Murphy-O'Connor, O.P., "The Second Letter to the Corinthians," in *The New Jerome Biblical Commentary,* ed. Raymond E. Brown, S.S., Joseph A. Fitzmyer, S.J., and Roland E. Murphy, O.Carm. (Englewood Cliffs, N.J.: Prentice Hall, 1990) 50:55, p. 828.

Homily 33

1. Ignatius, *Letter to the Romans* 4.1 (tr. James A. Kleist, S.J., in Ancient Christians Writers 1 [reprint New York/Ramsey: Newman, 1978] 82).

2. Robert Payne, *The Fathers of the Western Church* (New York: Viking, 1951) 30.

3. The occasion was a gathering of social, pastoral, and international ministers of the Maryland Province of the Society of Jesus.

4. Ignatius, *Letter to the Romans* 5.1.

5. Ignatius, *Letter to the Ephesians* 7.2 (see Kleist, ACW 1.63, with n. 24, p. 122).

6. Ignatius, *Letter to the Smyrnaeans* 1.1–2 and 2 (tr. Kleist 90–91).

7. Ibid. 2.

8. Ibid. 4.2.

9. Ignatius, *Letter to the Romans* 4.1 (tr. Kleist 81).

10. Ibid. 5.3 (tr. Kleist 82).

11. Ignatius, *Letter to the Philadelphians* 4 (tr. Kleist 86).

12. Ignatius, *Letter to the Ephesians* 20.2 (tr. Kleist 68).

13. Ignatius, *Letter to Polycarp* 3.1 (tr. Kleist 97).
14. Ibid. 4.1 (tr. Kleist 61).
15. Ibid. 10.3 (tr. Kleist 64).
16. Ignatius, *Letter to the Smyrnaeans* 6.2 (tr. Kleist 92).
17. Ibid. 12.2 (tr. Kleist 95).
18. Ignatius, *Letter to the Romans* 7.2 (tr. Kleist 83). Some commentators understand the Greek subject (*ho emos eros*) to mean "my earthly passions." Note, by the way, the keen insight of Hugo Rahner, S.J., *Ignatius the Theologian* (New York: Herder and Herder, 1968) 51–52: "Among the saints there is, surely, an affinity which reaches beyond the conditions of historical process, so that they have no need to back up everything they say with an appeal to literary sources—in other words, there is a reality of mystical interconnections between saints who, however remote from one another in time, were once permitted a glimpse into the luminous darkness of God. This alone can explain how Ignatius of Loyola was so much more profoundly akin than he could ever have suspected to Ignatius of Antioch, whom he so greatly revered—yet he knew of him only from the *Flos Sanctorum,* and it is hardly likely that he had read any of his letters. . . ."
19. See Spiritual Exercises, no. 104.
20. Spiritual Exercises, nos. 146, 147.
21. Harvey D. Egan, S.J., *Ignatius Loyola the Mystic* (Wilmington, Del.: Michael Glazier, 1987) 113; see 111–14.

Homily 34

1. See James J. Walter, "Conversion," *The New Dictionary of Theology,* ed. Joseph A. Komonchak, Mary Collins, and Dermot A. Lane (Wilmington, Del.: Michael Glazier, 1987) 233–35.
2. This homily, preached on the feast of St. Paul's conversion, was given at a five-day retreat/workshop within my project *Preaching the Just Word,* an effort to move social-justice issues more effectively into Catholic preaching across the country.
3. See Acts 9:1–18; 22:3–16; 26:4–23.
4. Here I am borrowing the four facets from a homily of mine, "What Shall I Do, Lord?", preached on January 23, 1982, to the Paulists and their friends celebrating their patron's conversion at St. Paul's College in Washington, D.C.; I am adding some fresh material. See my collection *Still Proclaiming Your Wonders: Homilies for the Eighties* (New York: Paulist, 1984) 163–67, at 163–64.
5. On this difficult issue, see Karl Rahner, "Grace II. Theological," in Karl Rahner, ed., *Encyclopedia of Theology: The Concise* Sacramentum mundi (New York: Crossroad, 1982) 592–94.

Homily 35

1. Ralph Waldo Emerson, "Divinity School Address," in Jaroslav Pelikan, ed., *The World Treasury of Modern Religious Thought* (Boston: Little, Brown, 1990) 252–53.
2. See "The Fundamental Constitution," no. I. See also the Prologue of the *Primitive Constitutions:* The Order of Friars Preachers "is known from the beginning to have been instituted especially for preaching and the salvation of souls."
3. J. F. Hinnebusch, O.P., "Dominican Preaching from a Historical Perspective," in *The Dominican Preacher,* ed. Office of the Promoter of Preaching (Washington, D.C.: Dominican Province of St. Joseph, 1986) 9–16, at 12.
4. Thomas Aquinas, *Summa theologiae* 3, q. 40, a. 1 ad 1m.
5. See J. B. Walker, "Vincent Ferrer, St.," *New Catholic Encyclopedia* 14 (1967) 680–81, at 681.
6. See K. Foster, "Savonarola, Girolamo," *New Catholic Encyclopedia* 12 (1967) 1106–8: "Savonarola was a great Christian and, in some sense, certainly a martyr" (1108).
7. See W. A. Hinnebusch, "Dominicans," *New Catholic Encyclopedia* 4 (1967) 974–82, at 977–78.
8. Gerard Manley Hopkins, "S. Thomae Aquinatis Rhythmus ad SS. Sacramentum," in *The Poems of Gerard Manley Hopkins,* ed W. H. Gardner and N. H. MacKenzie (4th ed.; New York: Oxford University, 1970) 211.
9. Yves Congar, O.P., "Sacramental Worship and Preaching," in *The Renewal of Preaching: Theory and Practice* (Concilium 33; New York: Paulist, 1968) 51–63, at 62.
10. Second Vatican Council, Decree on the Ministry and Life of Priests, no. 4; italics mine.
11. Bishops' Committee on Priestly Life and Ministry, National Conference of Catholic Bishops, *Fulfilled in Your Hearing: The Homily in the Sunday Assembly* (Washington, D.C.: USCC, 1982) 1.
12. From *Commissio II: De Praedicatione* 1, passed by the General Chapter of Oakland, July 1989; text kindly supplied to me by John Burke, O.P., Promoter of Preaching for the Dominican Province of St. Joseph. The General Chapter set the priorities for the Dominicans throughout the world.
13. See Hinnebusch (n. 3 above) 10–11.
14. See the sad stories by the director of Covenant House, Sr. Mary Rose McGeady, *God's Lost Children: Letters from Covenant House* (New York: Covenant House, 1991).
15. See Thomas McCarroll, "Down and Out: 'Discouraged' Workers," *Time* 138, no. 10 (Sept. 9, 1991) 56.
16. See Isa 1:11–18; 42:1–4; Hos 2:18–20; 6:6; Amos 5:18–25; Mic 6:6–8; Jer 7:5–7.

17. *Commissio II: De Praedicatione* 1 (n. 12 above).
18. 1971 Synod of Bishops, *De iustitia in mundo* (Vatican Press, 1971) Intro-
    duction, p. 5. One may argue whether "constitutive" in the document
    means "integral" or "essential." What is beyond argument is that the
    Synod saw the search for justice as inseparable from the preaching of
    the gospel.
19. 1974 Synod of Bishops, "Human Rights and Reconciliation," *Origins* 4
    (1974) 318.
20. See Abraham J. Heschel, *The Prophets* (New York: Harper & Row,
    1962) 5.
21. From the fifth version, which "perhaps represents as exactly as can be
    known the speech [Lincoln actually] gave" (Paul M. Angle, "Gettysburg
    Address," *World Book Encyclopedia* 8 [1975 ed.] 164).

Homily 36

1. See Mary Rose McGeady, *God's Lost Children: Letters from Covenant House*
   (New York: Covenant House, 1991) 31.
2. See the statement of the U.S. bishops, "Putting Children and Families
   First: A Challenge for Our Church, Nation and World," approved in
   the bishops' 1991 Washington, D.C. meeting; text in *Origins* 21, no. 25
   (Nov. 28, 1991) 394–404; figures on teenage suicide at 395.
3. From a National Women's Study, as given in the Cleveland *Plain Dealer,*
   April 24, 1992, 11-A.
4. Kevin M. Cahill, M.D., in Cahill, ed., *Imminent Peril: Public Health in a
   Declining Economy* (New York: Twentieth Century Fund, 1991) 3.
5. From the United Nations 1992 Human Development Report, as given
   in the Cleveland *Plain Dealer* (n. 3 above).
6. Roger Wilkins, "Looking Back in Anger: 27 Years after Watts, Our
   Nation Remains Divided by Racism," *Washington Post,* Outlook, May 3,
   1992, C1–2.
7. See the booklet *Catholic Social Services in Maryland,* ed. J. Kevin Appleby
   (Maryland Catholic Conference, 1992).
8. *Documents of the Thirty-second General Congregation of the Society of Jesus,
   December 2, 1974—March 7, 1975* I, 4 (Washington, D.C.: Jesuit Conference, [1975]) 35–36.
9. Michael Kramer, "What Can Be Done?" *Time* 139, no. 19 (May 11,
   1992) 41. The article was written in the context of the Los Angeles riots
   that followed on the acquittal of four white policemen charged with
   excessive brutality in the arrest of Rodney King.
10. An effort to transliterate the Greek word for "power," *dynamis.*

Homily 37

1. See the homily "Medicine as Mission," in my collection *Dare To Be Christ* (New York/Mahwah: Paulist, 1991) 185–89.
2. Richard Selzer, *Mortal Lessons: Notes on the Art of Surgery* (New York: Simon and Schuster, 1976) 94.
3. A reference to a widespread outbreak of violence in Los Angeles consequent on a jury's virtual dismissal of charges against four white policemen who had brutally assaulted a black man they were arresting. The brutality was captured unexpectedly on video by a witness to the incident and broadcast here and abroad.
4. Frederick Buechner, *The Hungering Dark* (New York: Seabury, 1969) 45–46.
5. New York: Twentieth Century Fund, 1991.
6. Ibid. 4 and 3.
7. Ibid. 3.
8. Mario M. Cuomo, "Public Health: Old Truths, New Realities," in Cahill, *Imminent Peril* 123–36, at 126.
9. See editorial in *National Catholic Reporter* 28, no. 28 (May 15, 1992) 32.

Homily 38

1. For information on St. Mary's past, I am indebted to the booklet, author(s) unlisted, *The Story of St. Mary of the Mills Church, Laurel, Maryland* (1976), a chronicle explicitly indebted to "the interest, energy, and zeal of the late Father Peter F. Manganaro, who compiled a detailed history [1953] of St. Mary of the Mills Parish while he was Assistant Pastor . . ." (Introductory Statement). I have also profited from an article, "Maid of the Mills," in the *Laurel Leader,* January 21, 1993, B-1 and B-3, dependent in part on the booklet mentioned above.
2. Second Vatican Council, Decree on the Apostolate of the Laity, no. 10 (tr. *The Documents of Vatican II,* ed. Walter M. Abbott, S.J. [New York: Herder and Herder/Association Press, 1966] 501).
3. Second Vatican Council, Declaration on Christian Education, no. 8.
4. Paul VI, *Evangelii nuntiandi* 27 (tr. *The Pope Speaks* 21, no. 1 [spring 1976] 16).
5. Ibid. 29 (*The Pope Speaks* 17).
6. Ibid. 30 (*The Pope Speaks* 18). Here the Holy Father is speaking specifically of the peoples of the Third World.
7. See Decree on the Apostolate of the Laity, passim.
8. See Robert N. Bellah, "Religion & Power in America Today," *Commonweal* 109, no. 21 (Dec. 3, 1982) 650–55, at 652. To be perfectly accurate, I should quote Bellah's exact words: "What is significant here is not

the Moral Majority . . . but something that comes closer to being amoral and is in fact a majority" (652).

9. William J. O'Malley, "The Goldilocks Method," *America* 165, no. 14 (Nov. 9, 1991) 334–39, at 338.

10. See, e.g., Patrick J. Bearsley, S.M., "Mary the Perfect Disciple: A Paradigm for Mariology," *Theological Studies* 41 (1980) 461–504.

11. See Raymond E. Brown, S.S., *The Gospel according to John (xiii–xxi)* (Garden City, N.Y.: Doubleday, 1970) 922–27.

12. This quotation from the document *New Evangelizations, Human Promotion, Christian Culture,* I take from an excerpt in *St. Anthony Messenger* 100, no. 11 (April 1993) 14.

Homily 39

1. The occasion for this homily was the 150th anniversary of the Holy Childhood Association, founded in 1843 by French Bishop Charles de Forbin-Janson of Nancy, with significant help from the founder of the Society for the Propagation of the Faith, Pauline Jaricot, who suggested appealing to the children of Europe to assist their counterparts in other countries.

2. Louis S. Richman, "Struggling To Save Our Kids," *Fortune* (Special Report) 126, no. 3 (Aug. 10, 1992) 34–40, at 34.

3. See Mary Rose McGeady, *God's Lost Children: Letters from Covenant House* (New York: Covenant House, 1991) 31. The figures in this paragraph are taken from that book; see p. 31.

4. See James P. Grant, *The State of the World's Children 1992* (published for UNICEF by Oxford University Press, no date), Summary of Issues at beginning, not paginated [6–7].

Homily 40

1. This homily was addressed to the Catholic Seniors Clubs of Nassau County, Long Island, N.Y.

2. See my article "The Import of Ecumenical Developments for Theological Education—A Roman Catholic View," *Theological Education* 3, 2 (winter 1967) 298–307, esp. 298–300.

3. See, for background, the illuminating article of Gerald Kelly, S.J., "The Morality of Mutilation: Towards a Revision of the Treatise," *Theological Studies* 17 (1956) 322–44, esp. 341–44.